COMFORT ZONES

FIFTH EDITION

PLANNING A
FULFILLING
RETIREMENT

ELWOOD N. CHAPMAN
MARION E. HAYNES

ISBN 13: 978-1-59200-990-9
ISBN 10: 1-59200-990-5

Library of Congress Catalog Card Number 2005927433
Printed in the United States of America
4 5 6 7 8 9 10 14 13 12 11 10

In Memorium

Elwood N. Chapman died October 7, 1995. He wrote the first edition of *Comfort Zones* during the time he and his wife, Martha, were making their own transition to retirement. Subsequent editions incorporated insights from the experience he gained along the way. Although he wrote more than a dozen books, he considered this one his most important effort.

Mr. Chapman retired in 1977 as a professor at Chaffey College and a visiting lecturer at Claremont Graduate School after 29 years of successful college teaching. He was a graduate of the University of California. At the time of his death, he lived with his wife at Morningside, a Continuing Care Retirement Community in Fullerton, California.

I met Elwood Chapman in Houston in 1989. During our visit, he invited me to carry on the tradition of *Comfort Zones* when he was no longer able. I'm dedicated to keeping it America's premier retirement planning book, in his memory.

He touched the lives of many through his teaching and writing. Though his typewriter is silent, he continues to speak to us through the books that remain as his legacy. We will miss his cheerful smile, twinkling eyes, and wonderful attitude.

—Marion E. Haynes

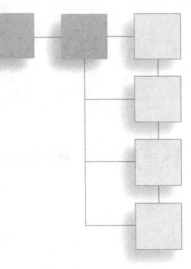

ACKNOWLEDGMENTS

Many people have contributed to the success of *Comfort Zones*. This group includes all of those who worked with Elwood Chapman on prior editions and our professional colleagues in the International Society for Retirement Planning. I thank each of you, even if I don't mention you by name.

The following made specific contributions to the development of this edition, for which I extend to each a special thanks:

Guy B. Mason
Manager, Pensioner Relations (Retired)
Shell Oil Company

Ms. Eddie Murphy
Manager, Retiree Relations (Retired)
Hughes Aircraft Company

Jay F. Rea, CPA
Personal Financial and Tax Advisor
Rea & Associates

Steven S. Shagrin, JD, CFP®
President
Planning for Life

ABOUT THE AUTHORS

Marion E. Haynes is a best-selling author. He has written nine books and 35 articles on management and supervisory practices, as well as retirement and life planning.

Mr. Haynes served for four years on the board of directors of Sheltering Arms, a social service agency assisting Houston's elderly. He also chaired the agency's personnel committee and served on its executive committee. A member of the board of directors of the International Society for Retirement Planning for eight years, he was also president of the society from 1991 to 1993. He has chaired the Editorial Board for the society's journal and served on its newsletter board.

Mr. Haynes retired from Shell Oil Company in 1991 after a 35-year career in human resource management. At retirement, he was the Manager of Pensioner Relations. Today he and his wife, Janice, live in Kerrville, Texas, where he pursues his interests in writing, community service, and travel. Visit Mr. Haynes' Web site at *http://members.aol.com/elvinhayns/books.htm*.

Elwood N. Chapman retired in 1977 as a professor at Chaffey College and a visiting lecturer at Claremont Graduate School after 29 years of successful college teaching. He graduated from the University of California. Mr. Chapman also co-founded Crisp Publications and authored more than a dozen books.

Preface to the Fifth Edition

Comfort Zones continues to be one of the most successful retirement planning books in America. It's used by hundreds of organizations for pre-retirement training, as well as by thousands of individuals working through their own transitions to retirement. This fifth edition retains the features that led to such wide acceptance and incorporates new ones that will make the book even more helpful.

Designed with you, the user, in mind, the primary objective of *Comfort Zones* continues to be to help you plan your retirement in a thoughtful, logical, yet manageable way. Exercises and questionnaires help you clarify your attitudes and expectations about retirement. Worksheets help you apply ideas to your specific situation. Each chapter ends with a list of key points and asks you to list things to do as a result of reading the chapter.

The appendix retains two popular exercises: Inventory of Retirement Activities (IRA) and Retirement Planning Guide. Use the guide to pull everything together into a specific plan after you complete the book. Program leaders as well as individual readers will find these activities helpful and easy to work with. A list of recommended resources has been added to assist you in further study and planning.

Comfort Zones is not a book to read once and put aside. Use it as a reference as you prepare for and live out your retirement. By applying the ideas presented, you will find fulfillment and joy in the years that lie ahead.

Good luck!

Marion E. Haynes, Kerrville, Texas

CONTENTS

Part V: Finances   183

Part VI: Living Arrangements   269

PART I

TAKING CHARGE

This section will help you prepare for your retirement adventure. After completing the first four chapters, you should be able to design a comfortable planning schedule; live with more style before retirement; make a smoother, more successful transition when retirement arrives; and recognize and adjust to the myths and misconceptions about retirement.

CHAPTER 1

WHAT LIES AHEAD?

The only reason you should retire is if you can find something you enjoy doing more than what you're doing now.

—George Burns

Retirement for ordinary people is a phenomenon of modern, industrialized society. At the turn of the Twentieth century, the at-birth life expectancy for American men was 45 years. This didn't leave much time for retirement. On the average, for the few who made it, retirement lasted fewer than five years.

Things have changed. Today, about a million Americans retire each year. This number will double as the 76 million Baby Boomers (those born between 1946 and 1964) begin to retire. Retirement is the goal that most workers and small-business owners look forward to as an appropriate conclusion to their careers.

People retiring today are finding a different experience than those who retired a generation ago. No longer is retirement a relatively short period at the end of life in which you take it easy and tend to household chores. Today, a substantial period of active living can span as much as a third of your lifetime. The image of retirement as idle time spent walking in the park, dozing by the fire, playing golf, or fishing has been replaced by a vision of unlimited opportunities for fulfillment.

CHANGES THAT ARE REDEFINING RETIREMENT

Today's concept of retirement has emerged as a result of several changes. The first notable change is the number of Americans who are living longer. Because of better medical care, improved diet, and increased interest in physical fitness, more people are reaching the ages of 65, 70, and older in excellent health. The activities and attitudes of today's 70-year-old are about the same as those of a 50-year-old a decade ago.

The next significant change is a well-defined trend toward earlier retirement. For example, in 1948, 50 percent of American men age 65 and older were actively engaged in the workforce. By 2005, this number had dropped to 13.8% and is projected to rise to around 15.2% by 2010.

Today, working until age 65 is more myth than reality.

Finally, the opportunities to prepare financially for retirement were greater for the average worker from the 1950s through the 1980s than at any other time in our history. While the 1990s and 2000s saw some erosion of employer-sponsored pension plans and retiree health insurance, careful planning through the years will still enable many to retire comfortably.

As a result of all these changes, a long life has become something to look forward to rather than dread. Many of today's retirees are younger, healthier, and more financially secure than their predecessors. Their children are reared, their careers are complete, and they are ready to enjoy the fruits of their labors. With careful planning, they can make these years the best years of their lives.

REQUIREMENTS FOR SUCCESS

If you want to retire soon, you need to plan to ensure that your future is truly golden. A meaningful, fulfilling retirement requires three basic ingredients: adequate financial reserves, good health, and emotional adjustment.

Your financial well-being will depend on your financial reserves, pension benefits including Social Security, and lifestyle needs. You can determine your financial well-being by inventorying your current reserves; developing a post-retirement budget that allows for the estimated impact of future inflation; and assessing your ability to make the necessary additions to savings to meet your needs.

Your physical well-being will depend on hereditary factors, where you live, how well you have maintained your health, and your commitment to your future health.

Eating and exercise habits and substance abuse can be assessed and their impact on your future well-being determined. Longevity is determined by heredity, lifestyle, and environment. Clearly, you can make a difference.

Your emotional well-being will depend on how well you make the transition from work to other activities. This includes developing a new personal identity apart from your career, leaving colleagues behind, making new friends, developing positive relationships with family members, and getting involved in activities that maintain and enhance your self-esteem.

Comfort Zones guides you through the process of planning your retirement in each of these areas and developing a plan that fits within your personal comfort zone.

PHASES OF RETIREMENT

Most people face retirement with apprehension. Some have such deep-seated fears that they extend their working years indefinitely. One reason this happens is because people see retirement as a fixed, linear period that offers decreasing fulfillment, instead of a succession of states, each with special opportunities.

The phases cannot be clearly separated and overlaps are to be expected—but knowing there are opportunities for fulfillment in each stage gives retirement a new, more exciting perspective. The bad news is that digging out the rewards may become more difficult as you move on to the next stage; the good news is that they may be enjoyed and appreciated more. When considering your retirement years, keep these factors in mind:

- There is no such thing as a completely predictable retirement. People are more individualistic during this part of their life cycle than in the youth and adult periods. Retirees are free to stretch or shorten some phases and eliminate others. Obviously, it would be unacceptable to prescribe or even suggest a retirement lifestyle for another.

- With health as the Joker in retirement planning, no specific time periods can be assigned either to retirement as a whole or to the separate phases. You are invited, however, to predict time periods for yourself. For example, you could go to a mortality table where annuity experts predict (depending on your age and sex) how many years you can expect to live. If the table should say 30 years, you might anticipate three years in transition, 15 years in active living, 10 years of slowing down, and two years in assisted living.

- ▪ Attitude is the psychological factor that stacks the deck in favor of a longer, more fulfilling retirement. To develop a positive attitude, anticipate getting the most out of each stage as it arrives, then recognize that each phase has its own inventory of pleasures and rewards. You must be determined to squeeze as much out of each phase as possible. With this kind of attitude, opportunities multiply in each stage, and with good health, it is possible to live up to your highest expectations.

Transition

Ahhhh...throwing off the frustrations of work, adjusting to greater freedom, and making the transition to a new, refreshing lifestyle! At the beginning it is bon voyage and honeymoon time, but major adjustments may be necessary later. Sometimes it's stormy at first, but once you find a new role and identity, retirement living is safely under way.

Few retirees move into retirement without going through some difficult times. Leaving a full-time career and adjusting to leisure activities, finding a part-time job or volunteer involvement, or embarking on a personal creative adventure is a far cry from preparing for an extended trip or vacation. We are talking about starting a new life! The old ego satisfactions are gone. The routine is gone. The security of the regular paycheck with all the benefits has been replaced with a new system. The old door has been closed and a new one needs to be opened. A new identity needs to be found.

A minimum of one year is usually required for an individual to make a safe passage into retirement. Sometimes it takes three or four, and a few never make it at all. This happens when one opens a new door (retirement) but refuses to close the old door (previous work) and winds up in limbo, often returning to full-time work and the possibility of a second retirement attempt down the line.

To make your transition shorter and more comfortable, here are five suggestions:

1. Realize that a honeymoon is just a honeymoon and cannot last forever. When it is over, expect a time of uncertainty, doubts, and disenchantment.

2. Leave all excess baggage from your previous work experience behind.

3. Anticipate some rocky days and devise a strategy to lessen the discomfort you may feel. Regular exercise can be a big help.

4. If you are making your passage with a life partner, talk openly about transition problems so you can reinforce each other.

5. If it is not already under way, do a better job of retirement planning by anticipating and preparing for four phases, instead of one. Where possible, know what you will do and what you want to be before you retire, then be aware that it is important to find your own comfort zone in each new stage. Retirement is never the same for two people.

Active Living

This is the time to achieve your retirement "thing," whatever it may be. Did you harbor a retirement dream during your working years? Have you always wanted to do something but your career prevented it? If so, now is the time to fulfill old dreams and create new ones. These are days of excitement, achievement, and risk-taking. You may not be able to get up the head of steam you could 20 years ago, but there is little out of your reach. Your battle cry should be: "Make the most of this period." If your plans suggest you should dip into your retirement nest egg, do it!

Almost everyone has one or more goals to fulfill during retirement. Although some goals (trips and so on) may be completed during the transition period, major projects are often best delayed until you have "found yourself" and feel comfortable in this phase. People who enter retirement without goals usually drift until they find something to fill their time—and thus miss the boat because they spend their time doing unfulfilling and boring things. Sometimes, however, you find a person who enters retirement without a goal but discovers one that turns out to be a lifesaver.

Most commonly, goals fall into such categories as consulting or part-time work for others, significant volunteer involvement, starting a small business, serious creative pursuits, and lasting hobbies. The range is as broad as the range of retirees themselves and once started, many surprise themselves with their success and enthusiasm.

Most retirees know that this phase provides the big opportunity for fulfillment in the more active pursuits. Later, some scaling down may be necessary. You hear people talking about getting a second wind and about needing to "retire to refire."

It is a period when late bloomers (those who may have been restricted in their work years) come into their own.

Under the old-fashioned concept of retirement, all years were to be "mellow" and "golden." Today, the early years are full of action, involvement, and accomplishment. Due to earlier retirements, better financial planning, and medical advancements, some retirees are successful in stretching this phase to 20 years. But sooner or later (often depending upon one's health), one is willing to think about moving into the next phase. When you hear someone say, "I've accomplished my major retirement goals," you may be getting a signal that this phase is drawing to a close. This does not mean that the next phase will eliminate travel, fulfillment, and laughter. It is just that the goals often are more modest and schedules less hectic. There will be different goals and different dreams in a different comfort zone!

The primary danger in the active living phase is moving into the next phase without recognizing the great opportunity this phase offers. This often happens when retirees are "worked out" or unable to come up with retirement goals they can be enthusiastic about. As a result, they drift through their active living phase without knowing what they are missing. At the other end of the spectrum, there is early retirement burnout. Some individuals get such a big second wind that they extend this phase beyond reason and often miss out on the rewards of the phases that follow. It is the old "die with your boots on" syndrome. Without knowing or accepting that there are worthwhile pleasures ahead, these individuals foolishly put all of their retirement eggs in this early basket.

Slowing Down

Sooner or later there comes a time for a new and slower direction. It is a period of shedding previous demands, learning to say no, and mellowing out. It is time to throw off pressures and think more of yourself. Staying home with simple pleasures may start to become as enjoyable as participating in social events or accepting strenuous outside involvement. Some of this occurs because of lower energy levels, some by preference.

Some individuals are happier in this phase than the prior one. These retirees don't like too much activity and when they start slowing down, they enter a comfort zone that provides more fulfillment, not less. Often one life partner reaches this stage ahead of the other.

This phase can last as long as the prior phase, and sometimes longer. Self-pacing and involvement balance seem to be the keys. You don't want to slow life down to the point where things begin to drag; on the other hand, anxiety is more difficult to handle. Often after making a commitment to do something strenuous, doubts appear. Of course, to the energetic retiree still in the middle of active living, a slower, more balanced pace may seem boring. Once there, these same people might think differently and appreciate their new comfort zone. To some, this phase can be the jewel in the retirement crown. For example, this is the period when grandparenting can be most delightful. With a more relaxed attitude, spending time with grandchildren and great-grandchildren can be as rewarding as the personal achievements of the earlier period.

The danger in this phase lies in misunderstanding just what balance means. For example, it does not mean a drastic change, but a slower, softer approach that retains some of the activity blended with more quiet times. Achieving just the right balance is an individual matter. Some can handle considerable social activity outside the home; others need only a sprinkle of the outside world to enhance their home-centered comfort zone. It can take a few years to reach a satisfactory balance because people keep frustrating themselves by trying to return to active living instead of relaxing and enjoying the new pace.

To help you fully understand (and achieve) the joys of this phase, here are some suggestions:

1. Waltzing can be as much fun as doing the samba.

2. The rewards of this phase may have less status but more pleasure.

3. Reducing the anxiety connected with active living (the constant need to achieve) can open the door to a more satisfying comfort zone with fewer demands but equally rewarding projects.

4. The right balance does not come easily—but don't give up.

5. Accepting this phase may not mean you are getting older as much as it means you are getting smarter.

Some retirees may be more motivated to stretch this phase than the prior one. This suggests three things. First, either rewards in this phase are yet to be defined or some people are lucky enough to discover a very special comfort zone for themselves. Second, those in this phase seem to take exercising and diet control more seriously. This may mean that, with less time left, they want to protect where they are more than they did in the past. Finally, you hear the phrase "simplify to beautify" more frequently at this stage. This could mean that the pot of gold in the retirement rainbow is most apt to be found here.

Toward the end of this phase may be the time to release some reins of control so that the "golden years" can become a reality. It is holding with humor, enjoying the sunsets, and memory time! The course has been set. Relax—many fulfillments are automatic. At this stage, home becomes one's castle, caution (safety) is king, and the court jester is needed more than in the past.

Here, a trip may be a Sunday drive instead of a flight to London, a celebration may be a quiet lunch with a close friend near home instead of a bash at a fancy resort, and an unexpected visit from a caring person might convert a routine day into a special event. Life remains good but it is a much slower pace. This does not mean, however, that you cannot take an occasional long trip or cruise.

When one reaches this point, active living may seem a long, long time ago and activities may remind you of the good times before retirement. In other words, you have the feeling that you have already made the most out of retirement. Everything else is icing on the cake!

Most individuals are motivated to maintain their physical and mental faculties so that they can enjoy this softer chair of retirement, but a few refuse to try and, as a result, move too quickly into the final phase. Although limited physical health improvements are within reach—those who have neglected to exercise and follow a reasonable diet in earlier periods can sometimes show the greatest improvement —the emphasis is on holding. For many it is a period when exercise diminishes, often being confined to taking care of personal needs, short shopping trips, and doing limited housework.

This phase is characterized by fewer but more enjoyable people contacts, an increase in pill taking, and more time in front of a television set. Sleeping is more erratic. Although personal pride is of utmost importance for most people, previous standards of behavior become less important.

Whether living alone or with others in a retirement center, holding patterns can be maintained for years. Apparently, the more success one has had with previous phases, the more determination one has to extend this one. Life remains precious.

Assisted Living

Memory time…golden thoughts…putting one's life in perspective. This is the unfinished-business-of-living stage. Although many things have been taken care of, some remain. Certain adjustments to wills or trusts may need to be made. This is also a time of reconciliation. There is little outside activity. Help from family and professionals is frequently required.

MYTHS AND MISCONCEPTIONS

Many myths and misconceptions get in the way of realizing the full potential of retirement. Following are a few of the most common ones. Watch for them and don't allow them to spoil your chances for meaningful retirement.

The Retirement/Early Death Myth

You probably know people who were not around long after their retirement parties. The unhappy news causes strange reactions.

- ▪ "It's too bad Joe didn't work longer."

- ▪ "The moment people retire, they grow old."

- ▪ "I'd still have Fred if he hadn't retired so early."

Retirement can be painful, but it is not lethal. It is, rather, a change not unlike others in life. Most people who die shortly after retirement probably had health problems before they stopped working. Retirement had nothing to do with their demise.

The only connection between retirement and early death may be that some retirees fail to stay active. They relax to the point that their bodies self-destruct. They give up. They fail to stay in charge. There are many reasons for retiring early, and there are just as many for retiring later, but staying on the job because you fear retirement will cause early death should not be one of them.

The Piece-of-Cake Myth

Retirement should be the dessert that follows the full-course meal of earlier life. Perhaps this is why some people view the transition as a piece of cake. Instead of thinking ahead to retirement, they make comments such as these:

- ▪ "My retirement plan consists of putting all of my work problems in my briefcase and presenting them to my boss as a farewell gift."

- ▪ "Retirement is a pot of gold at the end of the rainbow. You don't have to plan for something that beautiful."

Many people are so occupied with getting out of a career trap that they seem to care little about what happens after they leave their jobs. Despite the fact they have planned other aspects of their lives, they seem to feel retirement will take care of itself. The opposite is often true. Many retirees go back to work because they can't handle leisure time.

The Female-Exclusion Myth

Some people, including women themselves, continue to believe that only men retire. This misconception ignores career women who have the same retirement adjustment problems that men have. Also, it falsely assumes that women not holding down nine-to-five jobs can't retire. This may stem from the old saying: "A man works from sun to sun, but a woman's work is never done." Homemakers often have a more difficult transition than those who retire from other types of work. Women who have been homemakers all their lives need to insist on being a full partner when their spouses retire.

One reason this myth may continue is that women sometimes lose their spouses early. The transition to widowhood is so traumatic that it hides the equally important second passage they must make.

The Honey-Do Myth

Some folks put off retirement because they fear their life partners will control their free hours. It will be "Honey, do the dishes," "Honey, do the windows," and "Honey, take the dog to the vet." Normally these individuals need not worry because most partners don't want someone underfoot, monitoring their activities and invading their space. One woman expressed it well: "The only time you will ever hear me use that honey-do expression is when I say 'Honey, do something on your own, away from the house, so we can both have room to breathe.'" Both need the same autonomy after retirement that they did before—maybe more.

The Hobby Myth

Hobbies are a great idea. Those who can derive satisfaction from photography, gourmet cooking, stamp collecting, and so on are lucky. But hobbies must continue to be fun and interesting or they quickly become unsatisfying. Few people create a complete new life around hobbies. A few will be able to convert a favorite hobby into a small business or lifetime artistic involvement, but most are not this fortunate.

The Prior-Success/Easy-Passage Myth

It's not difficult to see why this misconception persists. It stands to reason that those who were successful before retirement should find retirement easier to cope with than those who did not do as well. Success breeds success; failure breeds failure. Translated, this means that corporate presidents should have an easy retirement.

True? Absolutely false! In fact, it often works the other way around. Those who earned high psychic rewards from their careers may have trouble finding replacements after retirement. It may be difficult to find a retirement role that provides enough ego satisfaction. All retirees can build a better lifestyle.

The No-Challenge-Needed Myth

Some conscientious individuals who have worked hard all their lives feel that they are home free when they retire. They say:

- ▪ "I've done my bit for society; now it's society's turn."

- ▪ "I've paid my dues through church work for 30 years. Now the church can take care of me."

These people operate under the premise that you pay your dues during working years and then draw interest during retirement. A pretty dream but, sadly, life doesn't work that way. In fact, happy retirees often pay more dues, not fewer.

They contribute more to charitable organizations and communities than when they were working. Perhaps the most successful retirees are those who have an opportunity to repay society by sharing their talents.

The Odd-Job Myth

If you ask friends who plan to retire in the next few years about their expectations, some will reply, "There are enough jobs around the house to keep me busy for at least 10 years." These well-meaning individuals, without knowing it, are using odd jobs as an excuse to avoid accepting a bigger challenge. They think about how satisfying it will be to catch up on all the little chores they have been avoiding. It usually takes only a few weeks to discover the truth. Having more time doesn't make a job any more fun to do. In fact, some retirees hate them so much they return to work to earn enough money to pay the plumber, gardener, and painter. All probably wish they had done more serious pre-retirement planning.

The Stay-Busy Myth

Keeping busy is a great idea after retirement, provided you are doing what you want to do and your activities are meaningful and fulfilling. If you keep busy simply to be busy, you are falling for the myth. Some people think that if they stay busy enough, their retirement problems will go away and they will be happy ever after. Others stay busy doing meaningless chores to anesthetize themselves against thoughts of aging or living alone.

These individuals seem willing to trade a life of challenge and fulfillment for a passive existence composed of busy work. Instead of slowing down to design a rewarding retirement strategy, they spend time and energy on meaningless tasks. They visit the supermarket daily when once or twice a week would do. They accept social invitations knowing they will be bored. Worst of all, they stretch dull chores around the house. You get the feeling these retirees are avoiding retirement. Are they afraid to face a new, more mature identity? Has life been so disappointing that they dare not hope for anything better? Are they afraid to get off the treadmill and search for late-in-life happiness?

THE BIG MISCONCEPTION ABOUT TIME

Most retirees grossly underestimate the amount of time they will have on their hands following retirement. Life exists within a 24-hour time box. Yesterday is gone, tomorrow is pending, today is center stage. To be happy, both before and after retirement, you must deal effectively with each time block—every day.

Retirees often don't understand how large a block of time 16 hours is. You can fly to London from San Francisco and still have time for a stage play—or drive across two or three large states. During this time period, it's possible to play 18 holes of golf, take a good swim, have dinner with friends, go dancing, and still read a few chapters before bedtime.

Yet, if not filled with meaningful activities, 16 hours can be forever. Compare the statements in the left column with those on the right.

"The days get longer and longer."   *"The days get shorter and shorter."*

"Time weighs heavily on my hands."   *"I need more time to achieve my goals."*

"I'm climbing the walls."   *"I need to squeeze out more time."*

These contrasting expressions indicate that some retirees not only treasure their time but know how to convert it into excitement. Others permit time to bore them to death. What's the difference?

KEYS TO RETIREMENT SUCCESS

- ▪ Accept the reality that your career is behind you and look at what lies ahead.

- ▪ Have a clear vision of the life you want to pursue and work toward achieving it.

- ▪ Get involved in something worthwhile and continue to grow knowledge, skill, and understanding.

- ▪ Maintain your health so you can remain independent and continue to stay active.

- ▪ Develop and maintain supportive relationships among family and friends.

The answer may lie in planning. Some retirees plan activities and events to maintain their excitement and motivation. Others with the same opportunity have no special events to fill their time and stretch uninteresting tasks just to get through the day.

YOUR RETIREMENT VISION

What do you expect life to be like in retirement? For many it is seen as a period of opportunity and options; a time to get on with fulfilling dreams; a window of opportunity characterized by more time, less responsibility, financial security, and the freedom to embark on new adventures. Clearly, you can continue to be productive and creative, and to grow intellectually for a number of years.

Reflect on your vision for your future and write a brief description of it in the space below.

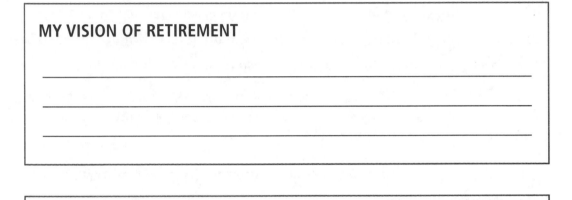

MY VISION OF RETIREMENT

_____

_____

_____

KEY POINTS

- Retirement can equal a third or more of your lifetime—30 or more years.
- As a result of increased longevity, earlier retirements, and greater financial independence, old age has become something to look forward to rather than dread.
- A meaningful, fulfilling retirement requires attention to your financial, physical, and emotional well-being.
- Retirement consists of distinct phases. Following a transition, there are periods of active living, slowing down, and assisted living. Each should be anticipated and enjoyed.
- Knowing the myths and misconceptions about retirement helps you avoid foolish, unnecessary mistakes.
- The challenge of retirement is knowing how to spend your time in rewarding ways.
- Retirement is freedom, opportunity, and choices.

MY UNFULFILLED DREAMS

Make a list of things you would like to do during your remaining lifetime. Then, mark the 10 that are most important.

1. _____
2. _____
3. _____
4. _____
5. _____
6. _____
7. _____
8. _____
9. _____
10. _____
11. _____
12. _____
13. _____
14. _____
15. _____
16. _____
17. _____
18. _____
19. _____
20. _____
21. _____
22. _____
23. _____
24. _____
25. _____

26. _____
27. _____
28. _____
29. _____
30. _____
31. _____
32. _____
33. _____
34. _____
35. _____
36. _____
37. _____
38. _____
39. _____
40. _____
41. _____
42. _____
43. _____
44. _____
45. _____
46. _____
47. _____
48. _____
49. _____
50. _____

CHAPTER 2

THE RIGHT TIME TO RETIRE

There is a time for departure even when there is no certain place to go.

—Tennessee Williams

As a rule, people tend to retire when they can afford to, when work is no longer fun, or when there is something else they would rather do. Some target a significant employment anniversary such as 30, 35, or 40 years. Others pick a birth date such as 55, 60, 62, 65, or 70. But some people don't have a choice. Ill health or workforce reductions may force them into retirement. Regardless of your circumstances, you face important soul searching and decision making as you consider leaving the comfortable and familiar day-to-day world of work.

Generally, this soul searching and decision making should prompt you to consider these major points:

- *Health:* What is the status of your health? Is your work physically strenuous? Are you in good health and want to retire while you're still able to do some of the things to which you look forward?

- *Career:* Honestly assess your career. How satisfying is the work you're doing? What are your prospects for the future? Would another line of work or a different work location provide greater satisfaction?

- *Family Responsibilities:* Are your children reared and educated? Are you responsible for the care of other family members? Would retiring allow you more time to handle these responsibilities?

- *Financial Status:* Can you afford to retire? If not, you may have to find ways to supplement your retirement income or delay retirement until you've built up a larger nest egg.

- *Alternative Activities:* What will you do all day? Do you have a well-thought-out plan to use your time productively and creatively as a means of maintaining your self-worth?

This chapter guides you through some considerations that may have bearing on your decision to retire, then directs your attention to factors involved in choosing the best time to close out your career. It also offers three plans for trying retirement before making a full commitment.

THE ECONOMICS OF WORKING VERSUS RETIRING

The first issue bearing on your decision to retire is whether you can afford to. A careful analysis may lead you to conclude that you'll have to work a while longer or that you'll have to supplement your retirement income. Or, you may find that you have sufficient resources to support your planned lifestyle. This topic is addressed fully in Part 5, "Finances." For the time being, compare how much income you have now to what you can expect after you retire.

People generally assume that they'll have more income by continuing to work. This may indeed be true, but it's important to know how much you will have after taxes and work-related expenses are taken into account. You may be surprised.

Use the following worksheet to compare your income while working to what you expect in retirement income.

	Working	Retired
Income		
Salary and Bonus	_____	
Pension		_____
IRA Income		_____
401(k) and/or 403(b) Income		_____
Savings Plan Income		_____
Social Security		_____
Other Income	_____	
Taxes		
Federal Income Tax	_____	
State Income Tax	_____	
Social Security or Self-Employment Tax	_____	
Work-Related Expenses		
Commuting Costs	_____	
Meals	_____	
Special Clothing	_____	
Laundry & Dry Cleaning	_____	
After Tax Net Income*	_____	_____
Marginal Net Income from Working**	_____	

*Total of all income items less taxes and work-related expenses.

**After Tax Net Income from Working less After Tax Net Income when retired. This is how much more you are getting from working than you would have if you were retired.

RETIREMENT GAINS AND LOSSES

As you contemplate retirement, you are likely to be pulled between the attraction of work and the attraction of retiring. Each has positive features. At the same time, each may have some drawbacks. To help you assess the impact of retirement on your life, complete the following worksheet. (If appropriate, have your life partner complete it as well and then discuss each other's responses.)

Instructions: List gains you associate with retirement, such as more free time, less stress, and more control over your schedule. Next, list losses you associate with retirement, such as enjoyment of the work, friendship of colleagues, and recognition for accomplishments.

Gains	Losses

ARE YOU A CANDIDATE FOR EARLY RETIREMENT?

Now that you have given some consideration to what you would gain and lose with retirement, both financially and otherwise, complete the Early Retirement Assessment Questionnaire that follows. It offers additional insights on whether you are a candidate to retire before earning full retirement benefits.

Early Retirement Assessment Questionnaire*

Answer all questions with the most honest decision possible. Total your Yes and No answers when finished.

	Yes	No
1. Would you be willing to retire early even if it means a reduction in your retirement income? (For example, you had planned on $4,000 per month but early retirement would drop it to $2,700?)	☐	☐
2. Is there an over-supply of qualified people in your career area or specialty?	☐	☐
3. If you retired now, would you find it easy to accept a part-time job at a much lower salary?	☐	☐
4. Would you find it easy to devote eight hours a day, every day, engaged in pure leisure activities?	☐	☐
5. Do you sense you are old enough to retire?	☐	☐
6. Is money becoming less important to you?	☐	☐
7. Will early retirement extend your longevity?	☐	☐
8. Do you feel you have met all of your career challenges?	☐	☐
9. Does your present job use up almost all of your energy?	☐	☐
10. If you retired now, would your estimated monthly income meet your future needs?	☐	☐
11. Will early retirement be accepted with enthusiasm by your family? (Will your life partner be pleased to have you around more of the time?)	☐	☐
12. Will you be able to adjust to the loss of ego involvements and social contacts your job has provided?	☐	☐

	Yes	No
13. If you took a one-year moratorium from full-time work, do you think you would find it difficult to return?	☐	☐
14. Are you willing to give a copy of this scale to a life partner or close friend and have him or her rate you so you can discuss answers?	☐	☐
15. If you were able to continue your present job until you reached your planned retirement date, would you be happy to do so?	☐	☐
16. Assuming you have lost your present job, would you accept a similar position with the same benefits but a 25 percent reduction in pay?	☐	☐
17. Do you figure you have already worked hard enough to deserve retirement?	☐	☐
18. Are you tired of carrying more than your share of family responsibilities and do you look at retirement as a way out?	☐	☐
19. Do you have a well-thought-out retirement plan that includes both financial and emotional contingencies?	☐	☐
20. Would you dread going through the job-hunting process at this stage of your life?	☐	☐
21. Are you ready to lead a more simple lifestyle even if it means fewer possessions and a lower standard of living?	☐	☐
22. Are you fed up with the rat race?	☐	☐
23. Do you feel it is time to live for yourself?	☐	☐
24. Would you feel secure enough to enter into retirement with a smaller nest egg than you had planned on?	☐	☐
25. Are you willing to accept the possibility that early retirement may not work for you?	☐	☐

_____ Number of *Yes* answers:

_____ Number of *No* answers:

*If appropriate, have your life partner complete this exercise independently and then compare answers and discuss differences in opinion.

If your Yes answers total 20 or more, it appears you are ready psychologically and financially for early retirement. You should be able to make it work.

If your Yes answers total 15 or more, you are getting a signal you may be ready but might encounter a few problems. You may need a part-time job to supplement your income or to keep you involved.

If you have 12 or more No answers, you appear to be getting a signal that it is too early for you to retire. You should consider making plans to seek a different full-time job so you can improve your retirement income and have additional time to use this book to complete a comprehensive retirement plan.

CHOOSING A RETIREMENT DATE

If retirement appears feasible at this point, here are a few things to consider when picking your actual retirement date:

- **Organizational Practices:** Find out when the best time is to retire from your organization. Some things you'll need to know are: How is accrued vacation handled? How are age and service rounded for pension calculation?

- **Project Completion:** Are you working on a major project? If so, is it practical to retire when it is completed rather than start something new?

- **Reorganization:** Is your group or department planning to reorganize? If so, would it be practical to time your retirement to coincide with the reorganization?

CLOSING OUT YOUR CAREER

In the days leading up to your retirement, you need to start weaning yourself both physically and emotionally from your work. During this time it is reasonable that you will become more emotionally invested in retiring than you are in working. You may find the days going by more slowly and find it difficult to concentrate on your work.

During this time, see that someone is trained to handle the work you've been doing, complete any pending projects that bring closure to your career, and reduce the amount of out-of-schedule time you spend on the job.

Cleaning out your work area can be a melancholy experience. You can reduce the impact by starting a few weeks before your last day. Begin by removing a few nonessentials such as books, pictures, and personal mementos. As time permits, clean out your files. This helps you disengage from your work and prevents the air of finality that comes with a one-day massive move out.

Save some meaningful personal items as a reminder of your career, but don't take home boxes of useless correspondence that will be in your way and take up space. If you can't face throwing it away, give it to someone at work.

CONSIDER A TRIAL RUN

A surprising number of people retire two or more times. Even some who reach 65 or over discover that they are not satisfied with themselves unless they are working. It is therefore wise to view retirement as an experiment—especially for those who retire early. Consider the options discussed in the following three sections.

Trial Period Without a Job

You hear a few individuals say, "I'm going to give retirement a year to see if I am ready. No part-time job. No volunteer involvement. If I discover I can't handle it, I'll come back into the labor market on a full-time basis. I need time to think, play, and gain a new perspective. I have everything to gain and little to lose."

A one-year trial period makes sense providing the following rules are honored:

▪ A strict retirement budget is followed for six months so that you can experience a realistic retirement lifestyle.

- Full- and part-time career possibilities are researched so that you know your chances of finding satisfactory employment if retirement doesn't work out.

- Optional living environments are explored.

Trial Period with Part-Time Job

Some people decide it is best for them to ease into retirement by having a part-time job. Those who possess skills that are in demand find it profitable and comfortable to work as consultants, freelancers, or temporaries. Many who follow this route like the arrangement so well they stay with it for years—long beyond the normal retirement age of 65. Others stay with the plan until they find even part-time work so demanding they give it up. Still others move into full retirement when they discover they no longer need the additional income or the contacts that work provides.

Another part-time arrangement that's growing in popularity is phased retirement. Under this arrangement, workers stay with their current employer but reduce the number of hours worked. This allows the employer to retain needed skills and the worker to try retirement—a win-win opportunity for both. To make phased retirement attractive, the Internal Revenue Service has proposed a rules change that allows workers 59 years or older who cut back on their hours to supplement their earnings with a partial pension from the same employer.

Trial Period with Owning a Small Business

This option has special appeal to those who have always harbored an entrepreneurial spirit but elected to work for someone else. Winding up without a job a few years before a planned retirement date forces many of these individuals to take the risk they should have taken earlier. In exercising this option, the following steps are recommended:

- Spend a full year doing research and do not make a final decision until near the end of that year.

- Recognize that it usually takes a period of three years to start and turn a new business of any kind into a profitable one.

- Follow the same rules as prescribed in the first option as protection against the possibility that your research does not produce a business compatible with your personality, training, and available capital.

If you find yourself out of a job and not fully prepared to retire, it might be wise to review these three options—talk them over at length with your life partner—and make a preliminary choice. In doing this, you may prefer a variation on one listed above or an option of your own that fits your special needs.

Make a preliminary choice of the option you intend to follow by placing a check in the appropriate square.

☐ Trial Period without a Job

☐ Trial Period with a Part-time Job

☐ Trial Period to Investigate Owning a Small Business

My own option, which is:

_____

_____

FORCED RETIREMENT

Sometimes a forced or unscheduled retirement eventually turns into an opportunity, but not always. Often it becomes a traumatic crisis period and what happens can depend upon the answer to a single question: "Am I willing to accept a new challenge?"

Some people can easily slip into a no-challenge retirement lifestyle and coast out their remaining years. With a few pleasures, a television set, and trivial keep-busy activities, they float along. Others, who desire more from their retirement years, seek and find a new challenge that can give them a second, rewarding life. Often this requires a new career on either a full- or part-time basis.

Most people who are forced into early retirement—perhaps with 30 years of life ahead of them—may need a challenge more than they are ready to admit. It's difficult to coast for 30 years.

KEY POINTS

■ Some people have the privilege of choosing their retirement date; others have it forced upon them by ill health or workforce reductions.

■ Deciding when to retire takes soul searching and decision making, and you must consider health, career, financial status, family responsibilities, and alternative activities.

■ Often the economic benefits of working, when compared to retirement, are less than expected.

■ Work provides more than just income. When considering retirement, look at other gains and losses as well.

■ Some people are prepared both financially and emotionally to retire early.

■ Consider retiring for a one-year trial period if you are unsure how you will adapt to retirement.

Things to Do

Instructions: In the space below, list the things you want to do as a result of reading this chapter. Then, choose a target date for completing each of your action items.

Action Item	Target Date

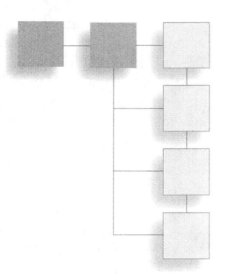

CHAPTER 3

A SUCCESSFUL TRANSITION

Even in slight things the experience of the new is rarely without some stirring of foreboding.

—Eric Hoffer

Although your retirement may still be years off, it's not too early to start preparing. Experts agree that the more advance planning you do, the better. If your retirement is close or already underway, retirement seminars and books like this one can still be helpful.

The transition to retirement is not always smooth. It can be a period of emotional ups and downs and psychological detours. Making the transition is like going from one safe harbor (career) to another (retirement).

A person makes many transitions on his or her journey through life. For example, from school to employment, from single to married, to parenthood, and from one job to another. All transitions have a common element. They require you to adjust to change as you move from one comfort zone to another.

The retirement transition can best be described as moving from the comfortable environment of work with its familiar surroundings and routine to a new environment and becoming comfortable. Most people make the transition successfully. However, a few do not. The key to success seems to be expectations. Those who look forward to new opportunities make better transitions than those who believe their usefulness ends when they leave the workplace.

For a successful transition to retirement, have realistic expectations based on your personal limitations—talent, finances, physical ability, and so on. Take your limitations into account, but don't use them as an excuse not to try something. A positive outlook helps. Your attitude strongly influences your experience, so go into retirement expecting the most. Then work to see that you are not disappointed.

Your emotional well-being is influenced by what you do with your time, where you live, and the relationships you have with friends and family. (These are all covered in later chapters in Part 4, "Relationships.") Planning for retirement gives you an opportunity to assess these issues and make whatever changes may be necessary. You can ease the trauma of retirement by attending to any concerns in advance so that there is minimal change when retirement becomes a reality.

This chapter helps you make a successful transition by presenting some of the issues involved and guiding you through a retirement planning model.

THE IMPORTANCE OF WORK

Work is a significant part of most people's lives. When retirement is equated to not working, it suggests a great void. Of course there are aspects of work that everyone looks forward to giving up. But, on balance, work is an enjoyable experience for most people. It is this significance of work that makes the transition to retirement so challenging.

To carry out a successful transition, you need to understand the importance of work in your life and consider alternative sources for replacing those contributions. Philosophers and behavioral scientists have identified five major contributions. Consider each of these and their importance to you personally. Then look for ways to build a retirement so that you can continue to receive these benefits in your daily living.

Income

The need for income is the primary reason people seek work. With retirement there is less need for income: The cost of educating children has usually been met, the home mortgage has been paid off, and daily living expenses are less. When you compare your income and expenses in retirement, you may find that you no longer need to generate income. However, if your retirement is not adequately funded, working either full- or part-time may be necessary.

Structure

Work structures your time. You have to get up in time to get to work. Days off, holidays, and vacations are set by your work schedule. You must be certain places at certain times. Many people look forward to being freed from the structure imposed by their work schedule. Others, however, feel a loss when they give up this familiar routine. When you retire you need to consider your daily routine: How much structure do you need? Do you prefer less routine than when you were working, or about the same?

Identity

Most people closely identify with their trade or profession and employer. What you do for a living is often the topic of casual conversations. Facing your identity, beyond your career, is one of the major challenges you face in retirement. How will you answer the question, "What do you do?" after you retire? One of the best ways to deal with this is to focus on current involvements such as community service, political, volunteer, or educational activity.

Social Contact

A very significant part of the work experience is the friendships that develop from close associations over long periods of time. These friendships become one of the major casualties of retirement. If you have social contact with colleagues outside the workplace, you can expect these friendships to continue. However, if you only see people at work, you can expect these relationships to end with your retirement. Single people who have not developed a social life beyond the workplace find this a particularly frightening prospect.

Psychological Needs/Satisfaction

A feeling of self worth is important for good mental health. Many people get this feeling through their work. They contribute and receive feedback that confirms and bolsters their self-esteem. Retirement destroys this system. How will you build a new system to provide you with a sense of purpose and an opportunity for self expression, accomplishment, growth, and recognition? Some people think these needs will change with retirement. They look forward to less pressure from work and more opportunities to relax, but they are bored after a month or so. The fact is, you are the same person on the first day of retirement as you were on the last day of work. You have the same needs. Without an alternative to satisfy these needs, you will become frustrated and depressed.

NEEDED: A NEW IDENTITY

The new roles of retirement fall into four major categories. In the next chapter they are identified as Plans A, B, C, and D. Plan A is leisure. You choose not to work (either for money or as a volunteer). Plan B involves working for money, either for someone else or in your own business on a part-time basis. You give up some of your leisure time, but not all of it. Plan C involves volunteer work, usually through an organization. It also replaces some of your leisure time. Plan D replaces leisure time with full-time work.

Prior to retirement, you have established yourself as a unique individual and probably felt good about it. You know who you are. You have an identity. To make a successful transition into retirement, you need to establish yourself as a somewhat different person. One identity will be left behind, and you will not be totally comfortable until you have established a new one. You can't carry your previous identity indefinitely. You need to find a new "self" with which you are comfortable.

Previous Experience Only Limited Help

You always know when you have a good identity because you have confidence in what you are doing. Others recognize and admire the role you play. You feel your life has meaning and purpose.

You have a lack of identity when you do not feel positive about the role you are playing. When you start to feel that life has little purpose and your goals are out of focus, you do not feel good about yourself. Often your relationships with others are not satisfying. This is typical for anyone going through a temporary loss of identity. Time seems to drag, and there is a loss of motivation. During this period there is often a great deal of self-assessment.

Moving from one phase of life to another can cause individuals to temporarily lose their identity. As a young person you may have struggled to "find yourself." You may have experimented with more than one identity during your life. Your adult identity may have come later. Even after finding a mature, adult self and feeling good about it, you may have lost it once or twice through a career change, marital change, or psychological trauma. For most people, searching for an identity is not new. These earlier searches can help you as you search for a retirement identity.

There is one big difference in making the transition to retirement—a difference that makes adjustment more difficult. As a mature adult, there were normally standards and expectations provided by the environment. There were acceptable work-oriented models. Success was more easily measured. You normally knew when you were on the right track and what to expect. By contrast, retirement takes you into a kind of no-man's land. There are few reference points; everything must come from within. You decide on your own activities. Your expectations are often your own, and there are few guideposts. You need to reach a destination to find a new identity, but don't know how far it is or when you will reach it.

Retiring to What?

Too many people retire to nothing and then wonder why they feel empty and disenchanted. They never sit down ahead of time to determine what they want from retirement. It's important to retire to something. The more you know about what you really want, the faster your transition will be. You will have a destination to work toward.

Without effective planning, it is possible to become stranded between your career and retirement. Some people are no longer effective or happy in their careers, but they refuse to move on. They are dissatisfied with what they are, yet they reject what they could be. They lose one identity but do not see the need to find another. Many in this situation fear retirement. They believe it will shorten rather than lengthen their lives. They see only the disadvantages. They refuse to accept the notion that there is a point where moving ahead makes sense.

What Lies Ahead?

What's ahead of you?

- More education?
- Second career?
- Special leisure activities?
- Church work?
- Recreational vehicle time?
- Late-in-life mission?
- Foreign travel?

- Volunteer involvement?

- Hobbies?

- Creative pursuits?

- Sports?

- Combination work and leisure?

There is a point in everyone's life when the advantages of the future outweigh the present. It's often difficult to know when this occurs, but a primary signal is an uneasy feeling that something has ended or a role has been played out. Holding onto the past prevents enjoyment of the future.

HOW TO MAKE A SUCCESSFUL TRANSITION

Assume it's time for you to retire. How can it be accomplished with the least disruption? First, you need to recognize the advantages of a new identity. Next, you must recognize and accept the disadvantages and learn to adapt to them in a graceful manner. These two steps add up to the word "adjustment." Capitalize on the good things and minimize the bad. Instead of resenting where you are in the life cycle, learn how to enjoy it.

Eliminate Excess Baggage

Most individuals unknowingly clutter up their lives during their working years. They surround themselves with unnecessary possessions, with social and community commitments, and with worn-out human relationships. When retirement possibilities appear on the horizon, many of these individuals are motivated to simplify their lives. This shedding process is a major part of retirement planning.

Retirement offers the promise of an uncluttered, non-pressure existence, but achieving this freedom takes some serious planning and action. When you think about simplifying your retirement in advance, consider the following three "clutter areas."

Simplifying your life is more than disposing of excessive possessions and counterproductive associations and relationships. It is a major and early step in preparing for a more positive, less demanding lifestyle. Here are three tips that may help you in your own pre-retirement shedding process:

Tip #1: Start at least two years ahead of the time. It takes time to dispose of possessions without unnecessary loss. Winding up community commitments should be done gracefully. Closing out any relationship should be done in a sensitive manner.

Tip #2: Go through the process as a team. All phases of retirement planning should include both partners. If you are alone, involve a family member or an important friend. Two heads do a better job than one.

Tip #3: Enjoy the excitement involved. View the undertaking as if you were preparing a long-awaited trip around the world. You are, in fact, moving into a new lifestyle and you don't want to be burdened with too much baggage.

Those who succeed in simplifying their lives are fond of the phrase "simplify to beautify!" They claim that the big dividend from the shedding process is the freedom and opportunity to find more beauty in life.

What a great attitude to take into retirement!

Clutter Area #1: Unused and Unappreciated Possessions

Some otherwise sensible people become slaves to their possessions. They surround themselves with more goods than they need or have time to enjoy. Only when retirement plans get under way do these pack rats face the inevitable discarding process.

Clutter Area #2: Too Many Organizational Involvements

Some nice people, in their desire to do good and gain acceptance, overextend themselves in social and community activities. To some of these individuals retirement offers an excuse to break away from many of these commitments.

Clutter Area #3: Overly Demanding Relationships

It may sound harsh, but most people have a few relationships that have run their course and need to be eliminated. Some of these are job-related that can be easily terminated upon retirement; others are neighboring relationships; still others may come from social contacts at bridge clubs, country clubs, and so on. Although one does not normally want to eliminate a family relationship, it is sometimes wise to distance oneself from those who may be leaning on you too heavily. Retirement provides the ideal time for this kind of shedding.

When You Change Your Living Environment

The good news about moving to a new geographical location is that it forces you into a new lifestyle. This makes it easier for you to leave excess baggage behind. The bad news is that it might make your transition more traumatic. It is seldom easy for people to pull up roots, distance themselves from friends, and start retirement from a new environment. More on this follows in Chapter 21.

Learn to Use Your New Freedom Wisely

People often have trouble making a good transition to retirement because they fail to understand the dimensions of their new freedom. They have enjoyed so little freedom in the past because of responsibilities that they are often over-whelmed. Instead of taking advantage of freedom, they flounder because there is so much of it. A few are destroyed by it.

People are not taught how to use freedom wisely. Nobody tells you it must be tempered with self-discipline. To be enjoyed, freedom must be respected and channeled.

In making your transition, you will have more freedom than you have ever had before. You can get up early in the morning or sleep late. You have more options than ever before—an opportunity to cut loose, fulfill dreams, and do some of those crazy things you have always wanted to do.

Freedom is beautiful! It's also a trap. If you're not careful, freedom will swallow you like quicksand. It's important not to lose control. You make the most of free-dom only with self-discipline. It is not an open door to unlimited pleasure, but an opportunity to use time wisely.

Before you obtain freedom, you should think about it. How should it be used? What are your leisure priorities? Do you want to read more? Socialize more? How you use your time will determine the quality of your retirement life.

When you have completed this chapter, please turn to Appendix A and complete the IRA (Inventory of Retirement Activities).

Use Your Natural Talents

Your transition will be more successful when you make use of your talents and skills in new ways. It is through the utilization of your unique abilities that you find new roles.

A former school superintendent began his career as a zoology teacher. Following retirement, he brought his previous knowledge of animals back into play by starting a wild animal museum. Similarly, a former mathematics teacher now holds private art shows. A retired executive is using his mechanical skills to repair boats. You can probably find similar examples among your acquaintances.

Everyone has skills and talents that have not been fully used because of limited opportunity or too little leisure time. These talents can be dusted off and put to use in retirement roles that are both exciting and fulfilling. Those who do not wish to utilize old talents can always go back to school to develop new ones.

HOW CAN YOU TELL WHEN YOUR TRANSITION IS OVER?

When you begin to feel good about being a retiree, and when you have learned to capitalize on your advantages, you'll know you've made progress. When you look back at your career and are happy with where you are, you have made the transition. When you think less about retirement because you are too busy enjoying the day-to-day adventures of your new role, you have entered a new comfort zone.

PLANNING YOUR TRANSITION

A realistic retirement plan can influence how you age. It can determine your happiness factor once the step has been taken. A plan, however, does not have an automatic success warranty; it must be implemented carefully. Many retirees spend hours rehearsing their plans only to let them atrophy once the day arrives. In addition to designing a good plan, you must make it work. Here are some psychological phases most individuals experience as they approach retirement.

Phase I: Pre-retirement

Gentle but increasing anxiety occurs as you approach retirement. This anxiety can be healthy if it produces sound planning. The more planned changes the better, so long as you do not lose interest in your work role and become less productive.

Phase II: Retirement

Psychologists claim people are capable of showing improvement during crisis periods. In this respect, the transition to a new lifestyle can be considered something of a crisis period. This is the best time psychologically to make changes.

Although some significant positive changes can occur shortly before retirement (especially during the last few months), they are more likely to occur after retirement. For most retirees, the first year is critical. Some seem to extend the honeymoon period and make their major changes after the euphoria disappears. Eventually the impact of retirement will be realized.

Phase III: Post-retirement

Sadly, the longer you wait for retirement planning the less likely change will occur. The habits and behavioral patterns you establish soon after retirement often lock in and determine the quality of retirement living for the rest of the journey.

Making necessary changes close to your retirement day is usually easier than doing so a few years later. This does not mean that an 80-year-old is incapable of making positive behavioral improvements; it's simply less likely.

This points to the need for solid pre-retirement planning. Design a good retirement plan during Phase I and make it operational during Phase II. If you wait until Phase III, it may be too late.

A FIVE-STEP PLANNING MODEL

To get you started, here is a hypothetical timing schedule. If you are 50 or older, you need to condense the steps into a shorter span of time. Either way, they can act as a guide. It is never too late to design a retirement strategy.

- *Step 1: Early financial planning is best.* An ideal time to start serious financial planning for retirement is between the ages of 30 and 40. This means deciding which financial vehicles (investments, annuities, etc.) to select to supplement Social Security and employer-sponsored pensions. The sooner you start building your private retirement nest egg, the more it can grow while you are living out your full-time career. And don't forget, whether early or late, partners should always work as a team!

- *Step 2: Preliminary investigation can help motivate your present career.* Forty is not too early to start a research and development file on what you might want to do in retirement. What are your personal goals? Can you make retirement the most rewarding period of your life?

■ *Step 3: Some major decisions can be made in advance.* When you reach 50 (or before) it is time to start making your retirement goals a reality. For example, if you decide you want to retire in a home by a lake, this may be the time to buy the land. If you want to live in a protected community with a golf course, you can buy now, use it as a vacation home or rental, and make a permanent move later. This is also an excellent time to plan vacations with your retirement location in mind. Also, if you have not had a solid physical exercise program and a good diet, now is the time to act. You don't want to approach or enter retirement out of shape.

■ *Step 4: Review and implementation time.* When you get within a few years of retirement, it is time to bring your financial plan and dreams into sharper focus to see if they will accommodate your tentative retirement date. After adjustments have been made, you should develop the confidence to set a final date and move ahead. You will know whether to keep or sell the old homestead, how to shed unnecessary possessions, and so on. Getting ready for the kind of retirement you desire often means taking several steps ahead of time. You need to address questions such as whether one partner will retire first.

■ *Step 5: Finalizing.* Save the last year or two before retirement to wind things up. Fine-tune any plan you started earlier. Bring your financial program up to date. Make adjustments based upon economic, family, and other changes. Knowing you have a sound, updated blueprint to follow helps your attitude. It helps you get pleasure instead of pain from this final stage in the planning process.

All retirement plans, partial or completed, require frequent adjustment to compensate for change. But the evidence is strong that those who enter the preparation process with a good attitude have more successful retirements. They not only have a more open mind as they do their preparation, but they make better adjustments after the plan has been launched.

YOUR PLAN WILL BE DIFFERENT

If you have decided to design a retirement strategy (even if you actually entered retirement without one), how will it differ from others? What factors in your life will make your retirement more difficult? What factors will make it easier? How will these factors determine whether you will need to work part time? To help you answer these and other significant questions, you are invited to complete the following questionnaire. You are encouraged to make a photocopy so that your life partner can complete the list separately. Then compare results.

Pre-retirement Questionnaire

1. According to my best estimate, I will need to work full time until age _____ before I will be comfortable with my financial package.

2. I would like to work part-time after retirement to supplement my income.

   ☐ Yes   ☐ No

3. Getting our/my children through college and helping them get started in their careers is important before retirement.

   ☐ Yes   ☐ No

4. There is a mortgage we/I want to pay off before retirement.

   ☐ Yes   ☐ No

5. We/I have an aging parent or parents who will need either financial or personal help after retirement.

   ☐ Yes   ☐ No

6. We/I will enter retirement with a health problem.

   ☐ Yes   ☐ No

7. My life partner and I have some basic differences of opinion on what to do with our time after retirement.

   ☐ Yes   ☐ No

8. Other factors that may make our/ my retirement different from others.

   _____

   _____

   _____

   _____

Many factors are involved in developing a strategy. Your plan must be designed to fit your personal situation. As you plan your retirement, keep in mind these three common mistakes.

Planning Mistake #1

Viewing retirement the old-fashioned way. Years ago, when people thought they would have less time after retirement, it was natural for retirees to plan for a single, continuous "rocking chair" existence. Today people often have time, energy, and financial means to design a second life. The modern retiree, with much greater opportunities and an attitude to match, says, "We expect to get much more out of retirement than our parents."

Planning Mistake #2

Refusing to take advantage of professional help. With more to gain from retirement, planning becomes more important. This is why more and more people are opening their minds to outside help. Today it is possible to attend seminars, engage a financial planner, utilize self-help books, and receive counseling assistance. It is true that a few individuals are capable of doing their own retirement planning, but the majority can benefit greatly from professional help.

Planning Mistake #3

Allowing misconceptions and unwarranted fear to get in the way. Although not everyone will admit it, many people in their forties and fifties already have serious misgivings about retirement. The following comments reveal some of the fears:

- "Inflation will eat up most of my retirement nest egg before I get there."

- "Social Security will go broke before I draw my first check."

- "I'm afraid to look ahead. Things usually do not work out for me."

- "I have a mental block about retirement so I'm not going to think about it."

Obviously, one must develop a positive attitude toward retirement before a productive plan can emerge. Although it is impossible to predict the future, those with the courage to plan usually do far better than those who do not. Drifting into and through retirement, as some people do, is a road to disappointment and regret.

KEY POINTS

- The transition from a career to retirement can be difficult.
- The process is easier when you retire to something rather than from something.
- Planning lays the groundwork for a successful transition.
- Part of a successful transition is learning to use freedom.
- The three common mistakes in retirement planning are:

   1. Viewing retirement the way people did in the past.

   2. Refusing to take advantage of professional help.

   3. Allowing fears and misconceptions to get in the way.

- It is never too late to benefit from a retirement plan.
- The transition is complete when you have a comfortable identity and a rewarding lifestyle.

Things to Do

Instructions: In the space below, list the things you want to do as a result of reading this chapter. Then, choose a target date for completing each of your action items.

Action Item	Target Date

CHAPTER 4

BECOME A MASTER SENIOR

Whatever you are, as you get older you become more so.

—Betty Broach

This chapter defines the requirements to become a master senior and the benefits that accrue as a result of attaining that status.

An individual who has a purpose for living is more apt to maintain a positive attitude than someone without similar direction. Such a goal need not be an all-powerful, all-consuming mission that reaches for the stars. Modest goals are fully acceptable! All that is needed is a purpose sufficiently strong to provide a reason for getting up in the morning.

Unfortunately, some individuals move into retirement without sensing the need to find a new challenge to fit into their comfort zone. Some make the mistake of thinking that retirement is an idyllic period of leisure that will last forever. These people reject the phrase "retire and refire."

Many people are programmed to reach retirement, but nothing beyond. They look back to goals already accomplished, but not ahead to new ones. Master seniors accept responsibility for their life experience and make decisions that lead to their fulfillment and satisfaction. They're not mired down in the past but look forward to the future with eagerness and anticipation.

YOU NEED A CHALLENGE

A mission or purpose for living provides direction at any age. Even a small one can provide focus, dissipate much uncertainty, and make each day an upbeat experience. All of this is just as important after retirement as before, and is a necessity to become a master senior. Why is this true?

Without a work career to fall back on, retirement brings so much freedom that many do not know how to deal with it effectively. Without a purpose and a challenge, they are apt to drift, feel unimportant, and wind up negative and bitter. The message is clear. Few people can become master seniors without something to challenge them.

ATTITUDE IS IMPORTANT

Attitude is simply the way you view things. If you want to see the beautiful and humorous side of life, you can focus on these positive factors, and that is primarily what you'll see. If you want to see the unpleasant side, all you need do is let your mind dwell on the negative aspects. This is true all through life, but accentuating the positive is immeasurably more important as you approach retirement. To be negative then can be disastrous. Master seniors maintain a positive outlook.

You should not anticipate dramatic changes after retirement. Most people retain the same way of viewing the world they developed earlier. If you have a positive outlook on life, retirement should be easier for you. The pattern is already set. Naturally, there will be a challenge, but it will be easier for you than for a pessimistic person. This doesn't mean attitude is impossible to change. Sometimes people with a negative outlook earlier in life "come into their own" after retirement. They find a way to make up for things they didn't accomplish earlier. But it isn't easy. While the opportunity is present, it takes determination and self-discipline to change.

Measuring Your Own Attitude

What about you? Which route will you take? To measure your attitude toward retirement, complete the following assessment by circling the appropriate number. Circling number 10 means you believe the statement in the left column is completely true for you; circling number 1 means you believe the statement in the right column is completely true for you. If neither extreme fits, select the number that best fits you. When finished, total your score and write it in the box.

If you score 80 or higher, it appears that you can make the most of retirement. If you score between 50 and 80, you're less enthusiastic but should be able to create a rewarding retirement. If you rated yourself under 50, complete the assessment again after you complete this book.

Attitude Assessment

Retirement is going to be the most exciting part of my life.	10 9 8 7 6 5 4 3 2 1	People with physical problems should give up. Why fight an uphill battle?
There is an abundance of exciting opportunities after retirement.	10 9 8 7 6 5 4 3 2 1	I dread every hour in the future.
I want to stay in charge and be an active, involved retiree.	10 9 8 7 6 5 4 3 2 1	After retirement, everything is downhill. Opportunities disappear.
I will turn changes into opportunities.	10 9 8 7 6 5 4 3 2 1	I just want to withdraw from it all.
I intend to expand my sense of humor.	10 9 8 7 6 5 4 3 2 1	I am not up to coping with changes.
Retirees have advantages over others in our society.	10 9 8 7 6 5 4 3 2 1	What's humorous about getting old?
I can make new friends of all ages.	10 9 8 7 6 5 4 3 2 1	Retirees have no advantages; society is cruel to them.
Retirement is the best time of life to have fun and take new risks.	10 9 8 7 6 5 4 3 2 1	Nobody wants to know me. I'm obsolete.
Now I can use my creative talents and contribute.	10 9 8 7 6 5 4 3 2 1	This is the time to draw back.
It's possible to have a positive attitude even with a physical problem.	10 9 8 7 6 5 4 3 2 1	I have nothing left to give.

Total Score _____

Accept Responsibility

The moment you retire you must take responsibility for yourself. You must accept responsibility for your retirement lifestyle. You provide the direction for your new life. Face it! Nobody is standing by to take you to retirement heaven. Nobody can help you as much as you can help yourself.

Taking charge means facing decisions—not backing away from your problems nor relying on others, but staying in control. Master seniors choose to experience life under their own steam, holding their head high with style.

Hold on to Your Freedom

Most people looking at retirement say that more than anything else they want to maintain their freedom. For master seniors, staying free means staying in charge. It means keeping control of the money you have as long as possible. If you give your money away, you lose certain options that can help ensure freedom: the freedom to live where you want, how you want, and taking part in the activities of your choice. It means you should postpone, as long as possible, the time when others step in to help. If you are happy living where you are now, delay moving. Do not give your estate away until you are sure it is not required for your own happiness. Avoid handing problems and responsibilities to others if you can still deal with them. There may be circumstances that make it difficult to follow this strategy, but generally, the longer you stay in charge, the better. The longer you maintain your freedom, the happier you will be. Freedom and responsibility for yourself are significant influences on your attitude.

Keep Your Sense of Humor

The best way to make the most of almost anything, including retirement, is to maintain a sense of humor. The ability to see the funny side of things helps people over some rough spots. When your retirement arrives, you will need your sense of humor more, not less. If you have always been a teaser, keep it up. If you like jokes, keep telling them. If you have the ability to look at the light side when things go wrong, work to maintain this trait. Switch your positive attitude into high gear and protect your priceless sense of humor.

Attitude and humor have a symbiotic relationship. The more you develop your sense of humor, the more positive you will become. The more positive you become, the easier it is to maintain your sense of humor. It is a happy arrangement.

Whether you recognize it or not, your sense of humor is the guardian of your positive attitude. So give it tender loving care, both before and during retirement. As you do this, consider the following tips:

Tip #1: Recognize that humor is an inside job. One individual is not blessed with a potful of humor waiting to be served while another is left empty. A sense of humor can be created and practiced by anyone at any time of life.

Tip #2: View laughter as therapeutic. Just as negative emotions can produce ulcers, headaches, and high blood pressure, positive emotions such as laughter can relax nerves, improve digestion, and help blood circulation.

Tip #3: Admit that a sense of humor can sometimes get you out of the problem and into a solution. Simply finding the humor in a situation won't solve a problem, but it can help to lead you in the right direction.

Your attitude and sense of humor are priceless possessions. Don't plan your retirement without them!

STAY IN CHARGE

As you prepare for a new stage of life, you might have a natural tendency toward withdrawing from the reality of your environment. Retirement has always had an escape connotation. People have been conditioned to expect their later years to be free of hassles. They anticipate a quiet, peaceful, wind-down period. Many dream about the day they leave the rat race behind.

Yet, the further from reality people get, the sooner they become dependent on others. So they have a problem. On one hand they want the relaxed environment anticipated. On the other, they want to stay independent and free. A real dilemma!

If you don't stay in charge by maintaining your health, protecting your living environment, and managing your money, you will be enveloped in a retirement marshmallow where everything at first seems soft and delightful but later turns out to be sticky and uncomfortable. You can lose your flexibility and find yourself in a state of semi-depression. Instead of being part of the parade, you will no longer have an identity. Retirement may mean leaving work behind, but it does not mean leaving reality behind. Retirement should be an opportunity to replace a work-oriented lifestyle with a new, equally or even more exciting lifestyle.

LIVE WITH STYLE

Living with style means living with some flair. It means doing unusual and unexpected things. It is staying involved, speaking up, and proudly defying the norm. Style means communicating a lively, positive image to others. It means looking and acting the part of a confident, involved person. People with style are noticed.

Style is an individual matter. You don't copy a style; you create your own. If you want to break out of your previous routine and be outlandish, do it. If you want to withdraw for a while to lead a quiet, creative life with fewer outside contacts, do so. Whatever direction you take, do it with conviction.

You may even decide to be anachronistic. An anachronistic person is one who can maintain values and style from an earlier period, but survives successfully in today's world. If you believe in certain standards that no longer seem to fit younger generations, keep them—but not to the extent of being distant and negative. Defend your values but participate. Anachronistic people may hold onto parts of the past, but they never let others put them on a shelf. They have a style that may shake others up but one that earns respect.

As you approach and enter retirement, you should resist pressures that push you into a form of rocking-chair conformity. You should march to your own drummer more than you did in the previous phase of your life, not less. Now that you are no longer constrained by the norms, policies, and expectations of your employer, you are finally free to be yourself.

There are newly retired people who contribute to the image of the passive, discarded, negative retiree. Upon retirement these folks become grouchy, defensive, unchanging, and unhappy. They often look bored, act bored, and are bored. They permit themselves to be pushed into old-fashioned retirement patterns because they refuse to seek new opportunities. They refuse to join the more dynamic retirees.

JOIN THE PARADE

A new generation of retirees is emerging. They are defying the traditional images so frequently portrayed. They refuse to accept the old stereotypes. They are creating new, more active lifestyles. Instead of sitting back and watching things happen, they make things happen. Instead of accepting the traditional roles that await them, they create new ones. Some of this is happening because medical advances help extend the active years. More, however, comes from the fact that they see themselves differently than previous generations did. As a result, they are more individualistic and diversified. They are creating a new kind of retiree—one who is proactive rather than reactive. Are you a committed environmentalist? Do you want to devote your time to advancing religion? Do you dream of traveling to exotic places? All of these are possibilities for today's retirees.

Today, for the first time, you see conservative retirees who still have traditional values but live with a modern, upbeat style. They kick up their heels more. They spend money with more abandon. This may not fit the mold their adult children anticipated, but these new retirees know they are not being ignored or taken for granted. You hear them say, "If other generations have the freedom to be different, so do we. We can design a new, more exciting lifestyle."

Most would agree that whatever the financial circumstances or state of health, simply surviving is not enough. Nobody wants to drag through retirement. If the hours sacrificed to achieve this stage of life are to be worthwhile, they must be lived with vigor, humor, and style.

The Image Connection

If you have a good feeling of self worth, you probably enjoy who you are—the way you look, talk, and act. You like to be unique. You have a good identity.

Image is how others view you. Do others think you have style? The image you transmit determines the quality of relationships you have. You cannot ignore your image. It is more important to you now than ever before. The way others perceive you determines the way they interact with you. This includes everyone you come in contact with—doctors, lawyers, neighbors, friends, and family.

As important as it is to look good to others, it is far more important to look good to yourself. Why? Because when you maintain a good self image, you have a more positive attitude.

The connection between having a good self-image and positive attitude cannot be ignored. Having a poor self image is like looking through a glass darkly. When you don't look good to yourself, nothing else looks as good to you as it could. In short, your negative attitude shows.

Here are three tips that may help you improve your self-image:

*Tip #1: **Play your mature-appearance winners!*** For example, if you have attractive white hair, make the most of it; if you look better in one color than another, play it up in the garments you purchase; if you are male, bald, and don't want a toupee, go with a hat that matches your personality, or buff your skull and go sans hat.

*Tip #2: **Look as healthy as possible.*** Follow an exercise program; avoid stooping; walk with as much spring in your step as possible; watch your weight and diet and make the most of your mature figure.

*Tip #3: **Enhance your image in your own way.*** Jazz yourself up from where you are. Have the same courage to be different at your present age as you had earlier—or do even more than you did before.

Don't forget: You are not doing all of this just to draw the attention of others. You are doing it to maintain a priceless possession—your positive attitude!

Image and the Aging Process

There's nothing wrong with trying to look younger than you are. Many mature adults work to look like young adults. The younger you look to yourself (identity) and to others (image), the better; but don't overdo it. You may try so hard to look younger that you subconsciously reject the phase of life you have reached in other ways—emotionally, physically, and psychologically. When we talk about image, we are talking about appearance, not lifestyle. You can be retired, accept a new lifestyle, and still look like a mature adult. Looking younger chronologically is worth the effort, but rejecting a phase of life that is better for you may create conflicts that you are better off without.

Stay in the Game

The better you look to yourself and others, the more involved you will probably be in activities. But some retirees, at the point in life where they have some excellent cards to play, tend to quit the game. Instead of hanging in and creating a new lifestyle, they take retirement literally and fall back too far.

You may want to enjoy a slower, less hectic pace, but don't let down and lose your spirit. If this happens, the last phase of life escapes without providing the rewards you have earned.

The Difference Is Pride

Those with style are proud of their age. They are active and can communicate. They appear proud to be involved with life. Beautiful, and that's the way it should be. What is the source of this pride? Why do only a select few possess it? What about those who don't transmit this sense of dignity? Most look worn down, defeated, or disinterested. The most significant difference is that those with greatest personal pride seem to have set standards for themselves. They apparently are living up to some self-imposed expectations.

WHAT IS A MASTER SENIOR?

Every phase of life should have special goals, and this includes retirement. It is a serious mistake to retire without certain self-imposed standards. Many lose pride because they don't have serious goal replacements. Their sole aim is to let down, which in itself does not provide the motivation that converts to pride. They don't know how to measure themselves as retirees, and thus many deteriorate. Assuming this is true, consider the following standards for becoming a master senior.

Master Senior Standards

Indicate whether you agree with the following standards. Write any changes you want to make under Comments in the left margin. Keep in mind you are establishing standards that you wish to reach yourself. You need not reach all standards to earn the title Master Senior; it is simply something personal between you and what you hope to make of your retirement years.

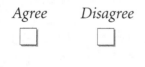

Agree   *Disagree*

Comments:

_____

_____

_____

_____

Standard 1: To become a Master Senior, you should strive to go as far as possible with the early phases of retirement and make the most of each stage. In doing this, endeavor to compensate for any physical loss through greater determination and mental effort.

Those who drift through the early stages of retirement putting off until tomorrow the things they hope to enjoy do not meet this standard.

Agree   *Disagree*

☐   ☐

Comments:

_____

_____

_____

_____

Standard 2: To be called a Master Senior, you must live with style. In this case, style means an individual has retained visible personal pride, maintained personal dignity, and been involved in some form of social or group activity.

Those who permit themselves to fall into a careless attitude in which they become inactive or unkempt do not meet this standard.

Agree   *Disagree*

☐   ☐

Comments:

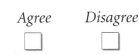

_____

_____

_____

Standard 3: This standard requires that some positive contribution be made to the lives of others on a regular basis. Some people call this paying your human dues. Others simply say it's being a good person. These individuals make a special effort to bring happiness to others each day. They often demonstrate their compassion by visiting those confined or making telephone calls that bring cheer to others.

Retirees who live only for themselves do not meet this humanistic standard.

Agree   *Disagree*

☐   ☐

Comments:

_____

_____

_____

_____

Standard 4: This standard demands a sense of humor—an ability to laugh at where you are, to see yourself in perspective. To qualify, individuals must consistently make a special effort to see the positive lighter side of life and communicate it to others. If you are considered good company, you probably have met this standard. If known as a positive force, you qualify. If you consistently make others laugh, you're setting a standard.

Retirees who constantly complain and focus exclusively on the negative side of life do not meet this standard.

Agree   Disagree

☐   ☐

Comments:

_____

_____

_____

_____

Standard 5: To achieve this, you must continue learning. This can mean returning to school, attending educational forums, learning from cultural involvement, or practicing a self-improvement program at home. These folks read books, watch television programs of substance, and enjoy intellectual conversations. They constantly attempt to understand society and improve their minds.

Those who seek only personal entertainment and refuse to stretch their minds intellectually do not meet this standard.

Agree   Disagree

☐   ☐

Comments:

_____

_____

_____

_____

Standard 6: This person must have handled one or more setbacks gracefully and with strength. Retirement years are not always easy. Serious health problems are common. There is always the risk of losing a partner. There can be a major geographical relocation or an agonizing problem with children. Master Seniors handle such problems without dragging others down. They bounce back and earn their stripes by facing difficulties with style.

Those who permit such problems to destroy their spirit do not meet this standard.

Agree   Disagree

☐   ☐

Comments:

_____

_____

_____

_____

Standard 7: To be a Master Senior, you must maintain personal independence. This can mean going it alone under trying circumstances—handling financial matters and making decisions as long as reasonably possible. Circumstances vary, but those who put up a strong fight can qualify. Master Seniors stay in charge of their lives.

An individual who prematurely gives away his or her independence does not meet this standard.

Agree   *Disagree*

☐   ☐

Comments:

_____

_____

_____

_____

Standard 8: Those who create and maintain good human relationships meet this difficult qualification. They not only maintain their inner circles but also reach out to meet new people. Some of these new relationships are with younger people. If a human-relations problem occurs, they repair it.

Those who nurse hurts and slights to the point where they chase others away do not qualify.

Agree   *Disagree*

☐   ☐

Comments:

_____

_____

_____

_____

Standard 9: To become a Master Senior, you must make a major effort not only to maintain your best possible state of health, but also to resist complaining about aches and pains. This often means experiencing discomfort in silence without becoming negative. It means controlling diet, exercising, and avoiding excessive medication.

Those who do nothing to maintain good health, and who dwell excessively and needlessly on present health problems, do not meet this difficult standard.

Agree   *Disagree*

☐   ☐

Comments:

_____

_____

_____

_____

Standard 10: This standard requires you to remain a positive force within the community as long as possible. You must continue to have an impact on others through speaking up and taking action when appropriate. Others must sense your presence. In certain situations, it may mean becoming a matriarch or patriarch within a family circle. Master Seniors are strong personalities.

Those who lose their individuality and, as a result, permit themselves to be ignored do not meet this standard.

To demonstrate personal pride—and be admired by relatives, friends, and strangers—is to become a Master Senior. What a challenge! If you talk with those who have met the challenge and made the successful journey into retirement, you hear expressions such as these:

- "Looking back, I'm glad I set such demanding standards. The payoff has been worth the efforts involved."

- "It took discipline, but these have been years of creativity and accomplishment."

- "My retirement years have not always been easy, but the respect and recognition I earned have made it worthwhile."

- "You either fight to make retirement work or you give up. I'm proud I made mine work."

- "Nobody told me retirement would take so much self determination. Nobody told me it would be this rewarding either."

If you stay in charge and have some luck with your health, you can become a Master Senior. Friends and family may not use this term, but you will see the admiration and respect in their eyes. You will realize that you have met your retirement standards and that your life has been a success.

MASTER SENIOR CARD

You may want to carry the following message with you. It can be a reminder to live up to the Master Senior standards presented in this book. Good luck!

Master Senior Standards:

- Stay in charge.
- Live with style.
- Pursue activities with enthusiasm.
- Maintain health through exercise and diet.
- Continue to learn.
- Develop an inner-circle support system.
- Contribute to others.
- Keep a sense of humor.

KEY POINTS

- A new kind of retiree is emerging—more active, more involved, and with more style.
- A key to retirement happiness is your attitude.
- You have a choice. You can take charge, accept the challenge, and make the most of your opportunities, or you can coast through retirement and never know what you've missed.
- To make the most of retirement take your sense of humor with you.
- It may take time and effort, but by meeting certain self-imposed standards, you can earn the right to be called a Master Senior.
- Master Seniors make the most of retirement regardless of their special circumstances.

Things to Do

Instructions: In the space below, list the things you want to do as a result of reading this chapter. Then, choose a target date for completing each of your action items.

Action Item	Target Date

PART II

ACTIVE
LIVING
CHOICES

If you have not already done so, before reading this section, turn to Appendix A and complete the Inventory of Retirement Activities (IRA). When this has been accomplished and you have read the chapters in this section, you'll be able to compare your high, average, and low retirement interest activities; decide if Plan A (leisure), Plan B (leisure plus part-time work), Plan C (leisure plus a volunteer activity) or Plan D (full-time work) is best for you.

CHAPTER 5

PLAN A:
PURE LEISURE

A perpetual holiday is a good working definition of hell.

—**George Bernard Shaw**

Leisure! To lounge and spend time in idleness…to slow the pace…to throw off responsibilities…to relax…to play. These are the rewards of retirement—the big payoff for working all those years.

Pure leisure (Plan A) is keeping all your retirement hours for yourself. It is refusing to work for money, run your own business, or accept a time-consuming volunteer job. It is tending to the business of living quickly (household chores, shopping, and the like) and then devoting the rest of your time to planned leisure activities. It is being free of entanglements with organizations.

No guilt feelings, please.

Some retirees react to total leisure as a selfish way to live—self-gratification without concern or compassion for others. Not so. You can adopt Plan A as your retirement lifestyle and still make contributions to the lives of others on a personal, one-on-one basis. You can continue to pay your human and social dues. Plan A just means that you refuse to have organizational connections that require responsibilities. Participate in church life, but refuse to assume a leadership role. Be a member of a fraternal organization, but refuse to accept an office. Enjoy country-club life, but back away when it comes to being on a committee. You have reached a stage in life where it is time for others to carry organizational responsibilities. You paid your dues. You carried the load long enough. It is time to enjoy.

It all sounds idyllic—the way retirement should be. But don't expect it to be easy; few people can pull it off. Many want Plan A, but eventually settle for B or C. A Duke University Center on Aging study revealed that more than half of 200 men (52 percent) said they got more satisfaction from work than leisure. And 55 percent of 200 women surveyed said they enjoyed working more than free time.

Can you make pure leisure work? Can you take full advantage of the opportunity? Can you use your retirement freedom without becoming so involved in a creative pursuit that it either turns into a business or becomes an obsession? Some signals will come from your activity profile (Appendix A, "Inventory of Retirement Activities"). If you scored low in both working (15) and volunteer work (16) and your leisure activities were high, Plan A may be your best bet. Give Plan A careful consideration. Also complete the Preference Scale in this chapter. After doing this you should have considerable insight into what is best for you.

If you scored above 80 on the Preference Scale, you have an excellent chance of making pure leisure work successfully. If you scored between 80 and 60, you may need a job of some type (Plans B, C, or D). Additional signals on this become available after you complete scales in the following chapters.

LEARNING NOT TO WORK

Many retirees have the work ethic so ingrained that no matter how hard they try, they cannot escape it. Work is what life is all about. Many may dream of a life of leisure—they have earned it and have all the money they need—but pure leisure provides too much time. Without work they feel frustrated.

Can people successfully learn not to work? What kind of retiree can wrap the work ethic into a neat package and leave it behind forever? Such individuals normally have one or more of the following characteristics:

■ They have exhausted their capacity to work. They have been at it so long and so hard that there is no motivation left. Work has become repulsive. The farther it is behind them, the better. Usually these people never liked the work they chose.

■ People claim they no longer need a feeling of accomplishment. They have fulfilled career and money goals. Except for a few humanistic desires, entertaining themselves is what retirement is about.

■ Some insist a life of leisure does not provide guilt feelings. In fact, Plan A gives them a feeling of pride and satisfaction.

LEISURE IS NOT INACTIVITY

The first thing successful Plan A people recognize is that leisure does not mean inactivity. Leisure is not idleness, although some time is set aside for total relaxation and meditation. Leisure, in a practical sense, is being able to choose among a variety of pleasures, such as those enjoyable, exciting activities in Appendix A's Inventory of Retirement Activities.

Plan A retirees have the unique capacity to substitute leisure activities for work activities. Don't think they turn golf, reading, creative efforts, or other activities into work. They don't. What they do is schedule their pleasures in such a way that these continue to remain challenging and pleasurable. When an activity begins to feel like work (pressures are mounting), it is discarded and another takes its place. There is always an activity they want to spend time on—one that will challenge their minds and keep them involved.

Kinds of Leisure Activities

Here are some ideas for various leisurely pursuits.

Hobbies: Hobbies result in an output of which you can be proud. This includes crafts, artistic endeavors, and collections. Hobbies are excellent alternatives to work, for a portion of your time. Through a hobby you can find meaningful use of your time, identity in what you do, and satisfaction of psychological needs such as achievement.

Social Activities: Social activities provide a means for satisfying your need for contact with others. The range of activities is very broad. It covers such things as card playing, dancing, participating in social clubs, and entertaining guests.

Travel: Traveling involves more than the trip itself. Planning the adventure and sharing your experiences with family and friends when you return are part of the total experience. Exploring other places and cultures gives you a new perspective on your life. And, you return home with memories that last long after the trip is over.

Pure Leisure Preference Scale

This scale is designed to help you discover how you might cope with a pure leisure lifestyle. Circle the number that indicates where you fall on the scale from 1 to 10. After you finish, total your score in the space provided.

I am worked out. When I retire I never want a job of any kind.	10 9 8 7 6 5 4 3 2 1	I admit I have the work ethic. I will always need to work a little.
After retirement I'll have all the money I'll need to live a life of leisure.	10 9 8 7 6 5 4 3 2 1	It will be necessary for me to work part-time to supplement my income.
I will never be a volunteer.	10 9 8 7 6 5 4 3 2 1	I look forward to volunteer activities.
I can organize my leisure time completely. Time will not be a problem.	10 9 8 7 6 5 4 3 2 1	I cannot plan or discipline myself. Too much time is my greatest worry.
It won't bother me to spend my life pleasing myself. I've earned it.	10 9 8 7 6 5 4 3 2 1	I'll never be happy in retirement without doing something in an organized way for others.
My psychological makeup is such that I can relax for days without any pressure from myself.	10 9 8 7 6 5 4 3 2 1	Two days of relaxation and I am climbing the walls.
I enjoy sports both as a participant and as an observer. This uses a lot of my time.	10 9 8 7 6 5 4 3 2 1	I've never been much on sports. It's too late to get involved now.

I would like to spend at least half of my leisure time traveling. I have the money to do it.	10 9 8 7 6 5 4 3 2 1	I'm a homebody. I've seen all of the world I want to see. Besides, I don't have the money.
I can think of several leisure activities that I will enjoy.	10 9 8 7 6 5 4 3 2 1	I can't think of any leisure activity I would enjoy.
I'm positive about my ability to cope with the leisure life.	10 9 8 7 6 5 4 3 2 1	I'm negative about making leisure work.

Total Score _____

Sports: Sports help keep you fit and at the same time add pleasure to your life. They bring you in contact with people who share a common interest and add the excitement of competition. Sports also provide a framework for achievement. Whether you are preparing to participate in the Senior Olympics or just enjoying a round of golf with friends, some sports activities should be included in your retirement plans.

Education: Retirement gives you the chance to look to the world of education with a fresh perspective. You may explore anything you want, at your own pace, for no other reason than your interest in it. You don't have to earn a degree unless you want to. You don't even have to take tests unless you want credit for the class.

Entertainment: This includes at-home activities like reading and watching TV. It also includes going to the movies and attending cultural and sporting events. With retirement comes the flexibility to enjoy many of the things offered in your community. Also, you may be interested in attending events in neighboring towns that you were unable to attend while working.

Go for Variety

Some experts maintain that the broader one's leisure activities, the more chance that Plan A will work. In other words, if you have a variety of activities, you spice up your lifestyle and keep from becoming bored. Here are some thoughts:

- Switch from physical activities (running, golf, tennis, walking) to mental activities (bridge, reading) and back.

- Move from an activity where you are happy alone (working on a craft) to a social activity (dancing, bingo).

- Have something new on the back burner, an activity you wanted to try when you had time.

Coming Up with the Right Activity Mix

Each person must design a personal activity mix. Experimentation will probably be necessary, and the right balance may not surface immediately. Some make Plan A work with three or four activities; others need more. Some can spend a majority of their time on one activity (travel), but others can't. It boils down to interests and aptitudes. One naturally spends more time on high-interest activities. As interests change, so should activities. Keeping the right mix so the mind is challenged is the key to success. Only a few people do it convincingly.

QUALITY LEVELS OF LEISURE ACTIVITIES

Some retirees claim a pure leisure lifestyle works for them when it really doesn't. The quality of their leisure is such that a great deal is left to be desired. They occupy time but their personal satisfaction is low. They are bored with certain activities. They seem to have excessive down periods. Some would be much happier with Plan B or Plan C, but they don't seem to realize it.

What is a satisfactory quality level? How do you know when the level is sufficiently high to make a leisure lifestyle effective? Here are some ideas:

Signal 1: Your leisure activities keep your mind challenged and you want to spend more time on them rather than less.

Signal 2: You receive satisfactory rewards from activities. They make you feel good. Competitive people often have good luck making Plan A work because they often win at the games they play—tennis, golf, bridge. Winning can be stimulating.

Signal 3: You keep in contact with the kind of people you enjoy. Good communication takes place. Your social contacts make you feel good about yourself.

Signal 4: Your creative nature is satisfied. You feel achievement even if you don't share what you do with others.

Signal 5: Your activity mix provides you with a sense of exuberance and richness.

KEEP YOUR OPTIONS OPEN

You may know people who have been successful in a quality leisure retirement. Talk to them about how and why it worked. Learn from their experiences. The more research you do, the more you will learn that Plan A is usually the most difficult. Very few can retire to pure leisure with style. Many try it, but few make it work. Those who do have a right to be proud. Before you can make your decision, consider the three alternate plans—B, C, and D. Follow these basic rules:

Rule 1: Keep an open mind. If preconceived ideas dominate, you may wind up with the wrong plan and get less from your retirement than is possible. For example, you don't abandon leisure activities if you accept Plan B or Plan C.

Rule 2: Be true to your desires. For most of us, retirement is the last chance to fulfill dreams. You have lived long enough to know yourself, so be honest. Remorse can occur when you look back and realize you spent your available time the wrong way.

Rule 3: If appropriate, work out a plan that will be best for you and your life partner. An open discussion of all four options is the way to accomplish this. It is possible for one partner to employ Plan A and the other to employ Plan B, C, or D. To succeed requires discussion ahead of time, and each person must have enough space in which to operate.

Guidelines for Meaningful Use of Time in Retirement

1. Allow leisure activities to add balance to your life. (You may have to alter your thinking about the value of leisure.)

2. Select activities that provide you with status, recognition, fellowship, accomplishment, and a sense of self worth.

3. Include a variety of activities. Few people can engage in even the most absorbing activity all day, every day.

4. Plan some activities you can do alone and some you can do with others. Everyone needs private time as well as social contact.

5. Commit yourself to an activity. Experts say it helps deepen your commitment to disclose your plans to others.

6. Make sure some of your activities are demanding enough to provide a challenge.

7. Consider activities that offer an opportunity to contribute to others so you can make a difference in someone's life.

8. Don't overextend yourself. Make quality, not quantity, your goal.

9. Put some structure in your life to replace the structure of work. Have a daily routine but be flexible.

10. Consider the possibility of slowing down in later years and plan some activities you can continue to enjoy when age takes its toll. Again, variety is the key. Include some physical, some creative, and some intellectual activities.

KEY POINTS

- Plan A is pure leisure. Except for routine living tasks, no work or organizational commitments are involved.

- Some retirees have a difficult time learning not to work.

- Leisure is not inactivity. It includes a variety of hobbies, travel, sports, educational entertainment, and social activities.

- Some retirees try a pure leisure lifestyle and move on to part-time work or volunteer activities.

- Those who can make a pure leisure lifestyle work at a high level have accomplished a great deal.

Things to Do

Instructions: In the space below, list the things you want to do as a result of reading this chapter. Then, choose a target date for completing each of your action items.

Action Item	Target Date

CHAPTER 6

PLAN B: LEISURE PLUS PART-TIME WORK

Think young, keep a positive point of view, stay active, enjoy your life, and never, never retire.

—Jerry Lewis

Work, to many retirees, is a good four-letter word. To some, work is the most meaningful part of retirement. To others, work is more satisfying than recreational activities. Because of these factors, many individuals work far into their retirement years.

ACHIEVING A SUITABLE BLEND

Plan B, when successful, is a special balance of leisure and work that fits the style of an individual. It is a compromise between working full time and a life of leisure. For most who choose this option, it means working 15 to 20 hours a week. If you approach 40 hours per week, you're moving into Plan D. You must design your own plan. When the proper balance is found, both work and leisure may be enhanced.

What is your situation? Would retirement be better for you under Plan B? Can you design a balance that improves your leisure hours? Is it important that you supplement your income to achieve the best possible retirement?

If you gave working a high rating (above 20) in the IRA profile (Appendix A, "Inventory of Retirement Activities"), you have a strong signal that Plan B might be the direction to take. You will know even more about yourself and Plan B if you complete the following Work-Leisure Preference Scale. If you score above 70 on the scale, it may be an indication that a blend of part-time work and leisure is for you. If so, this chapter can help. If you score below 60, you should explore Plans A and C more carefully.

It is not always easy to make Plan B work at a quality level. Some retirees, especially those who need additional income, can place so much emphasis on their job that leisure hours are neglected. Instead of using the extra dollars to create some excitement in their lives, they sit at home. They expect too much from their jobs. They say:

- "I'd be happier if I could work more hours."

- "My job is the only thing I look forward to."

- "By the time I work 20 hours a week and take care of my daily chores, there isn't time left for fun."

These people are not working to improve their leisure hours; they are working to use up time. They apparently don't realize that if they take charge of both work and leisure, retirement can be more exciting. Neither work nor leisure will do the trick; it is the combination.

WORK REWARDS

Why do so many retirees work part-time? What are the rewards that cause them to give up much of the leisure time they worked so hard to get in the first place? Below are 10 rewards. Check the box if you want that reward. The more boxes you check, the more satisfaction you would receive from Plan B.

☐ *Reward 1*   **Additional money.** Earning more money is often necessary to maintain or improve your standard of living.

☐ *Reward 2*   **Insurance benefits.** Having an employer pay for medical and other benefits and contribute to Social Security can be a compelling reason to stay on a payroll after retirement.

☐ *Reward 3* **Ego satisfaction.** Having a job, even at a lower organizational level than the one you held before retiring, can help your self image.

☐ *Reward 4* **Scheduled activity.** A job helps structure your day. You don't have to plan how to spend all of your time.

☐ *Reward 5* **More appreciation for leisure hours.** Working helps make leisure hours more important, fun, and exciting.

☐ *Reward 6* **Eliminated down periods.** Too much leisure can cause depression. A job helps you keep better control of your positive attitude.

☐ *Reward 7* **Better home life.** You appreciate home more when you are not there so much. Working provides more freedom for your life partner.

☐ *Reward 8* **People contacts.** A job helps you communicate with others, both at work and after work.

☐ *Reward 9* **Feeling of purpose.** Working is an excellent way to make a contribution to society. You feel you are paying your own way.

☐ *Reward 10* **Therapeutic.** A job involving activity keeps you in better shape mentally and physically.

Working should not be something to simply fill time. It should provide both tangible and psychological rewards.

Work-Leisure Preference Scale

This scale is designed to help you discover if you would be happier after retirement with a part-time job. You should gain additional insights by comparing this scale's score with that of the Pure Leisure Preference Scale in Chapter 5. Circle the number that best describes your situation and total your score in the space provided.

The work ethic is in my bones and I admit it. I hope a part-time job will satisfy this need.	10 9 8 7 6 5 4 3 2 1	I've squeezed the work ethic out of my system.
I need to have a feeling of accomplishment each day; only a job will do.	10 9 8 7 6 5 4 3 2 1	I can get a better feeling of accomplishment through a hobby, craft, or other activity.
Working for money is necessary to my ego; I need the recognition.	10 9 8 7 6 5 4 3 2 1	I can satisfy my ego in other ways.
I've got to have a job to wake up to; I can't fill my days on my own.	10 9 8 7 6 5 4 3 2 1	I love to sleep late and then enjoy leisure activities.
Work keeps me in the mainstream and in contact with younger people.	10 9 8 7 6 5 4 3 2 1	I can keep in touch with others without a job.
Work will keep my mind active. I can't do it on my own.	10 9 8 7 6 5 4 3 2 1	There are many things other than work that will keep my mind active.
I need the money or I need the good feeling that earning money gives me.	10 9 8 7 6 5 4 3 2 1	I'm tired of working for money. I don't even want to think about it.

Working part-time will help me enjoy my leisure far more. It's the combination I like.	10 9 8 7 6 5 4 3 2 1	Having to work for money would spoil my leisure time.
Work is pleasure for me— as long as I get paid for it.	10 9 8 7 6 5 4 3 2 1	I would get more pleasure out of leisure activities or a volunteer job.
Work is therapeutic; it will keep me alive longer.	10 9 8 7 6 5 4 3 2 1	Work tears me down, makes me a nervous wreck. I can't handle it.

Total Score _____

FINDING THE RIGHT PART-TIME OPPORTUNITY

Retirees have experience, knowledge, and skills that society needs. They constitute a giant reservoir of ability and talent. But finding the right part-time job is not always easy. It is estimated that for every two retirees who work part-time, at least one more person would like to work. With Plan B, you have some choices. For example, you can continue to use skills you already possess or learn to do something fresh and different. Here are some ideas to consider.

Service jobs help people. During the first decade of the twenty-first century, the U.S. economy is projected to added about 22.2 million new jobs. About half of these will be in service occupations. If other areas do not appeal, why not give service careful consideration? You might enjoy the contact with people, and your hours could fit into your free time schedule. Here are some areas to consider:

Health Services: Improved medical technology, coupled with an aging population, will cause this sector to add the greatest number of new jobs. Health care has traditionally provided part-time employment and flexible scheduling. The number of jobs is expected to grow 33 percent by 2010.

Business Services: Advances in technology and a continuing trend toward office and factory automation will fuel a healthy demand for workers in this area. Companies that supply workers to other firms are expected to see the most dynamic growth. Jobs are projected to grow 42 percent by 2010.

Education: Adult education and corporate training will become major growth areas, opening up opportunities for self-employed workers seeking part-time, seasonal, or flexible schedules. Job opportunities for teachers' assistants are expected to increase 24 percent by 2010.

Personal Care and Services: Childcare, eldercare, and family services are expanding rapidly. The number of jobs in this area is expected to grow 56 percent by 2010.

Sales and Related Occupations: Retail stores and restaurants have traditionally provided part-time employment opportunities to workers of all ages. By 2010, jobs in this area are projected to increase 19 percent.

Independent service is for those who want to work for themselves. Here again, the opportunities are many. You can start a business, do fix-it work, babysit, garden, or many other jobs on your own terms. Not only do you protect your freedom, but the contact with people is also excellent. If you like this area best, you can probably come up with a number of additional possibilities.

Some retirees desire to work only in creative pursuits. They hope to turn hobbies into money-producing activities. Often these individuals refuse to consider other opportunities. It is creative work or nothing at all.

Seasonal work often makes sense for two reasons. First, seasonal jobs are easier to get. Second, it is possible to work full-time for a few months and then pursue leisure activities with more freedom. For example, many retirees work in department stores around Christmas or at resorts during the summer.

Don't overlook the opportunity to stay with your profession on a part-time basis. If you are happy with your work before retirement and want to continue on a less-demanding basis, you may be able to mix work with leisure at your own design.

As you explore part-time opportunities, keep your satisfaction in mind. Examples of people who have selected Plan B include a corporate president who grows and sells flowers, a wealthy farmer who leases his land so he can raise exotic birds, and a retired CPA who charters his boat for fishing expeditions. If you plan carefully, you should be able to find the type of job that best fits your situation.

CONSIDER WORKING AS A TEMPORARY

Working through a temporary-help agency can provide you with the flexibility you need to enjoy your leisure activities and, at the same time, supplement your income and keep you active in your chosen field.

The best way to find a good agency is to talk to people who have worked as temporaries. Ask which agencies they liked to work for and why. Also ask about the ones they didn't like and find out why. You can read the help-wanted ads to see which agencies are looking for workers. In addition, the yellow pages has a list of temporary-help agencies.

There are specialty agencies for doctors, lawyers, nurses, accountants, pharmacists, childcare workers, business management professionals, computer professionals, and writers. In fact, if you are a professional, there is probably a temporary agency that specializes in your field.

Going to work for a temporary-help agency requires you to go through a selection process similar to what you'd encounter at any organization. Be prepared with a well-written resume and call for an appointment. You will be evaluated during an interview and may be required to take a battery of tests. If you have the skills the agency needs, you can expect to begin receiving calls for placements.

Advantages of Temporary Work

Temporary work has several advantages over regular part-time employment. Here are a few of those most relevant to retirees:

Flexibility: You can manage your work schedule to fit your personal life. If you want a few days off you can have them without pay. This allows you to accommodate leisure interests such as travel and visits from the grandchildren.

Less Stress: As a temporary, you can walk away from the work at the end of the day. None of the worry goes home with you. You get paid for the time you put in and all the problems belong to someone else. You don't have to put up with abusive people. If the situation is undesirable, simply call the agency and ask to be reassigned.

Variety: Temporaries work in different organizations, under different conditions, and meet a lot of people. If you like variety in your work assignments, you'll find the jobs and different work environments offered by temporary work enticing.

Disadvantages of Temporary Work

Temporary work is not the answer for everyone. There are a couple of disadvantages that must be taken into account.

Onerous Tasks: Every profession has its mundane tasks that regular staff put off doing. Frequently, these are the jobs that temporaries are brought in to handle. You may find your day filled with boring, repetitive work that presents little challenge.

Lack of Benefits: You do not participate in the benefits of the companies using your services, and few agencies have developed fringe-benefit packages for their employees. Therefore, temporary workers must provide for their own vacations and insurance needs.

GETTING THE RIGHT JOB

In a way, doctors, lawyers, dentists, and other professionals are fortunate when it comes to Plan B. They can reduce their work hours and expand their leisure hours. No career change is necessary.

Some retirees, including professionals, can convert a lifelong hobby into a Plan B that makes money. Others study themselves, look around their communities, and establish low-overhead businesses that provide both involvement and money but do not interfere with their leisure hours. The possibilities are endless, but most retirees are not in a position to create their own jobs. To get a job, they must sell themselves to an employer. They must find a firm that sees the value of having them on the payroll.

KEY POINTS

- If not overdone, a part-time job can enhance retirement for some.
- Plan B provides certain psychological rewards that deserve careful consideration.
- To some, work is more satisfying than leisure activities.
- Despite experience, skill, and maturity, not all retirees find it easy to secure a suitable part-time job.

Confidence-Building Exercise

This exercise is designed to help you have the confidence to take the first step. On the left are possible disadvantages to the employment of those over 65 (many are myths). On the right are the advantages. Check both your disadvantages and advantages. Your advantages should build personal confidence and help you communicate why an employer would be smart to hire you.

Possible Disadvantages

(check only if you agree)

☐ Slightly less strength for heavy physical work.

☐ Slightly slower in physical movements.

☐ Slightly slower in learning new skills.

☐ More difficult to fit into pension and benefit plans.

☐ Some co-workers and customers may equate age with being out-of-date.

☐ Too late in life to be a long-term career employee.

☐ Not interested in full-time employment.

☐ Under certain situations might be less flexible.

☐ Older value differences might create conflicts with younger workers.

☐ More accident prone, thus more of a risk.

Total _____

Advantages

(check only if you agree)

☐ More dependable, thus a better absentee record.

☐ More responsible than younger employees.

☐ Better at following directions and rules.

☐ Will appreciate job more, thus stay longer.

☐ Socializes less on the job.

☐ More productive.

☐ Requires less supervision.

☐ Distracted less by outside interests.

☐ Better with human relations and customers.

☐ More accurate.

Total _____

When seeking employment, follow these rules: stay close to home; make an interview appointment by telephone; communicate your confidence; mention your advantages during the interview.

Things to Do

Instructions: In the space below, list the things you want to do as a result of reading this chapter. Then, choose a target date for completing each of your action items.

Action Item	Target Date

CHAPTER 7

PLAN C:
LEISURE PLUS
VOLUNTEER ACTIVITIES

Wherever a man turns, he can find someone who needs him.
Even if it is a little thing, do something for which you get no pay
but the privilege of doing it. For remember, you don't live in a world
all your own. Your brothers are here, too.

—Albert Schweitzer

When you volunteer your services, you give more of yourself and you usually get back more. You interact with other dedicated people and involve yourself in worthwhile causes. Fellowship can add new dimension to your life, and your leisure hours can be enhanced.

Volunteerism is a big thing in the United States. It is estimated that more than one-third of all retired people do volunteer work, ranging from one hour per week up to a full-time commitment. Three out of four who do volunteer work are women. It is possible to provide your services free to several organizations. It is also possible to hold down a paying job and a volunteer position at the same time.

But volunteerism is not for everybody. Only certain people gain the true rewards it offers. Those most rewarded are usually people with a humanitarian attitude. They feel inadequate if they only satisfy their own desires. Pure leisure or working only for money is not satisfactory. They want to contribute something they feel is significant. They seek different retirement rewards.

If serving others appeals to you, you should give volunteerism a chance. A certain activity in your church, for example, might satisfy your needs better than pure leisure or a work-leisure combination.

The more you learn about those who donate their services, the more enthusiastic you will become. You hear a variety of positive comments:

- "My retirement didn't have meaning until I gave time and energy to a cause where I was committed."

- "Once you have led a full, beautiful life, you feel good about contributing to those less fortunate."

- "It's the time of life to deal with your special passions. Mine happens to be animals, so I donate my time to a pet shelter."

- "I'm putting good deeds instead of money into my bank."

- "All I gave my church before retirement was money; now I give some of myself."

You need to know yourself well to determine if volunteerism is right for you. If you rated yourself high in volunteer work (category 16 in the IRA exercise in Appendix A, "Inventory of Retirement Activities"), Plan C is a possibility for you. Know your personal values well if you seriously consider this choice. The following Volunteer-Leisure Preference Scale may help you in this respect.

Volunteer-Leisure Preference Scale

Many retirees find happiness through a combination of volunteer work and leisure. See if you fall in this category. Circle the appropriate number and total your score.

I recognize I can't handle leisure, but I don't want the pressure of working for money.	10 9 8 7 6 5 4 3 2 1	Volunteer work would provide as much pressure as real work to me— and no benefits.
I need a consuming mission in life; only volunteer work will provide this.	10 9 8 7 6 5 4 3 2 1	I do not need or want a big mission in life —just leave me alone.

I don't need money—just personal contacts for my mental health.	10 9 8 7 6 5 4 3 2 1	If I have to deal with group politics, I want to be paid for it.
I'm not the bridge-playing, country-club type; I've got to have a purpose to my life.	10 9 8 7 6 5 4 3 2 1	I want leisure, fun, and games, even if I have to make money to achieve it.
Volunteer work appeals to me—involvement without daily responsibility.	10 9 8 7 6 5 4 3 2 1	I'm just not the volunteer type and I know it.
I can't work for money, but if I don't do some volunteer work, I will climb the walls.	10 9 8 7 6 5 4 3 2 1	Volunteer work would cause me to climb the walls.
Organizational politics would not bother me.	10 9 8 7 6 5 4 3 2 1	I've had all the organizational politics I can handle.
Volunteer work is the only thing that will get me out of the house regularly.	10 9 8 7 6 5 4 3 2 1	My leisure activities will get me out of the house with ease.
Volunteer workers are the happiest of all.	10 9 8 7 6 5 4 3 2 1	Nothing I've seen convinces me volunteers are happy.
I don't want total leisure or a job. Volunteer work is my cup of tea.	10 9 8 7 6 5 4 3 2 1	I'm happy we have volunteer workers; I'm just not one of them and I know it.

Total Score _____

If you scored over 70, volunteer work may be part of your answer.

Reward Checklist

Below are 10 rewards that people receive from doing volunteer work. Check the ones that are important to you. The more squares you check, the more satisfaction you can expect to receive.

☐ *Reward 1*   Comradeship. Fellowship becomes increasingly important after retirement. When this need is combined with a worthy purpose shared by others, the rewards are multiplied.

☐ *Reward 2*   Recognition. When you are on a payroll, money itself can be the main form of recognition. In a volunteer position, recognition and ego satisfaction come from many directions. Certain groups, like a hospital auxiliary, carry considerable prestige.

☐ *Reward 3*   Freedom to withdraw. You are not tied to a volunteer role in the same way you are to a salaried job. You can come and go more easily.

☐ *Reward 4*   Sense of mission. Retirees who have a sense of mission are often the happiest of all. Giving time to something you believe in can be rewarding beyond expectations.

☐ *Reward 5*   Keeps mind active. A good volunteer activity is like a mental-health insurance policy. It keeps you alert and ready for other facets of your life.

☐ *Reward 6*   Beautiful substitute for work. In a sense volunteerism is work; but, if handled properly, pressures can be eliminated and enjoyment can be at a higher level. In short, you can get the values of paid work, including physical activity, but you don't have the pressure of satisfying an employer.

☐ *Reward 7*   Compatible people. In a paid job you work with employees or co-workers. In a volunteer activity you work with colleagues. The difference is significant.

☐ *Reward 8*　Chance to develop new skills. Volunteer work often provides opportunities to learn new things. This can strengthen personal confidence.

☐ *Reward 9*　Enhance leisure hours. The enthusiasm of meaningful volunteer work can spill into leisure hours.

☐ *Reward 10*　The give-back idea. Some retirees feel they have taken from society during their lives. They feel good when they are able to give something back.

SELECT VOLUNTEER ACTIVITIES WITH CARE

To make money, people sometimes select jobs that fall short of what they enjoy. A paycheck helps compensate for the effort. With no pay, a person should be careful. The key to the right volunteer activity is to know yourself and be honest with yourself. This means matching that which provides the most rewards for you with what is available in your community. If your rewards are right, you will probably stick with it. If the rewards are not right, you should leave. Your volunteer role should do something for the organization, but it also should do something for you.

If you are a religious person, you may want to contribute your services totally to your church. If you like to help people who are ill, and you would be comfortable in the atmosphere of a hospital or nursing home, look carefully at the opportunities in healthcare. If you love children and work well with them, you may want to make your contribution in the educational field. Cultural activities appeal to many, especially those who like activities with prestigious organizations. The opportunities are many.

Many national organizations accept volunteers. There are advantages to affiliation with these fine groups. Fellowship and prestige are usually present, and often there are some leadership opportunities. It is possible to start as a local volunteer and, in time, achieve a position on a national committee. Organizational membership and volunteer activities go together. If you join the right group, the organization will fill all the volunteer hours you want to give.

In selecting a volunteer position, consider all your interests, aptitudes, and desires. To discover new groups and learn more about available opportunities, contact your Senior Information Center or your local library.

HOW TO GET INVOLVED

To get involved in volunteer service, first decide the type of job you would like. This requires you to consider the wide variety of organizations and agencies that use volunteers. Then, you have to decide on the type of work you prefer. The opportunities fall into the following categories:

Client Contact: This type of work brings you in direct contact with the clients served by the organization. It often means daily contact with the down-and-out or the physically or mentally ill. This work is not for everyone, but those who enjoy doing it generally reap the greatest rewards.

Administrative Support: This involves the wide variety of office work required to keep an agency operating. This work is every bit as important as client contact work. If it were not done by volunteers, someone would have to be hired to do it, thus diverting money from the agency's primary mission.

Fund Raising: Perhaps you have a special talent that can help your favorite organization raise funds. This involvement usually occurs annually during a short time period, leaving you free to do other things during the remainder of the year.

Boards of Directors: Most charitable organizations have a board of directors made up of community leaders. This is an excellent way to put your professional or executive talents to work serving others.

Approach volunteer service with realistic expectations or you will be disappointed. Most nonprofit organizations get by on less. If you come from a business or corporate career, you may find many things missing that you took for granted. Adequate facilities, secretarial help, and equipment are often in short supply.

Organizations need volunteers that take their duties seriously, get the job done, and see that someone else fills in when they are unavailable. To get the most from volunteer service, your job must be as important to you as a paid position.

Volunteer with Confidence

It is estimated that for every two retirees who volunteer, an additional person has the desire but not the confidence to take the first step. If you are in the latter category, visit the organization directly after making a telephone appointment to learn more about opportunities to do volunteer work.

FITTING IN WITH PAID STAFF

As a volunteer, you have a special relationship with the people who are paid for their services. You are entitled to this status, but should not take advantage of it. The better you cooperate with others, the more rewards you will receive. The last thing you need is a volunteer job where there is a problem with paid staff.

Your sponsor or director, paid or not, is the key. This person is responsible for your contribution and should be the person you consult if problems arise.

You have a responsibility to get along well with paid employees. Always try to meet them at least halfway. Make an effort to know them and help them understand why you are a volunteer. If you make their job easier instead of more difficult, you will probably build a warm relationship. There are a few things, however, that you should not tolerate.

- If you are under the direction of an individual who devalues free work, take your services elsewhere. Volunteer work is not paid status and the difference must be clear. The fact that you work for free should bring sensitive treatment from others. Volunteerism should have dignity.

- If you are consistently assigned demeaning work that others avoid, you should talk to your sponsor. Because psychological rewards are the only pay you receive, they should not be withheld.

- Watch out for overloads. If you discover too much work is coming your way and pressures are mounting, discuss the situation with your sponsor. You did not volunteer for stress.

- If you discover, perhaps because your talents are exceptional, that you are resented by an employee, address the problem directly. Under no circumstances should you permit human-relations problems to build.

Take charge and protect your volunteer status. The moment you do not look forward to your volunteer activity is the moment to consider action. Your involvement should contribute to a better retirement, not detract from it.

KEY POINTS

- Volunteerism offers special rewards not found in paid jobs. When these rewards are not forthcoming, you should look elsewhere.
- Finding the right volunteer activity is as difficult as finding a good job.
- The right volunteer activity can and should contribute to a more enriching retirement.
- Sharing and caring benefit not only those served, but those serving as well.

Things to Do

Instructions: In the space below, list the things you want to do as a result of reading this chapter. Then, choose a target date for completing each of your action items.

Action Item	Target Date

CHAPTER 8

PLAN D:
FULL-TIME WORK

I go on working for the same reason a hen goes on laying eggs.

—H. L. Mencken

Retire to full-time work? Isn't that a contradiction in terms? Perhaps, but the fact is that many people retire from large organizations and seek other full-time employment. Their reasons for doing so vary. Some are forced to retire before they are ready. Others want to stay active and involved in work for financial reasons, emotional reasons, or both. Plan D meets these needs. Here are a few facts about working after retirement:

- Nearly 25 percent of retirees hold jobs—about half for financial reasons and the other half for emotional reasons.

- Of over 4,000 retiring executives, 49 percent became consultants or worked part-time, 13 percent took full-time jobs, and 12 percent went into business for themselves (according to a study by Drake Beam Moran, Inc.).

Some people shouldn't retire to a life of non-work activities. They are the ones who choose Plan D. You may be one of them. If so, you should view retirement as a time to work on your own terms rather than a time to stop working. This might mean doing something you've always wanted to do, such as starting your own business, teaching school, or moving to a favored part of the country and finding suitable work there.

If you gave work a high rating (above 20) on the IRA profile in Appendix A, you have a strong signal that Plan D may be the direction for you to take. You will know even more about yourself and Plan D after you complete the Full-Time Work Preference Scale. If you score high on the scale, this chapter can help.

It's essential that you spend enough time identifying your needs and interests and exploring the array of options open to you. While mistakes can be corrected, it's best to get started on the right track.

There are four options available:

- Employment with a typical for-profit organization.
- Employment with a nonprofit organization.
- Consulting.
- Going into business for yourself.

Look at each of these choices carefully. Then, consider the benefits and drawbacks of each before you make your final decision.

WORKING FOR SOMEONE ELSE

It is possible for those who are flexible and creative to find work after 50, but it is not an easy task. You may not be able to continue in your same line of work, but you have gained skills over the years that can be applied in a variety of settings. So, don't limit your search to duplicating the job you left. Look for new arenas where your skills can be put to good use.

Begin your quest with a careful analysis of what you have to offer a prospective employer and of what you consider an ideal position. Your task throughout your job search is to find where these two come closest together.

Few people are aware of the many job opportunities that match their individual skills and interests. Look for jobs that use your favored skills and present the types of problems your skills can help solve. Where would you like to work? What kind of organization do you prefer? Do you prefer to work alone or with others? These are the kinds of questions you need to answer as you attempt to match your skills and interests to employment opportunities. Finally, don't get caught up with status. If you are interested in keeping busy, making friends, and staying in contact with the public, a lower-level job might be right for you. Also, they're easier to find.

THE AGE DISCRIMINATION IN EMPLOYMENT ACT OF 1967

The act states that employers may not fail or refuse to hire, or discharge, or otherwise discriminate against any individual with respect to his compensation, terms, conditions, or privileges of employment because of such individual's age.

Full-Time Work Preference Scale

This scale is designed to help you discover if full-time work is appropriate for you in retirement. Circle the number that best describes your situation and total your score in the space provided.

I admit I have the work ethic. I'll always need to work to be happy.	10 9 8 7 6 5 4 3 2 1	I'm worked out. When I retire, I don't want a job of any kind.
I'm too young to retire.	10 9 8 7 6 5 4 3 2 1	I'm ready. Retirement is okay at any age.
I'll need to work to meet my post-retirement spending needs.	10 9 8 7 6 5 4 3 2 1	When I retire, I'll have enough money to meet my needs.
It's important to me to stay active and up-to-date in my field.	10 9 8 7 6 5 4 3 2 1	I feel I'm falling behind in my field. I'm no longer in touch.
I thrive on the recognition I get from doing my job.	10 9 8 7 6 5 4 3 2 1	I can meet my needs for recognition through other endeavors.
I have few friends outside my place of work.	10 9 8 7 6 5 4 3 2 1	I can make friends in different settings.

I need the structure in my life that comes from working.	10 9 8 7 6 5 4 3 2 1	I can manage my life without being tied to a work schedule.
My work defines who I am.	10 9 8 7 6 5 4 3 2 1	I am more than my work.
After a couple of days off, I'm ready to get back to the job.	10 9 8 7 6 5 4 3 2 1	I'm content when I'm away from the job.
I have little discipline in the use of my time. Too much time on my hands worries me.	10 9 8 7 6 5 4 3 2 1	I have no trouble planning my time. This won't be a problem.

Total Score _____

If you scored above 80, it may indicate that full-time work is the way for you to find fulfillment in retirement. If you scored below 60, explore the other three plans more carefully.

Attitude

If you think you're too old, you won't get the job. You will communicate your attitude and it will do you in. Recognize that most negative feelings about age are based on misconceptions of older workers. In reality, older workers can have more going for them than against them. When preparing for your job search, keep these real assets in mind—assets that more and more employers are finding attractive:

■ *Expertise:* Your expertise, gained over years of experience, far outweighs what younger candidates have to offer. As many recruiters are beginning to realize, academic study is not equivalent to on-the-job experience. Plus, you will not be concerned about promotions, and you can be a mentor to less-experienced staff.

- **Dependability:** You can be counted on. Older workers can be more dependable than their younger colleagues. They have better attendance records, take fewer sick days, and are more punctual.

- **Stability:** Older workers are less inclined than younger workers to leave the organization. For example, Days Inn reports that it loses about 40 percent of its reservation agents each year. The turnover rate for older agents is only 1 percent.

So, being past a certain age doesn't mean you're too old. It does mean, however, that you are experienced, dependable, and stable. In other words, you're a great job candidate!

Developing Leads

A Department of Labor study concluded that employees of all ages found jobs in these ways: 48 percent through leads from friends, relatives, and other colleagues; 24 percent through direct contact with employers; six percent from school placement centers; five percent from help-wanted ads; three percent from state employment offices; and 13 percent from a variety of other leads.

The majority of people over 50 find jobs by networking. Generally, it is a waste of time and money to mail resumes in response to newspaper ads. Here are some ideas on developing leads:

- **Talk to friends and colleagues.** Personal referrals are still the best way to land a job. Talk to anyone and everyone—friends, acquaintances, relatives, people you do business with. You never know who knows whom. When you talk with people, tell them you are looking for a job. Be specific about what you are looking for. People can't help you unless you give them enough information.

- **Maintain your memberships in professional associations.** This keeps you up-to-date on what's happening in your profession. In addition to talking to people you know, listen to conversations around you. You might overhear something worthwhile.

- **Draw on your contacts in organizations.** Hobby clubs, health clubs, church organizations, night school classes, and community organizations are good places to hear about job leads. Let your fellow members know of your interest.

▪ *Consider joining a self-help group.* Being around others in similar circumstances can provide support and motivation.

▪ *Use the services of Operation ABLE.* Operation ABLE provides assistance to older job hunters in Arkansas, California, Massachusetts, Michigan, Nebraska, New York, and Vermont. See them online at www.operationable.org.

▪ *Register with your state employment service.* These offices provide a clearinghouse for matching applicants and jobs. They also offer job skills training, job-search workshops, and individual job counseling. They tend to be more effective for those seeking middle- and lower-level opportunities.

▪ *Sign up with a private placement agency.* Private agencies are more effective with middle- and upper-level positions. Many agencies specialize in a specific profession or type of employment and therefore may be more familiar with opportunities in that segment of industry. Private agencies charge for their services. Be sure you know the full terms of your commitment before signing a contract. Some employers pay the agency fees, but you should not assume that your placement will be handled in this way.

▪ *Send out targeted sales letters.* Use a letter, rather than a resume, when you contact an organization directly. A well-written letter can get you an interview. Include only information that sells you. Outline the qualifications that make you right for a job at the organization and list your specific accomplishments.

Over 40?

For managers and professionals, membership in 40-Plus may be the best way back into the mainstream of your profession. 40-Plus is a private, nonprofit organization with 16 clubs in major cities. You must be 40 years or older to join and have an average income of $30,000 or more during the three prior years. AARP's Works program offers a series of job-hunting and career development workshops in 13 cities across the country. The Senior Career Planning and Placement Service specializes in finding jobs for retired executives. You can contact them at 257 Park Avenue South, New York City, NY 10010. These and other, similar organizations can be a tremendous help during your job search.

Interviewing Hints

You have three goals during an employment interview. First, you must determine if the available job is right for you. Second, if the job appears right, you must convince the interviewer that you are the person the organization needs. Third, you must determine if there is an opportunity to have a job created that will utilize your unique skills.

Remember, the interview is make or break time. It's up to you to prove that you are right for the job. The real key is believing in yourself. Here are some additional points that will contribute to your success:

■ *Maintain faith in yourself.* Even if you have experienced a number of unsuccessful interviews, continue to think of yourself as a winner. Review the high points of your life. Read uplifting books. Listen to motivational tapes. Interviewing is selling. Assertive, confident people sell best.

■ *Make a good impression.* People make judgments on what you appear to be. Your first impression is far more important than your credentials. The first five minutes set the tone for the rest of the interview. Be sure to look and act like a successful, polished professional.

■ *Do not apologize.* Older applicants frequently apologize for their age. This is a mistake. Start out positively and emphasize the advantages of hiring someone with your experience and expertise.

■ *Emphasize specific accomplishments.* Your experience is the greatest thing you have to offer. Bring up your accomplishments during the interview. Study a list of your achievements and be prepared to present detailed information on each.

■ *Don't overdo it.* The real skill of selling is to know when you have made the sale. All too often, sales are lost from overselling, rather than underselling. Don't dominate the interview or you may come across as overbearing. Present just enough information to close the deal.

■ *Delay giving your resume.* Hold off as long as you can. Sell the interviewer through conversation. Explain that you have the right background and the right combination of expertise for the job. After you have made the sale, hand over your resume.

CHARACTERISTICS THAT HELP AND HINDER APPLICANTS

Help	*Hinder*
Good first impression	Poor first impression
Confidence	Lack of confidence
Enthusiasm	Interruptive
Sincerity	Pushy attitude
Honesty	Evasiveness
Good communication skills	Talking too much
Pleasing personality	Arrogance
Applicable job skills	Lack of job skills

Based on a survey of 625 California business executives conducted in 1989 by Thomas Temporaries of Irvine, CA.

Consider Nonprofit Organizations

Retirees with less concern about financial rewards can find some very satisfying employment opportunities with nonprofit organizations. The varieties of opportunities are broad enough to accommodate just about any kind of experience.

Approximately 1.3 million charities, church organizations, foundations, schools, agricultural coops, quasigovernmental bodies plus arts, health, social service, and educational organizations operate on a nonprofit basis. They employ more than 20 million people and generate annual revenues of $750 billion. You can get a list of nonprofit organizations from your state commerce division or county clerk.

Tapping into the realm of nonprofits is as simple as deciding what cause you're motivated to support. Do you want to eliminate world hunger, provide homes for low-income families, help stamp out illiteracy, protect the environment, or feed the homeless? There is a place for you and your talents wherever your heart leads you. Generally, work opportunities can be divided into two major categories—direct involvement in the organization's mission and indirect involvement or administrative support. Pick your cause and your involvement. Then launch a job search to a truly fulfilling experience.

BECOME A CONSULTANT

A consultant provides technical or professional services to a client for a fee. As a consultant, you are free to work as much or as little as you wish. You work on a per-project basis, removed from the daily stress of a regular job. Meanwhile, you are able to continue using your skills. This makes consulting very appealing to retirees.

Many consultants get started by working for their former employer. They then expand their practice by adding other companies in their field—often companies that are suppliers or clients of their former employer. This is a logical extension of their background and an excellent way to use their experience.

If you are seriously considering consulting, make sure your capabilities are compatible with the requirements of the job. In addition to a marketable technical or professional skill, you need to be comfortable approaching people and selling yourself and your ideas. Not everyone is cut out to be a consultant. It requires a motivated self starter who is comfortable working alone.

RUN YOUR OWN BUSINESS

If you have dreamed of owning your own business, retirement can be the perfect opportunity to realize that dream. Your retirement income can provide a base of financial support to get you through the initial start-up and help you weather the inevitable ups and downs of a new venture. In addition to a financial base, you have both the time to invest and the experience of a lifetime to draw upon.

The business world is a demanding, unforgiving place. Being very good at what you do is essential to success. You have to be good to be a viable competitor. If you enjoy what you do so much that you would do it even if you do not have to, you can keep going when times get rough.

Working for yourself requires you to be organized and a self starter. It takes discipline to do what has to be done. You have to set schedules and stick to them.

Starting a business is risky. According to the Small Business Administration, three out of four businesses fail in their first year of operation, and nine out of 10 fail within 10 years. If you have an entrepreneurial spirit, you are willing to take this risk. Also, you have the drive and persistence to keep going when things get tough. You take charge of the situation and allow your creativity to overcome the obstacles. Above all, you believe in yourself and your ability to succeed.

Choices Available

There are more than 13 million businesses in the United States. The Small Business Administration classifies 97 percent as small businesses; 79 percent of these are home based. Many of these home-based businesses grow out of hobbies. Others grow out of special interests. The choices are limited only by your imagination.

You can start a business from scratch, buy an existing business, or team up with a franchiser. Each choice has pluses and minuses. You can get more personal satisfaction from starting and growing your own business from scratch, but your risk of failure will be greater because the business has no track record. There may not be enough of a market for another establishment of your type. Or, your product or service may not appeal to your potential clientele.

The most successful businesses fulfill special needs. Find a unique angle that gives your business an advantage; discover something different or a new twist to an old product or service. Think like a customer. Why would you, as a customer, want to buy your product or service, rather than patronize someone already in business? The answer may be your location, delivery, quality, hours of operation, customer service, product choices, price, or some other feature unique to your particular venture.

Sources of Help

The Small Business Administration has several ways to help you get started. A toll-free call to their answer desk—800-827-5722—gets information on how to develop a business plan, where to get training, and how to obtain financing, including Small Business Administration loans. They will send you a start-up kit containing a list of over 50 publications, planning guides, and other helpful information.

Small Business Development Centers are located in every state, generally as a part of a university or college. They offer management assistance, training, and counseling. The Service Corps of Retired Executives (SCORE) provides counseling and free advice, as well as workshops on how to start a business. SCORE will be listed in your local phone book, or your library can tell you how to contact them.

THE DOWNSIDE OF EARNING INCOME IN RETIREMENT

If you plan to earn income after retiring, you need to look carefully at the net effect of your earnings on your overall tax bill and plan your income to minimize any adverse effect. In addition to the graduated schedule of federal and state income taxes, consider the effect of earnings on Social Security benefits and the cost of self-employment tax.

Earned income may affect your eligibility for Social Security benefits. If you are at full retirement age or older, there is no earnings limitation. But, if you retire before reaching full retirement age, your benefits are reduced when your annual earned income exceeds the appropriate limit.

■ If you are age 62 but less than full retirement age, the earnings limit in 2005 was $12,000. The benefits reduction for those in this age group is $1.00 for each $2.00 earned in excess of the earnings limit.

■ If you attain full retirement age during the year, the earnings limit was $31,800 in 2005. The benefits reduction for this age group is $1.00 for each $3.00 earned in excess of the limit.

If you are self employed, you must also pay self-employment tax. This is the equivalent of F.I.C.A. withholding paid by you and your employer when you work for someone else. In 2005 this tax was calculated at 15.3 percent of net income up to $90,000 plus 2.9 percent of net income above that amount. When you calculate net profit, half of the tax is deducted as a business expense.

DECISION TIME

Before moving to the next section, think about which of the four plans would enrich your retirement years the most. It is a decision you can always change or modify. But, the sooner you feel committed to one plan, the sooner you will feel comfortable with retirement. To help in this decision, compare your scores on all four preference scales.

Score on Pure Leisure Preference Scale	Score on Leisure-Work Preference Scale	Score on Leisure-Volunteer Preference Scale	Score on Full-Time Work Preference Scale
———————	———————	———————	———————
Chapter 5	Chapter 6	Chapter 7	Chapter 8

KEY POINTS

■ Whether motivated by financial or emotional reasons, many retirees choose to work full-time in retirement.

■ Changing demographics and federal legislation have helped open up opportunities for older workers.

■ When seeking employment, be flexible and creative in your quest. Don't limit yourself by trying to duplicate the job from which you retired.

■ Consider the emotional rewards from working for a nonprofit organization.

■ Many retirees find satisfying post-retirement careers as consultants, drawing on the technical and professional skills developed prior to retiring.

■ Retirement can be the ideal time to realize a dream of going into business for yourself, although there are risks to consider.

■ There are costs associated with working in retirement. When the loss of Social Security benefits and the cost of taxes are taken into account, it may not be worth it.

Things to Do

Instructions: In the space below, list the things you want to do as a result of reading this chapter. Then, choose a target date for completing each of your action items.

Action Item	Target Date

PART III

WELLNESS

The number-one concern of retirees is health. When you complete this section, you'll be able to adjust your diet to achieve better health and implement a lifestyle that will reduce your risk of heart disease.

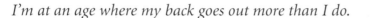

CHAPTER 9

HEALTH AND AGING

I'm at an age where my back goes out more than I do.

—Phyllis Diller

Which would you rather have as you approach retirement: health or wealth? What good would it be to have carefully planned and saved to be financially secure in retirement and then be in such poor health that you can't enjoy it? Fortunately, you don't have to choose between the two.

MYTH VERSUS REALITY

Growing older does not mean your health will deteriorate. Recent advances in medical research have separated myth from reality in the area of health and aging. Generally, it is found that many of the conditions associated with growing older are the result of abuse and neglect rather than the natural aging process. So, to a large measure, you are in control. Make the choices and take the action that will increase your odds for staying healthy.

Normal, healthy aging affects your vanity more than it does your ability to function. Your skin wrinkles, your hair turns gray, your hairline recedes, you can't see things up close, and you don't heal as quickly. Also, as you become older your muscles stiffen and the connective tissues become less elastic. Healthy aging may slow you down, but it doesn't stop you.

Unhealthy aging is a different story. One of the first signs of unhealthy aging is excessive weight gain. It is not unusual to put on as much as 20 pounds between the ages of 20 and 60. But if you have added 30 to 40 pounds, you have increased your risk of heart disease, stroke, and diabetes. Weight gain is tied directly to the next problem—lack of exercise. Do you look for the parking space nearest the mall entrance? Have difficulty lifting a bag of groceries or your grandchild?

Fortunately, even if you have neglected your health, you can start now to plan a lifestyle that takes you into a healthier retirement. How well you've taken care of yourself determines how much change may be required in your daily routine. This includes such things as proper eating habits, exercise, sleep, smoking, drinking, and the amount of stress you experience. Complete the following exercise to evaluate your current health practices.

FACTORS AFFECTING YOUR PHYSICAL WELL-BEING

The exercise "How Long Will You Live?" is designed to draw your attention to the factors affecting longevity and physical well-being. These factors can be grouped into three categories: lifestyle, environment, and heredity. The Center for Disease Control and Prevention estimates that the first two categories—lifestyle and environment—account for 75 percent of a person's longevity, while heredity accounts for only 25 percent. The obvious conclusion is this: Things over which you have control are major determinates of how long you will live and your physical well-being. People who exercise regularly, watch their diet, and don't smoke can look forward to longer, healthier lives.

How Long Will You Live?

Personal Factors

If you are male . . . . .score –3

If you are female . . . . .score +4   _____

If you live in a city of 2 million or more . . . . .score –2

If you live in a city of 10,000 to 2 million . . . . .score 0

If you live in a town under 10,000 or on a farm . . . . .score +2   _____

If you live in a city of 2 million or more ....score −2

If all grandparents lived to 80 or beyond ....score +6

If any grandparent lived to 85 ....score +2

If not ....score 0 _____

If either parent died of a stroke or heart attack ....score −4
   before the age of 50

If not ....score 0 _____

If you earn less than $50,000 a year ....score 0

If you earn $50,000 or more a year ....score −2 _____

If you did not finish college ....score 0

If you have a bachelor's degree ....score +1

If you have a graduate or professional degree ....score +3 _____

If you are 65 or over and still working ....score +3

If not ....score 0 _____

If you live with a spouse or friend ....score +5

If you live alone, score -1 for each 10 years alone since age 25 _____

Lifestyle Factors

If you exercise strenuously 5 times a week for ....score +4
   at least half an hour

If you exercise strenuously 2 or 3 times a week for ....score +2
   at least half an hour

If you don't exercise regularly ....score 0 _____

If you work behind a desk ....score −3

If your work requires regular, heavy labor ....score +3

If neither apply ....score 0 _____

If you sleep 7 to 9 hours each night ....score 0

If you sleep more than 10 hours a night ....score −4 _____

If you are intense, aggressive, easily angered . . . . .score −3

If you are easygoing and relaxed . . . . .score +3   _____

If you are happy . . . . .score +1

If you are unhappy . . . . .score −2   _____

If you got a speeding ticket in the past year . . . . .score −1

If not . . . . .score 0   _____

If you smoke more than two packs a day . . . . .score −8

If you smoke one to two packs a day . . . . .score −6

If you smoke one-half to one pack a day . . . . .score −3

If you don't smoke . . . . .score 0   _____

If you drink 1–1/2 oz. of liquor a day . . . . .score −1

If you drink less than 1–1/2 ounces . . . . .score 0   _____

If you are overweight by 50 pounds or more . . . . .score −8

If you are 30 to 50 pounds overweight .score −4

If you are 10 to 30 pounds overweight .score −2

If you are less than 10 pounds overweight . . . . .score 0   _____

If you see your doctor for annual checkups . . . . .score +2

If not . . . . .score 0   _____

Age Adjustment

If you are between 40 and 50 . . . . .score +3

If you are between 50 and 70 . . . . .score +4

If you are over 70 . . . . .score +5   _____

Total Score   _____

+72

Your Estimated Life Expectancy   _____

Source: *Lifegain* by J. Robert Allen, Ph.D. (New York: Appleton-Century-Crofts) copyright 1981 by J. Robert Allen, President, Human Resources Institute, 115 Dunder Road, Burlington, VT 05401. Used by permission of the author.

What is Your Reaction to Your Estimated Life Expectancy

Instructions: In the space below, write down your reactions to your score on the exercise. Can you identify the lifestyle, heredity, and environmental factors that affect your potential longevity?

_____

_____

_____

_____

_____

_____

_____

_____

_____

_____

TAKING CARE OF YOUR HEART

With heart disease being the number one cause of death among older Americans, you should pay particular attention to known causes of heart disease. A healthy heart can continue to function as well at 70 as it did at 30. If your heart is not affected by disease, your resting heart rate remains the same throughout your life. The question, then, is what can you do to keep it healthy? Here are five suggestions.

Stop Smoking

Smoking is thought to contribute to blood clotting, and researchers estimate that blood clots in the coronary arteries are responsible for more than 90 percent of all heart attacks. It's not surprising, then, that smokers are about twice as likely as nonsmokers to have heart disease and heart attacks. However, after 15 years of not smoking, the risk of heart disease is the same for former smokers as it is for those who never smoked.

Eat Well

A number of studies have shown a connection between diet and heart disease. The number one problem is cholesterol, which causes stiffening and narrowing of the arteries, thus increasing the risk of heart attack. By reducing fat in the diet to less than 30 percent of calories and keeping blood cholesterol below the 200 level, you help keep your heart healthy.

Limit Caffeine Consumption

Drinking five cups of coffee daily increases your chance of a heart attack by 50 percent over non-coffee drinkers. And, coffee is not the only culprit. Six cups of tea or six 12-ounce soft drinks can have the same affect. Break your caffeine addiction!

Keep Fit

The heart is a muscle, and muscles stay functional through use. A study of 3,000 men between the ages of 30 and 69 showed that the most fit were three times less likely to die of heart disease than the least fit. Any exercise is better than none. A brisk walk for 45 to 50 minutes, three times a week will make a big difference in your heart's ability to continue serving you.

Relax

Modern life is loaded with stress. While retirement takes you away from job-related stress, there will be other things like family, health, or money worries to upset you. Your heart becomes at risk when hostility is repressed or circumstances seem to overwhelm you. Participating in relaxation techniques such as resting quietly, breathing exercises, meditation, or yoga help keep stress under control.

Think Positively

Depressed people tend to eat too much, drink too much, and exercise too little. All of these have a negative impact on the heart. In addition to thinking positively, it helps to cultivate friendships as a way to lift the spirits. In a survey of 200 heart specialists, nearly two-thirds of them rated learning to enjoy love and friendship as an important factor in preventing heart trouble.

Rules for Healthful Living

When followed, these rules will contribute to a healthier lifestyle.

- Eat a balanced diet with no more than 30 percent of calories from fat.
- Eat breakfast every morning.
- Don't eat between meals.
- Eliminate added salt from your diet.
- Supplement your diet with calcium, if necessary, to obtain the daily recommended intake.
- Limit caffeine consumption.
- If you consume alcohol, do so only in moderation and don't drink distilled spirits.
- Don't smoke, chew tobacco, or dip snuff.
- Exercise daily.
- Consume plenty of fluids, eight to ten 8-ounce glasses a day. (Fluids containing caffeine or alcohol don't count.)
- Maintain your recommended weight.
- Get sufficient sleep each night to feel rested—usually seven to eight hours. For better sleep:
  - Stick to a regular bedtime.
  - Avoid caffeine after 2:00 PM.
  - Avoid strenuous exercise within three hours of bedtime.
  - Don't use alcohol as a sedative.

Rules for Healthful Living *(continued)*

- Consult with your doctor about a periodic colonoscopy.

- Visit your dentist twice a year for teeth cleaning and any other work needed.

- Have your eyes checked for glaucoma every two to three years.

KEY POINTS

- Many of the conditions previously thought to be a normal part of aging are now known to be caused by abuse and neglect.

- Normal aging affects your vanity more than it does your ability to function.

- The two major causes of death among older Americans are heart disease and cancer. Both are influenced by poor diet, smoking, and lack of exercise.

- A person can recover from years of abuse and neglect by adopting a healthy lifestyle.

Things to Do

Instructions: In the space below, list the things you want to do as a result of reading this chapter. Then, choose a target date for completing each of your action items.

Action Item	Target Date

CHAPTER 10

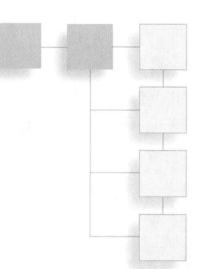

DIET AND NUTRITION

To safeguard one's health at the cost of too strict a diet is a tiresome illness indeed.

—François de la Rochefoucauld

The eating habits of most Americans lead to poor physical health rather than contributing to physical well-being. This chapter presents information on a proper diet. The following chapter deals with exercise. Together, they represent a program to improve your level of wellness so you are physically able to enjoy your retirement years.

In retirement, dietary needs will probably change. You will need less food and you will need different food. The extent of change will depend on your past eating habits and your present activity level. Regardless of your past eating habits, the challenges to attain a balanced diet take on a new dimension as you age. The following pretest lets you know how well you understand the key points of nutrition.

Nutrition Pretest

True   False

1. Water constitutes about one-third of body weight.

2. Fats are digested faster than other nutrients.

3. The Food and Nutrition Board has suggested that between the ages of 55 and 65, calories should be reduced by five percent; between the ages of 65 and 75, five percent; and 75 and older, another seven percent.

4. A calorie is a unit that measures the energy factor in different foods.

5. Excessive use of sugar is a major cause of obesity.

6. Osteoporosis is a thinning of the bones due to a loss of calcium.

7. The nutritive process (digestion) works better at night when you are asleep.

8. Very large meals can be stressful on the heart.

9. Water is not essential to good health.

10. Fiber is a form of carbohydrate that in itself is indigestible by humans and is therefore useless.

11. There is currently a rebirth of nutrition education in the United States.

12. Yogurt, apricots, and wheat germ are scientifically classified as "youth elixirs."

13. Long-lived people around the world generally have a lower caloric intake.

14. Fortunately, diet has nothing to do with the fact that 60 percent of older persons have dentures.

15. There is no evidence that nutritional deficiencies lead to decreased learning, performance, depression, disorientation, fatigue, general malaise, apathy, and headaches.

True	False	
____	____	16. RDA stands for Recommended Daily Allowance.
____	____	17. A potassium deficiency can easily be corrected by eating a banana every day.
____	____	18. A congressional committee in 1970 issued an educated guess that 2 million of the then 20 million seniors were malnourished.
____	____	19. The calories provided by sugar are loaded with vital vitamins and minerals.
____	____	20. When it comes to nutrition, more is not always better.

_____ Total Correct   (Answers on the following page.)

TYPES OF NUTRIENTS

Nutrients are classified into five main groups—proteins, carbohydrates, vitamins, minerals, and fats. Each plays an important part in keeping your body functioning properly.

Proteins

Every part of your body contains protein. It's the basic material used in the growth and repair of cells. Also, it helps you resist disease by forming antibodies.

Your body does not manufacture nor store protein. Therefore, you must take in your needs each day. Meat, fish, poultry, milk products, and eggs are good sources. Also, some plant foods are good sources when eaten in certain combinations. For example:

- beans with rice (red beans and rice)
- beans with corn (beans and cornbread)
- wheat with milk (breakfast cereal)
- peanuts with wheat (peanut butter sandwich)

Answers to Pretest

(1) F (water constitutes about two-thirds of body weight); (2) F (fats are digested more slowly and, as a result, keep us from getting hungry again so quickly); (3) T; (4) T; (5) T; (6) T; (7) F (it works better when we are active); (8) T; (9) F (water is essential for digestion, circulation, and other vital processes; we should drink more of it); (10) F (fiber is not digestible by humans, but it is vital to the elimination process); (11) T; (12) F (no single food or combination of foods can truly be called "youth elixirs"); (13) T (there is ample research on this); (14) F (there is a direct relationship between diet and the condition of one's teeth); (15) F (there is at least limited evidence); (16) T; (17) T; (18) F (their estimate was 8 million out of 20 million); (19) F (they are empty); (20) T.

Carbohydrates

Starches and sugar are the two forms of carbohydrates. Grains, cereals, peas, beans, potatoes, and wheat pasta are good starch sources. Fruits and milk products provide fructose and lactose, two beneficial forms of sugar.

Vitamins and Minerals

These nutrients help your body absorb and use food. They also influence gland secretion and maintain a proper balance in your body's chemistry. Fruits, vegetables, meats, dairy products, and whole grain or enriched breads and cereals supply you with essential vitamins and minerals. If you eat a balanced diet containing a variety of fresh and unprocessed food, you probably don't need extra vitamins or minerals. However, if you are neglecting a portion of your diet, see your doctor about a supplement.

Be cautious about overdosing on dietary supplements. Large doses of some nutrients act as drugs and prolonged heavy use can reach toxic levels. For example, too much Vitamin A can cause headaches, nausea, and diarrhea. High doses of Vitamin D can cause kidney damage. Too much iron can harm your liver.

Fats

While fat is essential to a well-balanced diet, you need only about a tablespoon a day. The average American eats six times that amount.

Fat comes in three forms—saturated, monounsaturated, and polyunsaturated. Eating saturated fats tends to increase the level of blood serum cholesterol, and the higher the cholesterol level, the greater the risk of heart attack. On the other hand, studies have shown that substituting mono- and polyunsaturated fats can reduce your cholesterol level.

THE STORY ON FATS

Type	Form	Found in	Tends to
Saturated	Solid at room temperature	Meat, dairy products, palm oil, coconut oil, and cocoa butter	Raise cholesterol
Monounsaturated	Liquid at room temperature	Olive, canola, and peanut oils, avocados, and most nuts	Lower cholesterol
Polyunsaturated	Liquid at room temperature and when refrigerated	Safflower, sunflower, soybean, corn, and vegetable oils	Lower cholesterol

THE FOOD GUIDE PYRAMID

One of the best tools for proper eating habits is the Food Guide Pyramid introduced by the U.S. Department of Agriculture in April 1992. The pyramid replaced the Basic Four Food Groups, which was the guide for over 20 years. In April 2005, the Pyramid was updated and coordinated with the *2005 Dietary Guidelines for Americans* released jointly by the U.S. Departments of Agriculture and Human Services. The new design incorporates four new features. The steps with a person climbing them are a reminder of the importance of physical activity. The width of the bands demonstrates proportionately how much to eat from each food group. The narrowing of the bands as they approach the top of the pyramid represents foods within each group that contain solid fats and sugars and suggests limiting consumption of these foods. Finally, the pyramid divides foods into five groups.

Grains: Grains include bread, crackers, cereal, rice, and pasta. Based on weight and calorie needs, an adult should have six to eight servings a day from this group. One serving is a slice of bread, six Saltine crackers, or 1/2 cup of cooked rice, pasta, or breakfast cereal. Make half of your servings whole grain.

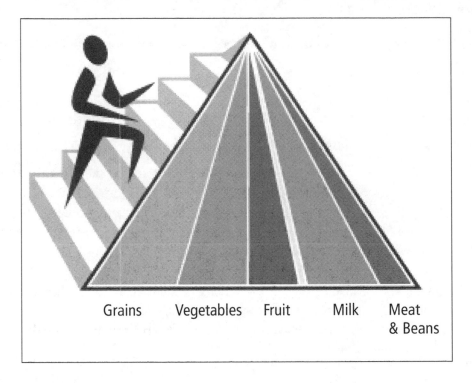

Grains   Vegetables   Fruit   Milk   Meat & Beans

Vegetables: The next food group is vegetables. These foods may be eaten either raw or lightly cooked. Be cautious about adding fat when cooking. Adults need three to five servings of vegetables a day. A serving is one cup of leafy vegetables or 1/2 cup chopped raw or cooked vegetables. You should eat more dark-green vegetables like broccoli and spinach and more orange vegetables such as carrots and sweet potatoes.

Fruits: You need two to four servings of fruit daily. A serving is 3/4 cup of juice; 1/4 cup of dried fruit; or one piece of fresh fruit or a melon wedge. Eat a variety of fruits which can be either fresh, frozen, canned, or dried. But, go easy on fruit juices.

Milk: This group contains dairy products. This includes milk, yogurt, and cheese. These are your calcium-rich foods. Two or three servings a day are sufficient. A serving is one cup of milk or yogurt or 1-1/2 to 2 ounces of cheese. Choose low-fat or fat-free milk, yogurt, and other milk products. If you don't or can't consume dairy products, choose lactose-free products.

Meat and Beans: This group contains meat, poultry, fish, dry beans, nuts, and eggs. Two servings a day are sufficient. A serving is three ounces of cooked meat, poultry, or fish, one egg, 1/2 cup cooked dry beans or peas, or one ounce of nuts. The major concern in this group is fat. This can be minimized by choosing low-fat alternatives. Choose the leanest cuts of beef and pork and substitute fish and skinned poultry.

When using the pyramid as an aid to planning your food intake, there are a few facts that help you make the right choices. A serving of starch has 15 grams of carbohydrate, three grams of protein, only a trace of fat, and no cholesterol. A serving of lean roast beef has essentially no carbohydrate, 21 grams of protein, and 15 grams of fat. If these nutrients contributed the same calories, you could cut back on any of them and expect to lose weight. But they're not equal. Carbohydrates and protein contain four calories per gram, while fat contains nine. By substituting carbohydrates such as pasta for the fat in your diet, you cut back on your calories while still having a nutritional and satisfying meal.

From a practical viewpoint, remember the five food groups of the Food Guide Pyramid and the foods they contain. Eat more servings each day from the groups containing grains, fruits, and vegetables. Supplement your diet with a limited amount of food from the milk and meat and beans groups. These foods are essential for the protein they supply, but must be eaten in limited amounts because of their fat content.

A BALANCED DIET

Most people don't eat a balanced diet. This leads to weight gain and other health problems. Average Americans get more than 40 percent of their calories from fat. (The National Heart, Lung, and Blood Institute recommends no more than 30 percent should come from fat.) This causes a major nutrient deficiency. Not enough fruits, vegetables, and whole grains are consumed and these foods are the primary sources of antioxidant vitamins, minerals, and fiber. If you follow the advice to eat five servings of fruit and vegetables and six from a variety of breads, whole-grain cereals, and pasta each day, you will easily get 100 percent of the Recommended Daily Allowance (RDA) of essential vitamins and minerals. Eat a bowl of cereal and a piece of fruit or a vegetable, either as a snack or with a meal, and you will be meeting your body's needs with less fat intake.

Measure your eating habits against these recommendations by checking the following that apply:

☐   I need to eat less fat.

☐   I need to eat fewer sweets.

☐   I need to eat more fruit and vegetables.

☐   I need to eat more whole grains and cereals.

NUTRITION EXERCISE

Listed below are 12 nutritional ideas. Read each statement and decide whether some action is required on your part. Place a ✔ in the appropriate box.

Action Required by Me	No Action Required by Me	
☐	☐	1. It is generally accepted that sodium (salt) should be restricted. Doctors normally limit salt consumption in cases of heart disease, kidney disease, hypertension (high blood pressure), and edema (swelling). An average person gets 15 to 20 milligrams of sodium per day—almost 10 times more than required. We do need sodium in limited amounts because it helps maintain water balance, but there is usually enough in the food we eat. You can learn to enjoy unsalted flavors and eliminate the need for a salt shaker.

Action Required by Me   *No Action Required by Me*

☐   ☐

2. Calcium is critical to your diet as you grow older. It may be too late for it to do much for your teeth, but you should do what you can to maintain strong bones. If you don't get enough calcium, the body secretes a hormone that causes the needed calcium to be taken from your bones. This process, called demineralization, causes bones to become porous. The medical word for this is *osteoporosis*.

The best sources of calcium are milk products. Most other foods contribute only small amounts. If you want to meet recommended daily calcium needs (800 milligrams), you need the equivalent of 2-1/2 cups of milk (whole, skimmed, or buttermilk) per day. One cup of yogurt or cottage cheese is the equivalent of one cup of milk. If you are trying to stay away from dairy products, you can eat large amounts of green, leafy vegetables, dried beans, and peas, or use calcium-supplemented soybean milk. Sardines provide calcium if the bones are eaten. Or, choose calcium-fortified foods and beverages.

Action Required by Me   *No Action Required by Me*

☐   ☐

3. Sugar, like salt, is more a habit than a necessity. The only contribution made by sugar is taste and calories. Certain foods, like ice cream, would not be tasty without sugar. Hotcakes, without syrup, would probably not be worth the effort. Sugar is basically a dietary luxury. The best way to avoid sugar is to resist candy, ice cream, cakes, cookies, and regular soft drinks. Also, you should be careful and select canned fruits and boxed cereals without sugar.

*Action
Required
by Me*

*No Action
Required
by Me*

☐   ☐

4. One of the best reasons for taking this exercise seriously is to help control your weight. Watching your food intake will help you avoid crash programs that provide short-term weight loss but can have serious side effects. As you get older, you need all the energy you can get, but you should not pay an exorbitant price for it. Although fat provides more than twice as much energy as carbohydrates or proteins, adding one pound to your weight means it takes 3,500 fewer calories to get it off. The problem comes down to balanced fat intake. The greater your ingestion of fat, the more you need exercise to maintain your weight.

*Action
Required
by Me*

*No Action
Required
by Me*

☐   ☐

5. You are aware when you shop that you have a choice of buying white bread or a variety of whole-grain breads that have rich, brown colors and a rougher texture. Wheat, rice, corn, rye, and barley are seeds of grasses. Each seed has a hull, bran layer, starchy layer, and germ. A whole-grain cereal or bread contains everything but the hull. This is what you want. In white bread, the nutritious, health-giving parts (bran layer, starchy layer, and germ) are refined out.

Of course, some bakeries put some of these back through enrichment. Most experts feel, however, that it's better to have all these vitamins and minerals naturally rather than through enrichment. What is put back, they say, is not always what is taken out.

*Action
Required
by Me*

*No Action
Required
by Me*

☐   ☐

6. Some say that four or five small, nutritional meals a day are better than two or three larger ones—especially if one is a big meal at the end of the day. The reasoning is that the digestive and assimilation process works better with more frequent but smaller amounts. The smaller meals, however, should not be junk food. Instead, good snacks should include fresh fruit, raisins, raw carrots, celery sticks, and so forth.

The idea is to discipline yourself away from bad snacks. The best solution is not to buy them in the first place, but it also means refusing them politely when they are offered at parties or other social events. If you have occasional snacks, make sure they are coordinated with your other meals so you don't consume excess calories.

*Action
Required
by Me*

☐

*No Action
Required
by Me*

☐

7. When the weather is hot or when you exert yourself, you become aware of your need for water. Thirst tells you when you need more and most people adequately meet their daily needs by letting thirst be their guide. To prevent dehydration, you must ensure that your body receives enough fluids. You need about three quarts a day to replace what is lost through respiration, perspiration, and urination. You get this fluid from liquids you drink and foods you eat. If insufficient fluid is taken in, thirst triggers a hormonal action causing the kidneys to save water by making your urine more concentrated. If you drink more fluid than you need, the opposite happens—kidneys produce a less-concentrated urine.

Water is good for your body. It is a lubricant for your joints as well as a regulator of body temperature. Maintaining the right balance of water within your system is critically important. This means getting enough fluids into your body every day through what you eat and drink whether or not you feel thirsty. (As a general guideline, the Institute of Medicine recommends 91 ounces of fluids a day for women and 125 ounces for men.)

*Action
Required
by Me*

*No Action
Required
by Me*

☐   ☐

8. Experts tend to agree that every diet should have sufficient fiber for good health. Because fiber can absorb many times its weight in water, its major benefit is that it creates large, soft stools that stimulate the colon naturally, thus eliminating constipation. Some researchers maintain there is good evidence that a fiber-depleted diet increases the incidence of certain diseases.

The best way to ensure that you are getting sufficient fiber in your diet is to eat plenty of plant fibers. This means having a variety of vegetables—consuming many of them raw—and having fresh fruits, which seasonally come on the market at a reasonable price. This takes planning.

Perhaps the best substitute, if fruits and vegetables are not readily available, is to consume bran on a regular, deliberate basis. Bran, the outside husk of wheat, can be purchased at most supermarkets and consumed as a cereal.

*Action
Required
by Me*

*No Action
Required
by Me*

☐   ☐

9. There is limited evidence that moderate use of alcohol might have some advantages. For example, it may promote relaxation and lessen symptoms of stress. But the disadvantages greatly outweigh any advantages, especially when alcohol is used in excess:

▪ Consumed before a meal, even a moderate amount of alcohol tends to stimulate the appetite and cause overeating.

▪ Alcoholic beverages are high in calories and low in nutrients; thus, drinking can rob one of needed nutrients.

▪ Excessive, chronic drinking promotes undereating because it acts as an appetite suppressant and throws a diet out of balance.

- Alcohol is toxic to the liver, stomach, pancreas, and intestines, causing them to act less efficiently in digesting, absorbing, and metabolizing nutrients.

- Taken in combination with certain other drugs, alcohol can cause life-threatening reactions.

Action Required by Me ☐   *No Action Required by Me* ☐

10. It is always a temptation to discard a diet when eating out. After all, there should be exceptions to everything, especially diets. Eating out is fun, especially if it doesn't happen often. But some folks overdo it to the point where they seriously cripple their diets and damage themselves needlessly. Some can overdo it at potluck dinners. Others lose all resistance in cafeterias. Those who eat out often may be unable to diet because it takes more self discipline than they can muster.

Other factors add to the problem. Starchy foods on menus are often less expensive. "Specials" are often tempting, but may not fit the diet. And a cocktail ahead of time can cause one to make food choices with wild abandon. Cafeterias have the advantage of offering a wide selection, which permits a person to adhere to his or her diet. But it is essential to have a dose of self discipline as an appetizer while standing in line.

Action Required by Me ☐   *No Action Required by Me* ☐

11. Although all diets are debated, most agree that a balance among the five food groups of the Food Guide Pyramid is important. A typical recommendation might be:

> *Milk group:* Equivalent of two servings a day, preferably nonfat.

Meat and beans group: Two 3-ounce servings a day. Fish and poultry are highly recommended. No more than three eggs per week. Avoid fatty meats.

Fruit group: Equivalent of two servings a day.

Vegetable group: Equivalent of five 1/2-cup servings a day. Dark green or orange vegetables every other day.

Grain group: Six to eight servings a day. A serving is one slice of bread or 1/2 cup of cereal—whole grain preferred.

It requires dedication and planning to have a balanced diet day after day.

Action Required by Me   *No Action Required by Me*

☐   ☐

12. Here are two factors to consider if you want the best possible diet:

The way food is cooked is a part of the nutrition game. Depending on the cooking method, a percentage of any nutrient is lost. When vegetables are boiled in water, vitamins disappear quickly. Much of their mineral content is also lost unless the water in which they were boiled is consumed.

A portion of fruits and vegetables should be consumed raw. Research indicates that pectin and bioflavonoids, natural parts of most fruits, lowers blood cholesterol levels more effectively than drugs. Both of these elements are found abundantly in unpeeled apples. There are many other positive reasons for eating some fruits and vegetables raw.

To ensure good nutrition, don't overcook vegetables and eat plenty of raw fruit and vegetables. You may also consider steaming vegetables, which saves most of the nutrients.

SOME INTERESTING FACTS

- Two quarts of strawberries or three honeydew melons have less calories than a cup of regular ice cream.
- The dark meat of chicken and turkey has more than twice the fat of the light meat.
- A five-pound sack of potatoes has less fat than ten roasted peanuts.
- A spoonful of corn syrup has nearly one-third more calories than a spoonful of sugar.
- Trimming fat from meat before cooking is better than trimming it after cooking.
- Most of an egg's cholesterol is in the yolk, while most of the protein is in the white.
- Canned beans can have as much as forty times the sodium of home-cooked beans.
- Drinking a 12-ounce can of regular soda pop gives you 10 teaspoons of sugar. (People get ten times more sugar from soda pop than from candy.)
- A cheeseburger has more than seven times the sodium of French fries and contains over 1,000 calories.
- Mushrooms have only five calories when eaten raw but have 73 calories when deep fried.

KEY POINTS

- The average American eats six times the amount of fat needed daily. Limit fat consumption to 30 percent of calorie intake.
- Eat more whole-grain bread and cereals, potatoes, pasta, vegetables, and fruit.
- Limit consumption of meat, eggs, nuts, and dairy products.
- Eat desserts sparingly.
- Use the Food Guide Pyramid as a tool for planning your food consumption.
- If you don't eat a balanced diet, take a vitamin and mineral supplement.

Things to Do

Instructions: In the space below, list the things you want to do as a result of reading this chapter. Then, choose a target date for completing each of your action items.

Action Item	Target Date

CHAPTER 11

EXERCISE

If you rest, you rust.
    —Helen Hayes

Only eight percent of Americans 50 and older get enough exercise to promote physical well-being. If your goal is a healthy heart and longer life, you don't have to run marathons—just avoid inactivity. There is unanimous agreement in the scientific community that regular exercise is essential for optimal body functioning. Aging is associated with decreased muscle strength, but strength can increase between 20 and 40 percent in the first weeks of an exercise program. Physical training can effectively postpone physical deterioration for 10 to 20 years.

There's nothing new about the idea that regular exercise is good for you, but research in recent years has added some new insights for older people.

- You don't have to wear yourself out for exercise to be helpful. Moderate exercise is more enjoyable, easier to maintain, less risky, and just as beneficial to your health.

- Life span is determined by heredity, environment, and lifestyle. By making healthful lifestyle changes, millions of people could live quality, enjoyable lives well past age 90.

- Exercise is now recommended as therapy for arthritis sufferers, even though years ago many doctors thought it was necessary to avoid exercise.

- Exercise does more than improve physical fitness. It also helps maintain mental and emotional health.

The effects of a sedentary lifestyle are gradual. Reaction time, balance, and digestion deteriorate. You begin to gain weight. As your body adds fat at the expense of muscle, deterioration increases. A pound of muscle needs 30 to 50 calories a day to maintain itself, while a pound of fat uses only 2. The bottom line: Regular exercise is essential to controlling weight and maintaining physical, mental, and emotional health.

Before starting any exercise regimen, check with your doctor for recommendations on an appropriate program for your age and physical condition.

TAKE YOUR CHOICE

Why are more people devoting additional time and attention to exercising? There are many excellent reasons, some of which are more important to you than others, but all are convincing. Read each of the reasons listed here carefully, and then rank them according to their importance to you. Place the number 1 in the box next to the reason that is most important to you, the number 2 for the second most important, and so on.

As you make your decisions, keep in mind the credibility of each reason. If you believe a statement is partially true or exaggerated, then give it a lower priority. There is no correct pattern. Your priorities will be uniquely your own.

☐ 1. A good physical exercise program will help you transmit a better image to others. You will project a more trim silhouette because exercising helps you stand straighter. This will enhance your personal pride and give you more confidence to take charge of your life.

☐ 2. Most medical specialists agree that exercise in the right amount and intensity strengthens your largest and most important muscle—your heart. Consistent, regular exercise—without overdoing it—is the key. Someone who has had a heart attack should rest until the heart has had time to repair itself, and then begin slowly exercising until a stronger heart can be rebuilt. If you have a strong heart, exercising the right way in the right amount will keep it strong.

3. It is generally agreed that exercising contributes quickly to a feeling of wellness. For example, if you do calisthenics, take a brisk walk, jog, or swim for 30 minutes before breakfast, you will enjoy your breakfast more and feel better all day. You will have a better attitude and be more sensitive in your dealings with others. You will achieve more and encounter fewer frustrations. Your day will go better because you have prepared your body to handle it.

4. Many experts claim that consistent exercising of the right kind helps prevent backaches. If you have suffered the excruciating pain of a back problem, you will probably give this one high priority. Exercise of the right kind helps your back muscles stay stronger and take strain better. Avoid unnecessary awkward or heavy lifting. To protect your back, the more preventive steps you take, including exercise, the better.

5. Exercising contributes to a more healthy-looking image. Those who do not exercise often have a pasty look. Those who exercise have a more vigorous appearance, with more color, better skin tone, and a younger look overall.

6. Some people believe exercising on a regular basis helps them stay mentally alert. They are convinced that a relationship exists between physical well-being and mental capacity. These individuals claim they make better decisions, are more creative, and stay motivated because of regular exercise. They say time spent exercising (30 to 60 minutes per day) is more than offset through better performance. Most runners and joggers will give this one high priority.

7. Researchers use the terms elasticity and joint lubrication to communicate the possibility that exercising can help prevent arthritis (or at least control its effects). The premise is that the more you use the various parts of your body, the more you can use them in the future (as long as it is not overdone). There are some exceptions; for example, deep knee bends or holding your hands above your head too long can do more harm than good. The older you are, the higher priority you may give to this one.

8. A reasonable premise is that the more you exercise, the more you maintain your strength. Muscle provides more strength to the body than fat, and exercising builds muscles. This means you can do more things (playing golf, dancing, walking, driving) longer. People who want to remain active understand the importance of exercise.

☐ 9. You may not give this one top priority, but many believe the stronger you remain physically and the more alert you remain mentally, the fewer accidents you will have. Home accidents, like falling in the shower or bathtub, are too common among retirees. Those who exercise regularly, even in modest amounts, are in better shape to avoid such accidents.

☐ 10. Combined with the proper diet, exercising can help you lose weight. Exercising replaces fat with muscle. A better balance can be achieved between the two. Excessive weight places additional strain on the heart and joints and has a negative impact on blood pressure. Almost everyone acknowledges that keeping slim has long-term health benefits.

☐ 11. Many doctors recommend exercise for patients who complain that they can't sleep. Insomnia can be a major problem. A brisk walk after dinner can help you relax, which in turn helps induce sleep. You can't buy exercise in a bottle, but it is an excellent antidote for insomnia.

☐ 12. Retirement does not guarantee a pressure-free existence. There is no way to isolate yourself from financial, health, or other worries. Here again, regular exercise can help. Exercise helps relieve tension and thus promotes serenity, insulating you from the negative effects of pressure. The more stress in your life, the higher priority this reason should receive.

TYPES OF EXERCISE

Exercise is divided into three types—aerobic, strength, and flexibility. A well-designed exercise plan includes all three types.

Aerobic Exercise

Exercise of this type develops the cardiorespiratory system, which delivers oxygen to every cell of your body and carries away waste. Aerobic exercise must elevate your heart rate to a target zone and maintain it for 30 minutes five times a week to be effective.

HOW TO FIND YOUR TARGET HEART RATE

Take your resting heart rate—60-second pulse rate when you first awaken. (This is required for the calculation.)

Start with _____220_____

Subtract your age _____

Maximum heart rate _____

Subtract resting heart rate _____

Multiply by fitness level* _____.60_____

Add resting heart rate _____

Your Target Heart Rate _____

*Beginner .60; Intermediate .70; Advanced .80

Swimming is considered the all-around best form of aerobic exercise. It works all the major muscle groups—arms, legs, and torso. And, since your body is buoyed in water, there is no stress on the joints. However, not everyone knows how to swim or has access to a pool. Therefore, another form of exercise may be right for you. The key is activity that is sustained for the duration. This includes:

- Handball
- Racquetball
- Cycling
- Rowing
- Walking
- Jogging/Running

You can add interest to your exercise program by engaging in more than one form of exercise. Machines are available that provide aerobic workouts either at a health club or in your home. These, too, can be alternated with outdoor exercise or reserved for inclement weather. Here are the most popular machines.

Treadmills.   Treadmills allow walking at a brisk pace, jogging, and running. These are excellent aerobic exercises that also improve lower-body muscle tone. The typical machine priced around $500 with a top speed of five miles an hour is designed for walking only. A beginner who wants to include jogging can expect to pay $600 to $1,000, while a machine that goes fast enough for running costs $1,000 or more. If you weigh more than 200 pounds, be sure to buy a treadmill rated for more than your body weight.

Stationary Bikes.   There are two types of stationary bikes—single-action models that pedal like a regular bicycle and dual-action models that also let you pump the handlebars with your arms. Recumbent models let you sit lower to the floor on a chair-like seat rather than on a bicycle seat. Single-action models work the lower body; dual-action models add an upper-body workout. A good single-action bike costs about $250, while the best dual-action model run $500 to $800.

Stair Climbers.   Simulating the exercise of climbing stairs, dual-action models work arms as well as legs. On some models, the steps are linked so that one goes up while the other goes down. Other models have independently working steps. Stair climbers offer lower-body muscle toning as well as an aerobic workout. Models for home use range in price from $200 to $800, with good dual-action models costing about $500.

Rowing Machines.   There are two types of rowing machines—single-action models that work the arms and upper-body and dual-action models that also work the legs. Both offer good aerobic workouts while dual-action models do a better job of total body toning. A good single-action model costs about $250, while dual-action models range from $300 to $500.

Skiing Machines.   Skiing machines simulate the exercise of cross-country skiing. This rhythmic action avoids the stress to the joints caused by other forms of aerobic exercise. In addition to an aerobic workout, skiing machines also provide upper- and lower-body exercise that contributes to strength and body toning. Machines for home use range in price from $300 to $800, with a good machine costing about $600. When shopping for a skiing machine, select one that has something to lean against. This is an important safety feature to help you maintain your balance —particularly while you are learning to use the machine.

Ellipticals. Elliptical cross-trainers are gaining in popularity. They provide an excellent aerobic workout while developing the leg muscles. The rhythmic motion, similar to pedaling a bicycle while standing up, avoids stress to the joints. The machines can be pedaled either forward or backward, providing a workout to different muscles. A good machine for home use costs $800 to $1,000 with top-quality machines going as high as $3,500.

Strength Exercise

As you grow older, you lose muscle fiber; and the less active you are, the more your muscles atrophy. One study found that 40 percent of women between ages 55 and 65 couldn't lift even 10 pounds! If you lack strength, everyday tasks such as lifting a bag of groceries, pushing a vacuum cleaner, or lifting a grandchild may tire you—or worse, cause a muscle strain or pull. You will start to limit activities and your weakness can interfere with getting up and walking, which can put you at risk of falling.

Strengthening techniques can reverse aging's effects on muscles. A strong back, firm abdomen, lean arms, and sturdy legs help you function not only under normal conditions, but abnormal conditions as well—that is, when you need an extra burst of energy or strength in an emergency.

Strong muscles go hand-in-hand with strong bones. Studies among healthy men and women between the ages of 64 and 84 have shown that those with higher muscle strength have higher bone density. Therefore, strength exercises may also help reduce the risk of osteoporosis.

There are three types of strength exercises—lifting free weights such as dumbbells or milk cartons filled with water, working out on weight-training equipment that uses hydraulic fluid or air rather than weight, and using your body's weight in exercises such as push-ups, sit-ups, and chin-ups.

The type of routine you choose depends on your preference, your access to a gym or health club, and the amount you are willing to spend.

As with any exercise program, you should get your doctor's okay. Blood pressure goes up during strength exercises, so if you suffer from high blood pressure or heart disease, be sure to ask if the exercise is safe for you. If you have arthritis, you should still be able to improve your strength, depending on how limited you are by the disease. Some authorities suggest that arthritis patients use weight-training machines rather than free weights. This allows them to limit the range of motion and provides better protection to the joints and the back.

Before lifting anything, warm up for about 10 minutes with light exercise. This increases blood circulation and warms your muscles. Afterward, spend another 10 minutes stretching to prevent muscle stiffness and soreness. These activities help prevent injuries.

If you work out three times a week, you can expect to see results in three to six weeks and significant improvement in 12 weeks. As you improve, you need to lift more weight or work out longer. More weight adds more muscles. Working longer with the same weight improves muscle tone and definition.

Flexibility Exercise

Think of the personal maintenance chores that require flexibility— for example, combing your hair, tying your shoelaces, zipping or buttoning a blouse that fastens in the back. When you lose flexibility you become dependent on others to perform these simple tasks for you. But, most people need not lose flexibility. They can keep tendons, muscles, and joints functioning through regular use.

Most active people routinely get enough flexibility exercise. The problem develops when people become less active in older age. Gardening, housecleaning, and washing the car keep you stretching and bending. If you add stretching exercises before and after aerobic and strength exercising, you will have a good flexibility routine.

If you find you aren't participating in these activities, you may need to add regular flexibility exercise to your schedule. Here are four exercises that stretch the major muscle groups. Because a warm muscle is easier to stretch, do 5 to 10 minutes of light aerobic activity before you begin. Then, stretch until you feel tension in the joint and hold at that point for 10 seconds. Return to the starting position and repeat the exercise three times. As your flexibility increases, gradually increase the duration of the stretch to 30 seconds and the repetitions to five.

Chest stretch. With your arm outstretched behind you, hold onto the side of a doorway with your hand at shoulder height and with your elbow slightly bent. Lean forward as you step through the doorway with the opposite foot, letting your weight pull your arm straight. Hold for a slow count of 10. Then do the same using the other arm.

Shoulder stretch. Stand with your feet shoulder-width apart and knees slightly bent. Place your right arm on your left shoulder. Use your left hand to pull your right elbow toward your left shoulder and hold it in a stretched position for a slow count of 10. Change arms and repeat the exercise.

Leg stretch. Sit on the floor with your legs straight out in front of you and knees slightly bent. Moving from the hips, slowly reach forward toward your toes. Hold for a slow count of 10, return to the starting position, and repeat.

Lower-back stretch. Lie on your back. Draw one knee to your chest by grasping your thigh under the knee with both hands. Hold for a slow count of 10, return to the starting position, and repeat with the other leg. Return to the starting position and draw both legs to your chest at the same time. Hold this position for a slow count of 10 and then repeat the complete exercise.

HOW TO START A WALKING PROGRAM

Walking is a safe aerobic exercise that can also increase bone density and help prevent bone loss. Before you begin, talk with your physician about your plan and any problems you may encounter. Then, follow these simple steps.

Follow Safety Precautions

Although walking is one of the safest ways to exercise, being attentive to some simple precautions reduces your risk of injury.

- Walk on smooth surfaces, such as dirt paths or sidewalks. You could trip and fall on an uneven surface.

- At night, walk with a buddy and wear reflectors so drivers can see you.

- Avoid neighborhoods with aggressive dogs.

- Never use ankle weights. The added weight can injure your back and joints.

- Always carry identification and change for a phone call.

Dress Appropriately

Choose comfortable clothing that will keep you warm but not hot. Layer your clothing so you can remove a sweater or jacket as you warm up and put it back on at the end of your walk. The only essential equipment is a good pair of walking shoes. Select a pair that fits properly, is sturdy, and supports your feet. Choose leather or nylon uppers to let your feet breathe, padded heel cup with good support, flexible sole, plenty of toe room, good arch support, and laces for a snug fit.

Walk with Good Form

When you start walking, be conscious of your posture. Keep your shoulders, back, and spine straight with weight centered over the hips. Keep your head parallel to the ground. By taking smooth, easy steps, your body will move fluidly through the walking motion.

Start Out Gradually

Begin by walking 10 minutes three times a week. Add five minutes a week until you are up to 45 minutes and then increase your number of walks to five a week. At the end of 15 weeks, you should be walking three miles per 45-minute walk, five times a week.

Stretch Before and After Walking

Stretching prepares your muscles and joints for exercise. After exercising, stretching prevents stiffness and increases flexibility. Before walking, lean against a solid surface (wall, tree, etc.) with one leg forward and one extended backward. Press your back heel to the ground and bend your front knee, keeping both knees pointed forward. Stretch each side three times slowly, holding for 20 to 30 seconds each. Next, while leaning with one hand against the solid surface, pull your foot up to your buttocks with the opposite hand, keeping your knee pointing straight to the ground. Repeat three times on each side, holding for 20 to 30 seconds each.

After walking, repeat the warm-up stretches and add two more. First, reach one arm over your head and to the side, keeping your hips steady and your shoulders straight to the side. Alternate arms and hold each position for a slow count of 10. Do three or four repetitions on each side. Next, place your leg out in front of you with your heel resting on an elevated support, knee slightly bent, back straight. Lean forward from the hips with hands extended toward the ankle. Like the warm-up stretches, these should be repeated three times on each side, holding for 20 to 30 seconds each.

GETTING STARTED

A well-rounded exercise program addresses three separate physical needs. Aerobic exercise develops the legs, heart, body composition, and stamina. Strength exercise develops the arms, upper and lower torso, and improves body appearance.

Flexibility exercise improves the range of body motion. A suggested combination program is 30 minutes of walking, jogging, or swimming; 10 minutes of stretching; and 20 minutes of weight lifting. This one-hour program should be repeated three times a week.

You can elect to exercise on your own or you might favor a group activity. You could join an organized exercise class, walk with friends, or buy a membership in a commercial club or gym where you have access to special equipment (perhaps even a pool or spa). This may help you define your visits, and may also provide supervision and group reinforcement to get you started.

These decisions are minor. Whatever fits your lifestyle best is the way to go. Whatever is least painful and most satisfying is the program you will probably stick with the longest. As you decide how to become more fit, keep these suggestions in mind:

Start out slowly. Give yourself time to reach the performance level (amount of exercise) you desire. You will know when you are there, because you feel better physically and feel proud for having reached your initial goal. If you have special health problems, be sure to check with your doctor. It is also a good idea to have a complete physical before you begin a fitness program.

To help, it must hurt a little. Although almost any exercise is helpful, some retirees are satisfied with so little that the benefits are insignificant. They never really reach a feeling of wellness and thus are not motivated to continue. Often they underestimate their capacity. Token exercising is not enough. It must tire you a little or you are deluding yourself. When you puff and strain in moderation, the trade-off is the minor temporary discomfort for a great feeling that can stay with you for hours.

Do it your way. It is not the purpose of this chapter to provide a formal pattern of exercise or recommend one routine over another. There are many fine books and articles that can help you. What is important is that you design a workable pattern that gives you personal satisfaction.

Avoid Negative Thinking

Many would-be exercisers talk themselves out of exercising with self-defeating excuses. When you think negative thoughts, you discourage yourself, develop a lower estimate of your ability, and end up not exercising.

If you want to exercise but can't seem to get started, you may be using excuses without even knowing it. Here is a list of excuses that typically run through people's minds when they are considering exercising. Check the ones you have used.

- ☐ I'm too tired.
- ☐ I don't have time.
- ☐ I'd rather relax.
- ☐ I have more important things to do.
- ☐ I'll do it later.
- ☐ It will take too long.
- ☐ I'd rather do something else.
- ☐ I'll eat less instead.
- ☐ I'll exercise longer tomorrow.
- ☐ Missing one day won't really matter.

When these kinds of thoughts prevent you from exercising, take a close look at your situation. Distinguish between excuses and real problems. If real problems are getting in your way, work to solve them. If it's just an excuse, make a commitment not to give in to it. Get up and get started!

THE BENEFITS OF EXERCISE

As you continue your exercise program, you will begin to notice several changes. Here are the most common.

Increased Stamina—Reduced Risk of Heart Disease

Your daily routine probably doesn't give you all the exercise you need to maintain cardiovascular fitness. When you are in good shape, you can walk up a hill and climb stairs without huffing and puffing, and you can keep up with your grandchildren.

Increased Strength

If you don't exercise, you lose 20 percent of your strength between ages 30 and 65. With regular exercise, you can maintain strength throughout your lifetime—and even improve it.

Increased Flexibility

Without regular, proper exercise you'll be ten times stiffer at age 60 than you were at age 10. Increased flexibility is the first benefit to show up after you start exercising. You will see and feel results in only two or three weeks.

Leaner Body Tissue

Muscle tissue converts to fat as a natural aging process. This reduces your basal metabolic rate, causing you to use fewer calories. Increasing your level of activity prevents some muscle from converting to fat, burns more calories, and helps keep your metabolic rate up.

Increased Bone Density

After midlife, you begin to lose bone tissue. This can result in porous, brittle bones. Exercise actually encourages the body to keep bone tissue dense and strong.

Lower Stress

Physical exercise increases brain endorphin, a powerful natural painkiller and tranquilizer. This increased endorphin helps reduce stress.

Improved Sleep

As you grow older, sleep becomes more erratic. The period of deep sleep becomes shorter and you awaken more often during the night. Exercise can lengthen the period of deep sleep and reduce the number of awakenings.

Increased Regularity

Exercise helps your body excrete waste.

Enhanced Self-Image

Regular exercise increases balance and poise and gives you a greater feeling of control and self-confidence. It improves your appearance and your attitude. It keeps you socially active, involved in life, and mentally fit.

KEY POINTS

- Only about eight percent of Americans get enough exercise to promote physical well-being.
- A well-rounded exercise program addresses three needs—aerobic conditioning, strength development, and flexibility.
- Swimming is the best form of aerobic exercise. Walking is a good alternative.
- Strength exercise develops bone density as well as muscles.
- Most active adults get enough flexibility exercise, but as people age, they tend to become less active.
- Exercise improves your mental health as well as your physical health.
- Consult a physician before starting any exercise program.

Things to Do

Instructions: In the space below, list the things you want to do as a result of reading this chapter. Then, choose a target date for completing each of your action items.

Action Item	Target Date

CHAPTER 12

A WEIGHT-CONTROL PROGRAM THAT WORKS

If someone's selling you sacks of diet pills, he's not in business for your health.

—**Public Service Advertisement**

Americans are among the fattest people in the world. More than 35 percent are overweight and, as a result, have increased risk of heart disease, stroke, and cancer. About 35 million need to lose 35 pounds or more for health reasons. Today, for many people, eating provides social and emotional fulfillment rather than physical needs. Weight gain has come about because of reduced activity and increased fat consumption.

The answer to solving this problem is not dieting. A diet is often seen as a short-term effort to lose weight. This program is a long-term lifestyle change to not only lose weight, but to keep it off and to make you a healthier person in the process. It consists of three components—a high-volume, low-calorie food plan; exercise; and water consumption.

YOUR IDEAL WEIGHT

The place to start on a weight control program is to determine what your weight ought to be. This becomes your goal. Take your height over five feet in inches and multiply it by five. Men add this number to 110; women add it to 100. The result is your ideal weight.

Calculate Your Ideal Weight

	Men	Women
	<u> 110 </u>	<u> 100 </u>
Inches over 5 ft. _____	_____	_____
	× 5	× 5
	+ _____	+ _____
Your Ideal Weight _____	_____	_____

THE HIGH-VOLUME, LOW-CALORIE FOOD PLAN

The average person, engaged in a moderate level of activity, needs 10 to 12 calories per pound daily to maintain body weight. If your goal is to lose weight, your calorie intake needs to be less. No one enjoys feeling hungry; therefore, rather than thinking of eating less, think of eating different foods—those that fill you up but are lower in calories. This means eating more foods at the bottom of the Food Guide Pyramid and fewer of the foods at the top.

Consider how your body functions. You consume food and drink containing calories. Your body processes this consumption and uses what it needs for heat, energy, and growth (including cell replacement). Anything left over is stored as fat. This process is shown in the following diagram.

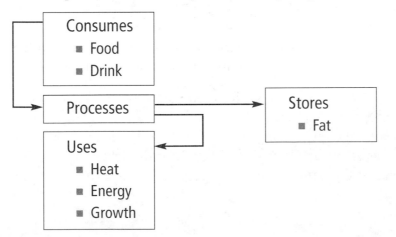

The challenge in any attempt to control weight is to balance consumption and bodily needs so there won't be anything left over to store as fat. Obviously, if you consume more than you need, you will gain weight. If you want to lose weight, reducing consumption below your body's needs forces it to draw on stored fat to meet its daily requirements. The concept is simple, but putting it into practice requires you to rethink the function of food in your life. Commit to a healthy food plan, and be disciplined in your eating habits. The payoff is worth the commitment.

Many considerations are relevant to a healthier food plan. In general, the rule should be moderation. You probably won't want to make sudden, dramatic changes in your eating habits. So, move gradually toward your goal. Start by looking at little things that add weight. For example, a tablespoon of half-and-half in two cups of coffee a day adds up to 14,600 calories and four pounds of weight gain in a year. Two cans of beer a day beyond your normal calorie requirements adds 20 pounds in a year. Snack foods such as candy, nuts, and ice cream can be unsuspecting sources of gradual weight gain. Start by eliminating or cutting back on these. Here are some further guidelines:

- Move toward eliminating all high-fat fast foods. This includes hamburgers, fried chicken, fried fish, French fries, and pizza.

- Choose lean meats and skinless poultry and trim away any visible fat before cooking. Fish and other sea foods are very low in fat and provide some beneficial fatty acids for a healthy heart.

- Increase significantly your intake of carbohydrates. This includes whole-grain breads, cereals, pasta, rice, fruits, vegetables, legumes and grains such as barley.

- Limit alcohol consumption to no more than two drinks a day.

- Avoid large amounts of fat from butter, cheese, cream, fatty meats, poultry skin, chocolate, rich desserts, pastries, many cakes, and biscuits.

- Avoid deep-frying. Broil fatty foods such as red meats. If you fry or sauté, use polyunsaturated vegetable oil.

- Use skim milk rather than whole milk and use low-fat yogurt.

- Limit egg consumption to less than three a week.

- Eat unsugared dry cereals, and use them as snacks.

- Eliminate or reduce your consumption of desserts that are high in sugar content. Eat fresh fruit and melon instead.

- Eliminate bacon, sausage, fried eggs, and biscuits from your breakfast menu. Eat cereals and fruit instead.

- Don't skip meals. Rather, adjust the amount of your meal. If you eat lunch out, eat a lighter dinner.

USE CALORIES BY EXERCISING

You must use up or give up 3,500 calories to lose one pound. By adjusting your eating habits, you can easily give up 200 to 300 calories a day. If you increase your level of exercise, so that you use up 200 to 300 additional calories, by the end of a week you will have lost a pound. A lifestyle change that nets a weight loss of a pound a week will have you 50 pounds lighter at the end of a year and, as a side benefit, you will be in better shape physically. Use the chart to pick how you will use up additional calories.

CALORIES USED IN 30 MINUTES

Activity	Your Weight					
	120	140	160	180	200	220
Slow Walking*	87	102	114	129	144	159
Moderate Walking*	123	144	162	183	204	225
Brisk Walking*	159	186	213	240	267	294
Swimming	237	276	315	354	396	435
Cycling	135	156	180	201	222	246
Aerobics/Dancing	168	195	225	252	282	309
Rowing Machine	195	228	258	291	324	357
Hiking	198	234	267	300	333	366
Household chores	114	132	153	171	192	210
Yard Work	150	168	201	225	252	276

*You use the same calories to walk a given distance whether you walk slowly or rapidly. The difference is how long it takes.

The most difficult part of regular exercise is working it into your schedule. It is often a challenge to find the time. But, be willing to be unconventional if necessary. Could you get up an hour earlier? What about immediately upon arriving home from work? Is there time during your mid-day break? When you find the right time for you, stick to the schedule. View it as a necessary part of maintaining a healthy body, much the same as brushing your teeth and bathing.

WATER—THE SECRET INGREDIENT

The human body is about 70 percent water. Water is involved in nearly every body process, including digestion, absorption, circulation, and excretion. Blood is about 90 percent water; it transports nutrients to the cells and washes out lactic acid and other waste products.

Muscles are about 75 percent water, and without it they wouldn't be able to expand and contract. Water continually moistens the lungs, enabling proper breathing. In addition, water controls both internal and external temperatures, lubricates joints, and allows organs such as the kidneys to do their jobs.

As a rule of thumb, women need about 3 quarts of fluid a day and men need about 4 quarts for their bodies to function properly. Most people meet their fluid needs from food, other liquids consumed, and drinking water when thirsty. An estimate of fluid need (water plus other liquids) can be calculated by multiplying body weight by 1/2 ounce. When your body experiences a water shortage, it automatically retains what it has. But when retention occurs, the stored water becomes more and more contaminated with waste and the kidneys become overburdened. The liver is the backup organ when the kidneys can't handle the task. This creates a further problem, however. When the liver is trying to deal with the toxic overflow, it can't do its own job well. It becomes less efficient at metabolizing stored body fat as usable energy. As a result, body weight begins to build since stored-up fat is not being used and, since the body is on drought alert, it is retaining water.

The solution to this problem is to drink plenty of water. This means routinely quenching your thirst plus drinking extra when exercising or in hot weather. This allows your kidneys to do their job of ridding the body of wastes and your liver to do its job of metabolizing stored fat.

Along with a move to low-fat food and increased exercise, adequate water consumption will add exciting results when you step on the scales. Lost weight won't be just the loss of retained water. It will be the loss of fat due to your body's increased ability to transform calories to energy and a reduced appetite due to the increased water intake.

You may consider fluids from foods, such as soups and broth, fruit juices, milk, and noncaffeinated soft drinks as part of your total fluid consumption. However, alcoholic and caffeinated beverages can't be counted because alcohol and caffeine dehydrate the body, thus increasing its need for water.

Choosing the Right Foods

Foods to Avoid	Substitutes
Whole milk	Skim or 1 percent milk
Fried egg	Poached or boiled egg
Biscuit	Hard or whole-grain roll
Croissant	Whole-grain bread
Prime rib	Pork loin
Rib-eye steak	Top sirloin or filet mignon
Fried chicken	Grilled skinless chicken breast
Barbecued ribs	Flank steak with barbecue sauce
Caesar salad	Caesar salad without eggs
Potato salad	Roasted potatoes
Marinated pasta salad	Pasta salad with low-fat dressing
Tuna salad with mayonnaise	Tuna salad with nonfat yogurt
Ground beef hamburger	Hamburger with half lean ground beef and half ground turkey
Regular sliced ham	Extra-lean sliced ham
Salami	Smoked turkey breast
Corned beef	Lean roast beef
Beef hot dog	Turkey hot dog
Regular ice cream	Fat-free ice cream or yogurt
Strawberry shortcake	Strawberries with lite pound cake
Ambrosia	Fresh fruit salad
Piña colada	Strawberry daiquiri

KEY POINTS

- About 35 percent of Americans are overweight.
- People eat for social and emotional reasons as well as to meet their physical needs.
- An effective weight-control program has three components—a low-fat food plan, exercise, and water consumption.
- The average person needs 10 to 12 calories daily per pound of body weight to maintain weight.
- The average person needs 1/2 ounce of fluid intake daily per pound of body weight.
- You have to give up or use up 3,500 calories to lose one pound of weight.

Things to Do

Instructions: In the space below, list the things you want to do as a result of reading this chapter. Then, choose a target date for completing each of your action items.

Action Item	Target Date

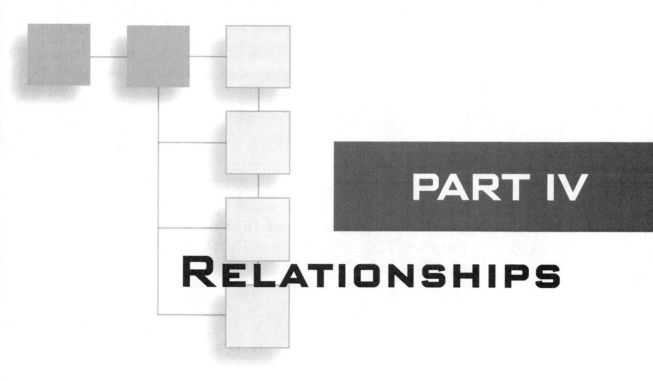

PART IV

RELATIONSHIPS

This section discusses personal relationships during retirement. When you complete it, you should be able to build better relationships, create a strong inner-circle support system, do a better job of handling family demands, and explain the difference between the two languages of love and decide which best fits your comfort zone.

CHAPTER 13

RETIREMENT RELATIONSHIPS

You can always tell a real friend; when you've made a fool of yourself, he doesn't feel you've done a permanent job.

—Laurence J. Peter

You generally get back the kind of behavior you send out. If you want better service at a restaurant, you're more likely to get it by being patient, pleasant, and positive. If you want help from a telephone operator, you'll have better luck if you put a smile in your voice as you make the request. Good relationships with others start with you, not with the other party.

If you want better treatment from others and want to set the stage for new friendships, learn to send out positive signals. You must earn, through your actions, the kind of behavior you seek from others. You should do this even when you are tempted to respond differently.

SHARING YOUR POSITIVE ATTITUDE

Here are some ideas that will improve your positive attitude by sharing it.

- When you give part of your positive attitude to others, the recipient feels better, and so do you. *You keep your positive attitude by giving it away.*

- Staying positive by giving your positive attitude to others works at any stage of life, but it seems to work better and mean more after retirement.

▪ Although some retirees don't need social contact as much as others, to stay positive through retirement most need at least a few opportunities a week to give their positive attitudes to others. And, strange as it may seem, the results to the giver are best when the giving is toughest.

▪ The less you feel like giving part of your positive attitude away, the more giving it away can do for you. Sometimes it can get you out of a deep, negative rut.

▪ Everyone winds up a winner when you share your positive attitude with others. Of course, you must do this in your own way. As you do, do not get the "guilts" when you discover you are the big winner. That is the way the system works!

YOUR HUMAN-RELATIONS CHALLENGE

Retirement is a time when you may need more human companionship, not less! The reinforcement you receive from others will mean more and more to you. Often retirees leave some of their best relationships behind in the workplace. Others reduce relationships further by moving.

What does this mean? It means that when you retire you have a new human-relations challenge. It means you should work harder to keep current friends and make new ones. How good you become at this can make a difference during your retirement years.

If you accept the challenge of building better relationships, you should consider that in a relationship both you and the other party must benefit somewhat equally. There must be a balance in reward. You should get something you need from the other person, and that person should get something he or she needs from you. In this way, both parties come out ahead.

You have heard that it's better to give than to receive. Giving should be its own reward. This may be all that is needed by some people. Ultimately, however, the person who constantly gives without receiving starts to back away. Everyone needs something out of a relationship. This is a human-relations fundamental. Those who ignore it usually spend a lot of time alone.

THE ART OF CONVERSATION

Communication is the lifeblood of any relationship. Relationships prosper almost entirely through your ability to communicate. No matter how good your other human-relations skills may be, without good communication skills, your life will be lacking.

People need affirmation that they are all right—that they are in tune with life. A good conversation is highly rewarding. Like good wine, the older we become the more pleasure we should find in our conversations.

Yet, at the very time when communication becomes more important, some people seem to lose their communication skills. Have you experienced being in a perfect environment for a meaningful conversation—such as a restaurant setting with a private table, good food, and ambiance—and then wasting the evening because your partner is insensitive? Maybe you did all the listening. Or perhaps your dinner partner introduced all the topics for conversation. What was your feeling when you realized you were not being heard? After such an experience, one cannot help but wonder how many potentially good relationships never developed because one party failed to understand the importance of a dialogue.

How can you improve your art of conversation? How can you improve your present relationships and build new ones? Here are some suggestions:

Give out more rewards. It starts with your behavior. Be an outstanding listener. Make your comments fit into the fabric of the conversation. Listen with your eyes as well as your mind. Work hard to implement the process.

Be sure that you receive rewards in return. Be an involved rather than passive conversationalist. If you are doing most of the listening, take action. Intervene in a sensitive manner. With a smile on your face and a twinkle in your eye, say:

"That's interesting—I once had something similar happen."

"To add to what you just said . . ."

"Would you like a reaction to that?"

If you are consistently on the short end of a conversation with an overly talkative person, you have only yourself to blame.

View conversation as an art. Set the stage for each opportunity by eliminating interference. Give each exchange your best effort, and take pride in your skills as a conversationalist.

Intervene when others start to repeat themselves. You do your friends a disservice when you pretend to listen to their jokes, problems, or stories a second, third, or fourth time. Stop them with the admission that you often do the same thing. Say with a smile:

"I remember that—you covered it the last time we met, remember?"

"I've heard that somewhere before."

Then quickly get the conversation on a different track, making certain it has a positive effect. If you are guilty of repetition yourself, ask your friends to help you get out of the habit. Make a game of it. They should be happy to play because they are the primary beneficiaries.

Redirect negative conversations. Positive conversations are rewarding; negative ones are debilitating. If you sense that a conversation is becoming negative, don't hesitate to ask a question or make a point that will get the conversation on a more positive track, such as:

"I understand you had a great time in San Francisco. Tell me about it."

Rehearse difficult conversations ahead of time. If someone you care about has been negative during recent conversations, say at the beginning that you have something exciting to share. This should help guarantee some equal time. The idea is to make sure at the beginning that there will be a balanced exchange before the meeting is over.

Send a special reward when you have been guilty of overtalking. There are times when you need to dump problems on another person. When this happens, send a thank-you card, flowers, or whatever expresses gratitude for being a caring listener. This way you can start the next conversation without feelings of guilt.

Avoid too much alcohol. A glass of wine can often make a positive contribution to the art of conversation. In moderation, it is not unusual for both parties to relax more and communicate better. Too much alcohol, however, can cause a person to talk too much, too loudly, and too incoherently. Everyone loses.

Feed your mind fresh, positive conversational material. You cannot be a good conversationalist unless you have a reservoir of thoughts from which to draw. If you like jokes, make certain you have new, appropriate jokes for those you frequently see. If you are a storyteller, keep in mind that it is fun to hear a well-practiced story the first time, but not the second. If you enjoy intellectual conversations, avoid talking about the same theme too often. Also, be sensitive in expressing opinions on controversial subjects. Those who constantly get on the soapbox risk adding an emotional dimension that will distort a relationship.

Some Additional Thoughts on Improving Communications

Here are some additional thoughts to help you fine-tune your conversational skills. Check the ones you need to practice.

- [ ] Pay attention when someone is talking to you. Focus your attention and energy on listening.

- [ ] Maintain eye contact during conversations.

- [ ] Concentrate on what is said. Don't be distracted by style, appearance, or mannerisms.

- [ ] Verify through questions and restatements your understanding of what you are told.

- [ ] Avoid slang, jargon, and acronyms unless you know the other person will understand you.

- [ ] Minimize defensiveness when someone tells you something that threatens your self image.

- [ ] Check out your understanding of things you see rather than assuming or drawing incorrect inferences.

- [ ] Maintain a tentativeness in your conclusions rather than taking a dogmatic position.

- [ ] Be cautious about judging or blaming others. Check your facts and state your own position, then examine any differences in perception.

☐ Use indefinite pronouns carefully. You communicate much more clearly when you refer to someone or something by name rather than using "he," "she," or "it."

☐ Stay with a topic long enough to develop understanding, rather than flitting from topic to topic.

☐ Be willing to set your topic aside until the other person's has been discussed. Then, return to yours.

☐ Explore feelings and reactions to the topic under discussion.

☐ Use broad questions to open conversations and gain information. For example, you might ask, "What did you have for dinner?" rather than a series of narrow questions such as "Did you have turkey for dinner?"

Some Thoughts on Being a Friend

Friends are special people. You may have several acquaintances, but only a few friends. Some friends are "best" friends while others are just "good" friends. Generally, friends are not family members, but they might be. A special aunt, uncle, cousin, brother, sister, or even a parent or spouse may be a friend. What makes a friend different from other people? Here are a few suggestions. Check the ones you need to work on.

☐ Friends spend time together. By being together, you have the opportunity to get to know each other.

☐ Friends share common interests. Interest in the same things facilitates enjoyment of time together.

☐ There is a feeling of equity between friends. Neither feels taken advantage of by the other.

☐ There is trust between friends. You can say what you think or feel and you won't be ridiculed or rejected for your thoughts. Friends do not talk to others about things revealed to them in confidence.

☐ Friends are available when needed. When you want to talk about something or need help, a friend finds a mutually agreeable time to be there.

☐ Friends support each other. You can disclose your dreams and hopes for the future to a friend without fear of embarrassment.

☐ Friends can resolve their differences. When disagreement or conflict occurs, friends are able to reach a conclusion that is satisfactory to both of them.

☐ Friends are comfortable together. There is an easy flow of conversation supported by a lack of tension.

☐ Friends are dependable. When a friend agrees to do something, you know it will be done or you will be advised ahead of time.

☐ Friends remain individuals. Friends allow each other the freedom to do things without them and to have other friendships without feeling left out or jealous.

BUILDING A SUPPORT SYSTEM

Without planning, it is possible, especially for those without family members close by, to wind up almost alone. By taking charge, you can create a human support system. A human support system consists of those who provide frequent spiritual, emotional, psychological, and occasionally, financial support. This group constitutes your inner circle.

The word *support* simply means that when you need help, these people will see you through your problem. You would probably not have to ask them, because they would voluntarily come to your aid in one way or another. They keep in touch and do things for you.

There is a tendency for people to seek friendships among people their own age. While this may contribute to compatible values and interests, it limits the kind of support these friends can offer. So, as you participate in groups where a range of ages is represented, look for opportunities to develop friendships with younger people. When called upon, these friends may offer a different perspective on your problem and be physically able to assist when needed. It is often said your doctor and lawyer should be younger than you. This will increase the odds that your doctor can provide care through your lifetime and your lawyer will be around to settle your estate after your death.

When it comes to human response, there are no guarantees, which is why any inner-circle system should include several people.

It goes without saying that you must help earn any support you may require before you need it. This means you should start working now to build sustaining, mutually beneficial relationships. Often you will be on the support end more than the receiving end. Love and compassion must be the bedrock of your support system.

The accompanying illustration demonstrates one inner-circle support system. The system is unique, but it serves as an example, especially if you are working on one of your own.

The squares indicate family relationships, and circles signify friends. A double line around a square or circle indicates the relationship has been neglected. Not all family members qualify as inner-circle members. Distance often makes it impossible to include a relative, and sometimes an irreconcilable conflict is present. Even in ideal situations, a balance between relatives and friends is a good idea. The closer a relative or friend is to the center of the circle, the more important the relationship.

There are 18 people in this example. This is a large number. Generally, a system should have between 5 and 20 people.

If you like the concept of the inner-circle support system, you should evaluate what it will take to develop one or to improve one that you already possess. These considerations are significant.

Each Inner Circle Is Different

We are all individuals with special support needs. Some people are loners and settle for a small human support system; others are more socially inclined and are happier with a large support system; still others may decide to confine their support system exclusively to family members. In all cases, it is important to real-ize that a human support system is a necessary part of a fulfilling retirement.

The example can be a guide, but your inner circle will be uniquely your own. It will have its own composition and design.

Start from the middle and work to the outside. If you have a life partner, you and your partner should consider doing one together. If you are alone and have only a few relatives to put into your circle, it will be necessary to build it primarily with friends and professional people. Whatever you eventually design should provide a new perspective on relationships and help you focus on the human side of your life.

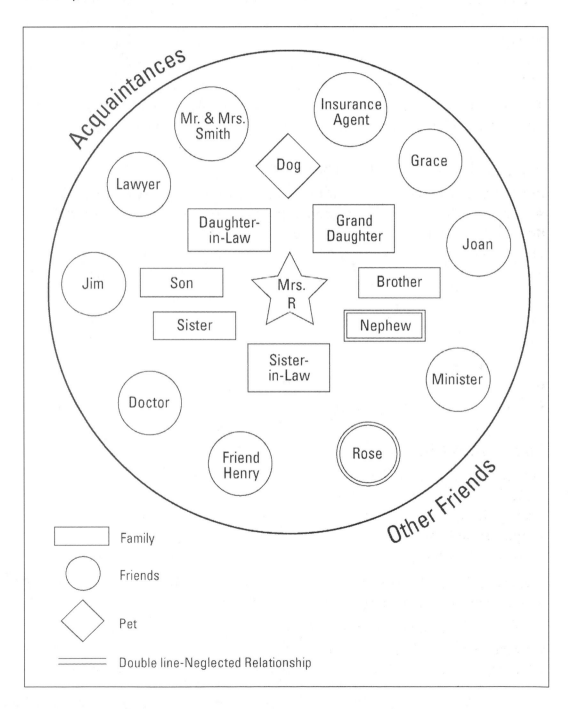

Keeping Your Inner Circle Private

Once you have completed your circle, it isn't necessary to broadcast the results. You might share the information with those closest to you, but generally it's best to keep it contained.

Building an inner circle may appear to be self-serving, but it isn't. It is nothing more than a way to help you focus on your most significant relationships. It is not meant to encourage an exclusive club that would cause you to ignore other friends. In fact, inner circles often motivate people to work toward building new, quality relationships.

Adding People to Your Inner Circle

After you choose those you want to include in your inner circle, you will occasionally add a person who has become special in your life. Don't, however, bring someone into your circle simply because you suddenly like him or her. A mature, durable, two-way relationship takes time to develop. In fact, when a new member is added, you should be proud because you helped it occur by building a relationship.

With new members, you must ensure that you maintain each relationship. Ask yourself these three questions:

- Can I spend adequate time to keep the relationship alive and active?

- Can I take care of new members without neglecting older ones?

- Am I willing to provide, if necessary, the same kind of support I would anticipate receiving if I needed it?

Remember, it's usually better to have a small, well-kept garden than a larger one that you are forced to neglect.

Strengthening Your Inner Circle as You Prepare for Retirement

Retirement should give you time to strengthen present relationships, restore those that have been neglected, and add new friends. Those who have already established such a group have a jump on retirement, because once an individual leaves the workplace, friends take on increased importance.

Knowing those you want to spend more time with after retirement constitutes a human-relations plan. When new members are added, excitement is added. The nice thing about working on your circle is that you don't have to wait years for it to pay off. The rewards are immediate.

You Cannot Hoard Relationships

One nice thing about a paid-up financial endowment is that you can depend on it. A check will come every month. Wouldn't it be nice if you could depend on relatives and friends to provide human support in the same manner?

Unfortunately, it doesn't work that way. Relationships are often capricious. For example, even when you have developed an outstanding relationship, that individual might move away. You could have a highly supportive child living nearby one day and across the country the next. People also have changes in their lives that can cause them to pull away. This is why you must work constantly on your inner circle. Thus, if you lose members, for whatever reason, you will not be alone.

Satisfying Now—Supportive Later

The ideal inner-circle support system is one that is enjoyable and fulfilling before and during the early stages of retirement, and supportive down the road should it become necessary. Of course, one cannot fully anticipate the future, so any system contains risk, just as any financial plan contains risk. But those who enjoy and feel secure with their support systems early in their development can feel good, even though their plans may not produce the results they anticipated. Their lives have already been enhanced!

KEY POINTS

- When you retire you need to develop new friendships to replace the ones left behind at work.
- Retirees who wind up lonely often ignore building relationships until it's too late.
- An important quality when making new friends is a positive attitude. You get back what you send out.
- One way to keep a positive attitude is to give it away.
- Communication is the life blood of any relationship.
- Improving your conversational skills is critical to building and maintaining relationships.
- Properly implemented, an inner circle enhances the quality of your life and the lives of those you love.
- You can improve your conversational talents and increase your circle of friends, but it takes work.

Things to Do

Instructions: In the space below, list the things you want to do as a result of reading this chapter. Then, choose a target date for completing each of your action items.

Action Item	Target Date

CHAPTER 14

FAMILY RELATIONSHIPS

The thing that impresses me most about America is the way parents obey their children.

—Duke of Windsor

Your career has had a powerful impact on your family. A successful career may have added to an overall sense of well-being and contributed to a rewarding family life—or the demands of your career may have contributed to the breakup of your marriage. Work is sometimes used as an escape from unhappy family relationships and may be blamed for causing them. Retirement can be a time for reassessing family relationships and doing whatever is needed to develop them to the desired level of closeness.

As you anticipate retirement, it is easy to become preoccupied with your own concerns. However, your retirement will have a profound impact on your life partner. To a lesser degree, other close family members will also be affected. You can moderate this impact through open discussions. Keep family members involved in planning your retirement. Let them know they are not being left out of your plans for the future. Don't hesitate to explore feelings about post-retirement budgets, schedules, where to live, and what to do. Here are some suggestions:

- Ask family members to tell you how they feel about your retirement and how they see it affecting them.

- Express understanding and concern for those feelings.

- Be curious. Try to understand the underlying reasons for their anxiety, rather than dismissing their comments as unimportant. Ask questions for clarification and repeat what you hear, in your own words, for verification.

- Be open and honest about your own feelings, both with yourself and others.

- Remember, there is no right or wrong when discussing feelings—they simply are.

- Be flexible and willing to compromise to accommodate the concerns of family members.

TIME TOGETHER

Time together is important to all relationships. The average worker doesn't spend much time with family members—maybe four or five hours each evening, when not traveling, and a few hours on the weekend. Sometimes, even when physically home, attention is consumed by work-related problems. Retirement can dramatically alter both the amount and quality of your time with family members. Think about this time and how it will be used. Couples who are not prepared, especially if the retiree has nothing to do, very quickly can get on each other's nerves.

It's unrealistic to expect both members of a life partnership will enjoy all of the same activities. Therefore, it is unrealistic to expect you will spend all of your time together. The challenge is to identify what each wants to do that the other does not; then give each other permission to engage in those activities alone. If you can do this in a way that neither party feels left out, you will be successful. One way to get there is to schedule individual activities at the same time. For example, one can go to a ball game while the other visits a museum.

To ensure that your time together is positive, discuss the following items with your life partner:

- Which of your partner's present activities does he or she wish to continue after your retirement?
- What new activities is your partner interested in pursuing?
- What activities will you engage in together after you retire?
- What activities will you engage in individually after you retire?

FAMILY ROLES AND HOUSEHOLD CHORES

During your working years, certain roles evolved within the family unit. At retirement, these are open to reexamination. Who is in charge of what? One partner may handle outside chores such as car, yard, and house maintenance while the other handles inside chores such as cooking, cleaning, and laundry. In two-career families, less traditional roles may exist, but role adaptation still evolves.

When you retire and have more time available, problems may develop around who handles various chores. If you try to get more involved, your partner may see it as an invasion of his or her turf. If you don't get involved, your partner may resent your extra time. There is no way to resolve these problems other than talking them through. Here is an outline that will help facilitate such a discussion:

- Which chores do each of you identify as your responsibility?

- Which chores would you like to swap with each other? For example, in retirement, some couples take turns, week to week, handling the evening meal.

- Which chores could you do together? Gardening, housecleaning, and grocery shopping are examples.

- Which of you handles family finances? How can you educate the other in this responsibility?

IMPROVING RELATIONSHIPS WITH ADULT CHILDREN

You can't be happy in retirement if you walk away from your children or grandchildren. Rather, you should take a positive view and build better relationships with adult children while simultaneously protecting your own freedom. Provide your family with the required support (financial or otherwise), but don't neglect other members of your support circle. Your adult children may require more from you than they are currently in a position to return. Things may change later and, when you need it, their support will be there.

In reviewing relationships with adult children, three myths must be dispelled.

Myth 1: First is the idea that the generation gap is wider today than ever. Evidence suggests the opposite. The gap has been closing for the past several years. Families are getting together more, not less. Communication is improving.

Myth 2: The second myth is that conflict within families is always bad and should be avoided. Some conflict and negotiation is present in all relationships and should be anticipated. Too often parents avoid problems that need to be discussed because they fear conflict. The same is true, perhaps more so, with adult children. Confronting problems can be healthy; otherwise they may remain unsolved for years.

Myth 3: The third myth is the belief that love will solve all problems. As a parent, all you need do is love your children enough, and eventually everything will turn out all right. The truth is that love can sometimes be a barrier to good communication. Love is the most beautiful emotion, but it can make both parties so sensitive that both sides bury problems that should be confronted and solved.

Anything you can initiate to improve relationships with your children will strengthen your support system. No matter how good you think the relationships are, some improvement usually can be made. If a relationship is bad, it can usually be turned around with effort. Here are four commitments you can make to help with your family relationships. Check those you feel to be important.

- [ ] Nothing positive will happen unless I become a good listener. I must endeavor to understand how my children feel and what their problems may be.

- [ ] I should forget old misunderstandings and start with a clean slate. I understand we can't discuss new problems if we continue to allow old wounds to be opened. Even if time has proven me right, old problems need to be buried.

- [ ] More communication on serious matters needs to be initiated with my children. When such sessions are necessary, I will not be talked out of them.

- [ ] I intend to discuss the inner-circle concept with my family and explain why a balance is necessary between family and friends. In this way, I can explain why my freedom is important.

BECOME A PARENT EMERITUS

There comes a times in the life of all parents when, to keep from being victims, they should change their style of parenting. They should continue to love and enjoy relationships with their adult children and accept suggestions and support from them, but they should discontinue assuming responsibility, even when it is needed. How, as a parent, can one separate love from responsibility, when you want to help (and you have done so in the past), but know that it will take away from your opportunity to enjoy retirement? Why not become a parent emeritus?

When a college professor retires, he or she is often given the designation of professor emeritus. When this occurs, the professor withdraws from active service (responsibility) but retains rank and title. One with emeritus status is often consulted on problems, but active involvement is over and responsibility is fully transferred to others.

Of course, emeritus status for professors is bestowed by an educational institution. If adult children would do the same to their parents, the problem would be solved. But adult children do not always do this.

So what is the answer?

Bestow the honor on yourself. Declare your own emeritus status openly so that all family members will know! To back it up, start refusing "old-time" responsibilities. Continue to love and enjoy adult children and grandchildren to the fullest, be available for consultation, but back away from stepping in or bailing out. Like a professor moving away from teaching responsibilities, move away from parenting in the old sense. Keep in mind that you are taking two steps (financial and health areas) to make your retirement years as carefree and fulfilling as possible. Now you may need to take a third step.

How do you go about declaring emeritus status? Everyone should do this based upon individual family situations and his or her own comfort zone. The following examples might provide some techniques and, more important, the courage to take action of your own.

> *"When Jean and I were getting close to retirement we had a family party and discussed our plans openly with our four children. We communicated that we had worked hard to establish a retirement nest egg and that we had a health program in place. We would do everything in our power to maintain our independence as long as possible. We told them we would always love them, but we wanted and needed the freedom to fulfill our retirement dreams without additional responsibilities. It worked."*

"We did it with our attitudes. Rather than communicate with words, we implied through our actions that we intended to be free and creative, to travel a lot, and be different in the future. We showed our love in every way possible, but we gave no signals that we would assume further responsibilities. Our problems have been minimal."

"We used an oblique approach. We told our gang that we would not worry about them if they would not worry about us. We said we intended to deal with the aging process to the best of our abilities and maintain our independence as long as possible. Then we really declared our new status by saying that if we needed help we wouldn't hesitate to ask for it."

To put oneself in an emeritus, or no-responsibility role, is more difficult for some than for others. Many fail. For example, some individuals (perhaps without knowing it) mess up their retirement years by holding on to family responsibilities to fill a void that they cannot fill from normal retirement activities. Others continue to provide unneeded emotional and financial support to maintain control. Still others fear that if they do not continue to provide support (whatever form it may take), they will lose their children's love—which may or may not be there in the first place.

So, for many people, becoming a parent emeritus is more complex than it appears. Yet the payoff is far greater than most retirees with children expect. It can even boil down to a happy retirement versus one fraught with guilt and resentment.

HOW TO HANDLE A CHILD'S DIVORCE

Divorces occur at all ages, but they're most common among younger people. You may face an unexpected divorce with your children. If grandchildren are involved, things can be traumatic.

Comparatively little attention has been paid to the impact of divorce on grandparents. Yet, like losing a spouse, discovering you have a serious health problem, or getting a divorce yourself, it can be devastating. The shock could cause you to behave in a way you could regret later. How might you accept their trauma and disappointment without damaging your own happiness? Here are some tips:

▪ No matter how upset you are, don't close the door. Keep communication open. Remember that your children have their own life and, as adults, are responsible for their actions. You don't have to like it, but you must respect that it is their life—not yours.

■ Protect your freedom. Don't rush to open your home or bank account until you are sure what you want to do. It's easy to overreact and regret it later.

■ Accept the premise that they are paying enough of a price without your making them pay more.

■ Make every effort to maintain good relationships with both parents. Avoid, when possible, taking sides.

■ Keep in mind a daughter-in-law or son-in-law can be very special.

■ When grandchildren are involved, think about family continuity. Decide what role you want to play with your grandchildren. A new alignment of relationships may be required.

■ Try not to cut off access to your grandchildren.

■ Keep an open mind on any new partners that develop on either side.

This advice does not mean a passive role on your part is best. You are not required to simply sit back. You have a need to talk about the problems with others and also to express your feelings with those immediately involved. It is essential that you handle the problem openly. You should remain determined to stay in charge of defining your own role in future relationships.

SITTING ON YOUR MONEY

Some retirees feel guilty about holding their money. Often the more they have, the more guilt they feel. They see themselves in an excellent financial position while their children are still in the process of building. Often these folks accelerate the giving process when it would be best for both parties not to do so. They shell out to soften guilt feelings that should not be there in the first place. This causes both parties to keep roles that should be left behind. Retirees often fail to give their children space to build their own lives. Adult children often fail to understand the new roles their parents want and need.

REDEFINING YOUR ROLE AS A PARENT

How can you get the most out of retirement and still be the kind of parent you should be? How can you make the transition and maintain excellent relationships with your children? Here are some thoughts that may or may not apply (or appeal) to you. Check those that do.

☐ Declare yourself a parent emeritus.

☐ Do not subordinate yourself to the needs of your children. Consider yourself first. It is your turn now.

☐ Generate activities away from your adult children. Demonstrate that you are in charge and want to live your own life. Be with your children when you want to be with them.

☐ Give your children the freedom to live their own lives. Refrain from intervention. If you give too much, it can be awkward for them—especially if there are strings attached, real or implied. Give them the privilege of handling their own problems.

☐ If your children ask for more help than they should, learn to say no in a loving but firm way. The reward-reversal process will not start until this happens.

☐ Keep in mind that you have had enough worries in previous stages of your life. If your children do not ask you to assume their worries for them, why do it?

☐ Work to see your children as adults—not the children they used to be. Recognize that they are capable of handling their own problems. Provide support only when necessary.

☐ Discuss how reward systems can change over the years. Anything you can do to help them understand your new role will help.

☐ Discuss why, as a retiree, you need to stay in charge, why you need to protect your nest egg, and why you may develop a new lifestyle.

☐ Don't use your children or grandchildren as time fillers. Enjoy them and have fun, but maintain your own leisure activities.

☐ Don't bypass your children just to enjoy your grandchildren.

It is not easy to build an ideal relationship with your adult children. You want them as pillars in your inner-circle support system, but you don't want to lean on them too soon, nor do you want them to lean on you. It is a delicate balance. Tell them you love them and respect their need to be free. Make sure they respect yours.

Assessing Family Relationships

Write a brief assessment of your relationship with each of the following family members. Note where improvement is required.

Life Partner: _____

_____

_____

Children: _____

_____

_____

Grandchildren: _____

_____

_____

Parents: _____

_____

_____

Siblings: _____

_____

Others: _____

_____

KEY POINTS

- Retirement affects family members as well as the retiree.
- Retirement presents an opportunity to improve family relationships, especially with adult children.
- It is unrealistic to expect both partners to enjoy all of the same activities.
- Family roles and responsibilities for household chores should be reexamined at retirement.
- As children mature, you need to become a different kind of parent.
- There are advantages to becoming a parent emeritus.
- Problems with adult children need to be handled openly, especially those relating to divorce.

Things to Do

Instructions: In the space below, list the things you want to do as a result of reading this chapter. Then, choose a target date for completing each of your action items.

Action Item	Target Date

CHAPTER 15

The Two Languages of Love

To grow old is to pass from passion to compassion.

—Albert Camus

The need for caring, sharing, loving, and intimacy begins at birth and continues throughout life. This need does not disappear as you age—you don't outgrow it. In fact, intimacy may be more critical in later years when meaningful relationships are fewer and loneliness may begin to invade your life.

There are two dimensions to love. Both are exciting and have their own special rewards. Each can be a beautiful manifestation of affection and love between two people.

Physical love starts out with touching, kissing, teasing, massaging, and can culminate with the exciting climax of sexual intercourse. It is an experience most adults can achieve regardless of age. It is the primary language of romantic love. It adds to the quality of life.

But love is also enjoying the company of another, with little or no physical contact. It is intimate conversation and the sharing of private thoughts. It is candlelight dinner with romantic overtones. It's doing fun things together. Mature people have a way of making the most of this so-called second language of love. Some enjoy it as much as the first language. This chapter discusses both, but first it dispels some of the myths and misunderstandings about sex and age.

MYTHS ABOUT SEX AND AGING

Social scientists have begun serious research in this vital area and only recently has the subject been covered openly. To measure your knowledge in this subject, answer the questions on the following pretest. Correct answers follow the questions.

A significant segment of society assumes that older people don't have sexual desires and are unable to do anything sexually, even if they wanted to. Some even believe that sexual activity in old age is perverse. Other common myths include: sexual desire ends with menopause, older people are unattractive and therefore sexually undesirable, and impotence is common among elderly men. Sexual activity among older people is generally considered taboo.

The problem with these myths is that they are often believed by the elderly themselves. As a result, older people adopt a negative view of their own sexual feelings, desires, and fantasies. The myth of sexless older years held by young people becomes a self-fulfilling prophecy when they reach old age. As a result, many elderly people are overwhelmed with guilt and shame when they have sexual desires.

Reality Is Different

Both men and women are interested in sex and participate in sexual activities in their 70s, 80s, and beyond. Studies have documented that sexual desire, interest, and activity may continue well into the ninth decade of life.

While it is true that the frequency of sexual intercourse decreases with advancing years, cessation is most often the result of a decline in the physical health of one or both partners. A decrease in frequency is typically accompanied by an increase in embracing, cuddling, and holding as expressions of intimacy.

Past sexual interest, enjoyment, and frequency are the three indicators that correlate positively with present sexual interest and activity among both older men and women. In other words, your present level of activity will probably continue as long as you are physically able and have a capable partner.

Pretest on Sex and Age

True *False*

_____ _____ 1. Female sexual activity knows no age limit.

_____ _____ 2. A new partner will keep a male's sex activity at a higher level indefinitely, regardless of his age.

_____ _____ 3. The sharp decline in sex interest for women after menopause has a sound physical foundation.

_____ _____ 4. Biology has established a mandatory age for sexual retirement among men.

_____ _____ 5. There is a greater loss of sexual ability in men than among women who are past retirement age.

_____ _____ 6. Casual sex becomes more desirable with age.

_____ _____ 7. Fifty percent of men over 70 function sexually.

_____ _____ 8. Few changes are more threatening to the male ego than loss of ability to function sexually.

_____ _____ 9. Cardiac energy expenditure during a sexual climax is approximately equal to climbing two flights of stairs.

_____ _____ 10. The decline in sexual activities is steeper than other physical levels such as endurance, mobility, or general health.

_____ _____ 11. A Duke University study found that approximately 15 percent of subjects over 60 years of age grew sexually over the 10-year time span of the study.

_____ _____ 12. Much impotence diagnosed as organic, attributable to aging, is actually attributable to psychological factors.

_____ _____ 13. Primary opposition to sexual freedom among seniors comes from adult children who have already accepted greater freedom for themselves.

_____ _____ 14. Some retirees foolishly abstain from sex to avoid painful feelings of frustration, anxiety, or depression over their declining sexual performance.

True	False	
____	____	15. Sexual problems experienced by aging males are often reversible.
____	____	16. It is not important to your identity to feel good about yourself sexually.
____	____	17. Sex is totally a physical thing.
____	____	18. The sexual activity of females is directly related to their partners.
____	____	19. Lack of interest is the main cause of declining sexual activity.
____	____	20. Some retirees, who have negative attitudes and want to forget about sex, use age as an excuse not to participate.

Total Correct _____

Answers: (1) T (there is some decline in late, late years only); (2) F (may be responsible for higher level on a temporary basis only); (3) F (reverse is true in many women, because there is no longer a fear of pregnancy); (4) F (a few men over 90 years of age are still potent); (5) T; (6) F (less desirable; as a rule, the relationship becomes more important than the act); (7) T; (8) T; (9) T; (10) T; (11) T; (12) T; (13) T; (14) T; (15) T; (16) F; (17) F; (18) T; (19) F; (20) T.

Although research and education are eliminating some of the misunderstandings surrounding sex, others remain. For example, a few would like to perpetuate the myth that sexual activity will extend life. This is hard to substantiate and probably has no basis in fact. That romance can add spice to life is a different matter. Many individuals who have existed in a chronically depressed state change dramatically when they are suddenly attracted to another. Result? A resurgence of life with some amazing behavioral changes. Hope is restored. This romantic involvement may not extend lives, but it increases a desire to live.

AGE AND SEXUAL FUNCTIONING

Now that some of the myths have been dispelled, here is what you can expect as you age. Some of these changes can actually enhance the sexual experience.

Changes in Men

Aging brings about changes in the male reproductive system. While testosterone output continues, it reduces in amount. Thus, the amount is increasingly inadequate and affects the genital tissues as aging progresses. A gradual decline in sexual energy, muscle strength, and viable sperm result from this hormone depletion. The testes become smaller and less firm. As the prostate enlarges, its contractions become weaker. There is a reduction in volume and viscosity of seminal fluid and the ejaculation force decreases. None of these changes is a major event, but together they are responsible for some real and apparent changes in the total expression of male sexuality.

As men reach age 60, the speed of attaining an erection, intensity of sensation, frequency of intercourse, and force of ejaculation are reduced slightly. Each of the four phases of sexual response—excitement, plateau, orgasm, and resolution—depart from the youthful pattern.

An advantage of age is that ejaculatory control is far better among older men. Because arousal is slower, the older man is likely to engage in more foreplay. During penetration, older men are liberated from the ejaculatory urgency of youth. And they have had time to overcome sexual inhibitions and have gained skill in lovemaking.

Changes in Women

Physiologically, older women seem to experience little sexual difficulty. Principal changes are caused by the decline in estrogen and progesterone after menopause. The vaginal wall atrophies and becomes less elastic and the vagina shortens and narrows. About five years after menopause, vaginal mucous secretion during sexual arousal declines. Consequently, intercourse may be painful for older women unless they use one of the lubricating gels readily available at drug stores.

As women age, both the duration and intensity of the physiological responses to sexual stimulation gradually diminish. As a result, older women need more and longer stimulation during sexual activity. Despite these changes, the four phases of the sexual response cycle can be experienced. Most older women maintain their multiorgasmic status if they are in good health and receive regular, effective sexual stimulation.

VALUE OF ROMANTIC RELATIONSHIPS

Not everyone needs romantic involvement to be happy and fulfilled. Many do, however, and those who let the opportunity pass may be making a mistake by foolishly avoiding relationships that could enrich their lives. To discover some of the hidden benefits of romantic relationships, review the reasons in the following checklist that have value and meaning to you.

How many times did you answer Yes? If five or more, it would appear a romantic relationship at either level would add to the quality of your life. If you do not now have such a relationship, perhaps you should do something about it.

Value Checklist for Romantic Relationships

Yes   No

☐ ☐   1. It is or would be important to me to express my romantic feelings in intimate ways with another person.

☐ ☐   2. I value affirmation from another that I am still attractive.

☐ ☐   3. It would improve my sense of self worth to know that someone enjoys being seen in public with me.

☐ ☐   4. Knowing another person intimately is like a port in a storm. I would be protected from certain anxieties.

☐ ☐   5. A sex-oriented relationship is a kind of defiance against stereotyping as an aging person.

☐ ☐   6. It would help me be more assertive. I could express myself more openly on subjects important to me and know the other person would listen.

Yes	No	
☐	☐	7. I take pleasure from being touched.
☐	☐	8. A sense of romance would give my life a lift.
☐	☐	9. I would have a feeling of sensual growth.
☐	☐	10. Having a close, sex-oriented relationship would be an affirmation of life. I would feel more alive.

Totals: Yes _____   *No* _____

THE ART OF BEING AVAILABLE

Many mature people who are alone reject the idea that they should take any initiative to make themselves available for romantic involvement. Some of this reluctance is based on the way things were in the past. Some fear that a relationship with another might destroy a valued memory. Often it is nothing more than a lack of confidence.

Any person who honestly believes a better life would be possible with a romantic involvement should not hesitate to make him or herself available. This normally means looking as attractive as possible, mixing in groups, sending friendly signals to prospects at the right time, and receiving signals from others in a friendly and welcoming manner.

Some retirees who acknowledge that they would enjoy a romantic involvement do not have the self-confidence to do anything about it. They envy others, yet hesitate to take the first step. They feel awkward about sending out signals and use the excuse that it wouldn't be proper. In some ways, it is unfortunate that we don't mirror certain cultures where women wear a flower over one ear if they are interested and over the other if they are not. Such signals could eliminate frustration. It's hard to believe, but even after six decades of living, some people are too shy to receive friendly signals from others, even though they would like to.

Another excuse you hear is, "I might get involved in something I can't handle." These people seem to fear that any relationship that starts out innocently will automatically escalate to a sexual relationship. These people do not consider that the other person may fear such an escalation as much as they do. Once friendly signals have been exchanged, a timely follow-up is desirable if a new relationship is to blossom. The initial psychological barrier must be overcome to allow a relationship to develop. What happens after a relationship develops should not be anticipated in advance. Retirees should be able to develop rewarding second-level relationships without needless anxiety about what might happen later.

To throw away the beauty of close companionship because you fear physical activities is foolish at any stage of life. For mature people, it is ridiculous.

What Mature Men Like in Mature Woman

Why one individual is romantically attracted to another has always been a mystery, sometimes explained by the phrase, "in the eye of the beholder." If you talk openly with men, they will tell you what they appreciate most in women. Following are some of the comments you will likely hear:

"I like a woman with style—one I can be proud to take out socially."

"I appreciate a woman who is satisfied to be her own age."

"It is great to talk about common interests, not about children or problems all the time."

"At our age it is an opportunity to have fun together."

"I love a woman who looks like she has spent time getting ready for me and then doesn't keep me waiting."

What Mature Women Like in Mature Men

Women like in men most of the same characteristics that men like in women. If you talk to women, you will get statements such as:

"I like a sensitive man who listens well and is interested in me."

"A man should look healthy and strong."

"I like a man who takes me to nice places I wouldn't feel comfortable going to alone."

"I like a man who takes charge."

"Give me a man who is polite and considerate."

"I like to be flattered."

ROMANCE AND MATURE WOMEN

There is a country and western song that says "Older women make beautiful lovers." If you feel younger women hold all the aces when it comes to attracting and holding a man, listen to this ballad. It says that older women also have some excellent cards—if they play them properly.

Some mature women think that there is an unwritten law preventing them from competing with younger women. Those who believe this are saying their experience and capacity to love is lost simply because they have aged. They are quitting without understanding what most men want. These comments tell the story:

"It bothers me when mature women let younger ones establish the rules. It often happens for two reasons. First, older women downgrade their charms. Second, they feel it is inevitable they will lose out so they don't even try.

"I have a better time socially and sexually with mature women. I don't have to prove myself with them."

"Mature women can give you the best time in the world, if they allow it to happen."

"Some women needlessly tie themselves up with old-fashioned ideas that younger women have discarded. If they learn to accept some of the new freedom, they can better compete with the younger women."

When it comes to love, mature women have their own aces to play. Many men have learned that a young woman may enhance their sexual performance temporarily, but in a long-term relationship they often lose more than they gain. Of course, some men will not discover this unless they are fortunate enough to meet women their age who have confidence and finesse.

KEY POINTS

- The need for caring, sharing, loving, and intimacy begins at birth and continues throughout life.
- One language of love is physical; the other involves sharing private conversation and thoughts in a romantic setting.
- Many men and women continue to enjoy sexual activity into their 80s and some even into their 90s.
- For some, the second language of love is sufficient to meet their needs for intimacy.
- Both languages of love contribute to the quality of life.
- There should be no guilt feelings attached to enjoying either language.

Things to Do

Instructions: In the space below, list the things you want to do as a result of reading this chapter. Then, choose a target date for completing each of your action items.

Action Item	Target Date

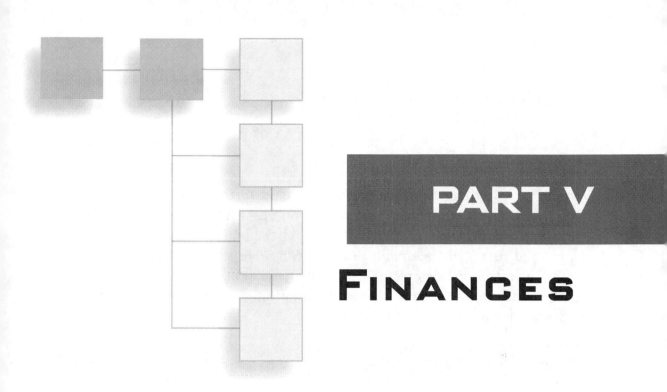

PART V

FINANCES

More than any single factor, money determines when people retire. This major section will help you accomplish your financial planning. After completing it, you'll be able to prepare and interpret a personal financial statement; design a workable, effective budget; improve your investments; determine the best financial strategy for your personal situation; complete your estate planning; and prepare the best possible insurance package for yourself.

CHAPTER 16

FUNDING YOUR RETIREMENT

Money is what you'd get along beautifully without if other people weren't so crazy about it.

—Margaret Case Harriman

Your ability to enjoy retirement will depend, to a great extent, on how well you have prepared financially. It's reassuring to know that you can meet the expenses of the lifestyle you choose and that you can meet unforeseen expenses as well. While a financially secure retirement does not guarantee fulfillment, it builds a foundation that frees you from worry and concern. Therefore, you can get involved with things you enjoy and that will bring you fulfillment in your later years.

It's fairly easy to assess your current financial condition. However, it becomes more difficult the further into the future you must look. There are a number of unpredictable factors to consider: the rate of inflation, changes in tax laws, your health, how long you will live, return on investments, health care costs, and changes in Social Security benefits.

To deal with these uncertainties, you need to make some assumptions based on either historical data or statistical averages. Then you need to update your plans from time to time as new information becomes available. It's important to recognize that your plans are only as accurate as the assumptions that go into them—and they are never final.

This chapter guides you through analysis of your current and post-retirement financial conditions. It is not intended to replace the service of a qualified expert. Rather, it provides a general overview and prepares you to meet with a financial planner.

YOUR PRESENT FINANCIAL STATUS

The place to begin an analysis of what you need to do for a financially secure retirement is to look at your finances today. This will give you insight into how you are spending your money, whether you're getting ahead, and how much you've been able to save.

Determine Your Net Worth

The first step in your analysis is to determine your net worth. This is a summary of your spending and saving habits. It shows the cumulative effect of your financial decisions. It not only shows how you're doing, but also gives clues to potential changes to improve your financial future.

In simple terms, your net worth is the difference between what you owe and what you own. If you come out owning more than you owe, you have a positive net worth. If the opposite is true, you have a negative net worth.

Net worth statements have common categories of assets and debts. Debts are generally divided into two categories: secured and unsecured. Assets are generally divided into the following categories:

Cash Reserves. This includes funds that are readily available in checking accounts, money market accounts, certificates of deposit of one year or less, U.S. Government Series EE and HH bonds, and U.S. Treasury bills.

Invested Assets. These are certificates of deposit of more than one year, stocks, bonds, mutual funds, business interests, partnership interests, mortgages, real estate, annuities, and retirement plans.

Personal Use Assets. This includes your home, furnishings, automobiles, recreational vehicles, furs, jewelry, collections, tools, and equipment.

To compute your net worth, gather all your financial records such as checkbooks, statements from banks, mutual funds, credit unions, and brokerage houses, and your loan balances. Check the value of your residence, automobiles, tools, and equipment by reading the classified section of your daily newspaper. You are now ready to compute your net worth using the following worksheet.

Net Worth Statement

ASSETS

Cash Reserves

Cash $ _____

Checking accounts   _____

Money market accounts   _____

Savings accounts   _____

Short-term CDs   _____

U.S. Savings bonds   _____

U.S. Treasury bills   _____

Life insurance cash value   _____

   Total Cash Reserves $ _____

Invested Assets

Long-term CDs $ _____

U.S. Treasury notes & bonds   _____

Bonds & bond mutual funds   _____

Stocks & stock mutual funds   _____

Notes & mortgages receivable   _____

Partnership interests   _____

Business interests   _____

Real estate   _____

Retirement plans   _____

Annuities   _____

Other   _____

   Total Invested Assets $ _____

Personal Use Assets

Residence $ _____

Furnishings   _____

Automobiles   _____

Recreational vehicles   _____

Collections   _____

Furs & jewelry   _____

Tools & equipment   _____

Other   _____

    Total Personal Use Assets $ _____

   Total Assets   _____

LIABILITIES

Secured Debt

Home mortgage $ _____

Automobile loans   _____

Recreational vehicle loans   _____

Life insurance loans   _____

Other   _____

    Total Secured Debt $ _____

Unsecured Debt

Credit card balances $ _____

Household furnishings loans   _____

Home repair loans   _____

Personal loans   _____

Medical bills   _____

Income taxes owed   _____

Property taxes owed   _____

Other   _____

    Total Unsecured Debt $ _____

Total Liabilities $ _____

Net Worth (Total Assets minus Total Liabilities) $ _____

ANALYZE YOUR CASH FLOW

If a review of your net worth suggests something needs to be done to improve your financial situation, the best way to understand the problem is to compare what you earn to what you spend. This is called a cash flow analysis. It gets to the basic question of how much of your income is spent on debt service, consumption, and savings. It also answers the question of how much more you are spending than you have coming in—or vice versa.

It is not easy to get the necessary information to do a good cash flow analysis. Start with your checkbook, credit card statements, and tax records. The most difficult information to get will be what you spend on cash purchases. The best approach is to keep a journal for a couple of weeks to get a pattern and then estimate the amounts factoring in your personal experience. Income information should be available from your tax records.

Cash Flow Statement

OUTGO

Taxes

Federal and state income taxes $ _____

Social Security   _____

Property taxes   _____

Housing

Rent or mortgage payments   _____

Repairs and maintenance   _____

Homeowner's insurance   _____

Transportation

Auto loan or lease payments   _____

Repairs and maintenance   _____

Gas, oil, and license   _____

Auto insurance   _____

Public transportation   _____

Operating

Food at home   _____

Clothing   _____

Laundry and dry cleaning   _____

Grooming and personal care   _____

Household supplies   _____

Professional fees   _____

Family allowances   _____

Family gifts   _____

Utilities

   Gas and electricity   _____

   Water   _____

   Telephone   _____

Medical

   Life and health insurance   _____

   Doctor and dentist bills   _____

   Medications   _____

Entertainment

   Admissions   _____

   Eating out   _____

   Vacation   _____

   Subscriptions   _____

Financial

   Contributions   _____

   Personal loan payments   _____

   Savings and investments   _____

      Total Outgo $ _____

INCOME

   Earnings   _____

   Savings and investments   _____

   Gifts, inheritances, etc.   _____

      Total Income $ _____

      Difference Between Income and Outgo $ _____

From an analysis of your cash flow statement, you will know where your money goes and whether your outgo exceeds your income. Also, you can set goals and plan to overcome problems in your personal finances. These goals and plans become a budget, or working guideline, for the coming year.

It is estimated that two-thirds of American households live paycheck to paycheck. This creates a problem. They are never able to save anything to meet future financial needs. As a result, they may never be able to retire or, if they do, they will be faced with a meager existence. By getting your income and outgo in balance, you can have a brighter financial future.

If you're having trouble putting enough aside to fund your retirement, here are some ideas that will help.

Summarize your spending. Look over your cash flow analysis and summarize your spending in three categories. First, calculate the amount of your monthly fixed expenses. This includes rent or mortgage payments, utilities, car payments, gas and oil, and operating expenses. Second, calculate your necessary variable expenses. This includes taxes, insurance, car and home repairs, and doctor and dentist bills. Third, calculate your discretionary expenses. This includes gifts, contributions, and entertainment.

Set up three bank accounts. The first account should be a money market account with check-writing privileges, the next a regular checking account, and the third another money market account.

1. Deposit all income into a money market account.

2. Write two checks. Deposit an amount to cover your monthly fixed expenses into the checking account. Deposit 1/12 of the annual total of your variable expenses into the other money market account.

3. Allow savings to build up in the money market account until you have a balance at least equal to three months', and preferably equal to six months', net take home pay. This is your emergency fund. Save it to cover times when your income is interrupted by illness, disability, or unemployment. When your emergency fund is in place, consider investment alternatives for your savings.

As you search for extra income to free up for savings or to retire debt, you may want to take a close look at discretionary spending. Consider such things as entertainment, clothing, food, personal care, and allowances. Monitor expenditures and set monthly allotments in areas you are scrutinizing. This will help you limit spending in one area so you can allocate those dollars to another priority. For example, if you have a monthly entertainment allotment of $100, you simply stop spending in this category when you reach that amount.

TIPS TO CONTROL SPENDING

Here are several additional ideas to help you get spending under control.

- Write checks for expenditures of $5.00 or more. This gives you a better record of where your money goes.
- Spend less for certain things such as gifts, convenience foods, and entertainment.
- Cut back on tobacco products, liquor, and gambling such as lottery tickets and bingo.
- Do things such as wash your car and mow the lawn yourself rather than hiring them done.
- Take your lunch to work rather than eating out.
- Take advantage of free community services for education and entertainment.
- Plan large purchases and save for them.
- Don't buy bargains that you don't need.
- Shop for gifts throughout the year.
- When in crisis, eliminate some, or all, discretionary expenditures.

DEBT REDUCTION

Consumer debt (for example, credit card, credit union, and in-house financing) is a very expensive way to spend your money. Interest is no longer deductible on your income tax and the interest rate is substantial. If you want to make 15 percent to

20 percent on your money, simply pay off consumer debt. And, clear all credit card balances at the end of each billing cycle. As a rule of thumb, don't buy anything on credit that will not last at least as long as the payments required to pay for it.

Reducing debt increases net worth. But where do you start? Logically, the debt bearing the highest interest should be paid off first. This includes all of the credit card balances you have been carrying. Another way to solve the problem brings greater psychological rewards: pay off the smallest balances first. Otherwise, you may become too discouraged over the seeming lack of progress.

If your consumer debt is substantial, you may need to consider paying off high-interest debt with less expensive money. Here are some potential sources of lower interest loans.

■ Borrow against securities in your brokerage account. You can deduct the interest as long as it doesn't exceed net investment income.

■ Borrow against the cash value of your life insurance.

■ Refinance your home mortgage or add a home equity loan to turn nondeductible debt into deductible debt.

■ Borrow against your bank CDs.

■ Borrow against your retirement account.

SAVING FOR RETIREMENT

How much do you need? How much do you already have? How much time do you have to save? These are the questions that lead you to a saving plan. A well-thought out and diligently followed plan leads you to your goal. This section walks you through the major steps in planning for your post-retirement financial needs.

Step 1: Estimating Your Needs

The starting point is to estimate the income level you will need in retirement to live the lifestyle you have become accustomed to, taking into account changes retirement will bring. Start by working up a detailed budget for your current living expenses, then adjust each item based on how you think your retirement lifestyle will affect it—will it go up, remain the same, or go down? The following worksheet can be used to prepare a detailed post-retirement budget.

Step 1: Post-Retirement Budget Worksheet

	Current Expenditures	Post-Retirement
Food at home	_____	_____
Household supplies	_____	_____
Clothing	_____	_____
Laundry & dry cleaning	_____	_____
House payments or rent	_____	_____
House & yard maintenance	_____	_____
Home furnishings	_____	_____
Medical & dental expenses	_____	_____
Grooming & personal care	_____	_____
Car payments or lease	_____	_____
Depreciation (car)	_____	_____
Gas & oil	_____	_____
Car maintenance & repairs	_____	_____
Property taxes	_____	_____
Federal income taxes	_____	_____
State income taxes	_____	_____
Medical & dental insurance	_____	_____
Life insurance	_____	_____
Automobile insurance	_____	_____
Homeowner's insurance	_____	_____
Entertainment	_____	_____
Eating out	_____	_____
Travel & vacations	_____	_____

	Current Expenditures	Post-Retirement
Education	_____	_____
Subscriptions	_____	_____
Club memberships	_____	_____
Hobby & craft supplies	_____	_____
Family gifts	_____	_____
Donations & contributions	_____	_____
Professional fees	_____	_____
Other	_____	_____
Total	_____	_____

Step 2: The Impact of Inflation

You now need to adjust your estimated post-retirement needs for inflation. Although you can't know what future inflation will be, you can look at what it has been in the past and use your judgment to pick a rate for planning purposes.

The highest 10-year period in U.S. history for inflation was 1973 through 1982. During this period, it averaged 8.3 percent per year. By 1986, it had dropped to 1.1 percent. The 1990s started off with a rate of 6.1 percent but ended with an average of 2.2 percent. From 2000 to 2003, it further dropped to an average of 1.6 percent and then began trending upward to 3.5 percent in 2005. From 1914, the overall average is 3.5 percent. Given this history, a rate from 3–5 percent seems reasonable for planning purposes.

Step 2: Inflation Adjusted Retirement Income Needs

Assumed Rate of Inflation _____   *Years to Retirement* _____

1. Estimated Retirement Income Needs in today's dollars   _____

2. Times Factor from Table 1   ×_____

3. Estimated Retirement Income Needs in future dollars   _____

Table 1: Inflation Adjustment Factors

Years to Retirement	Assumed Inflation Rate		
	3%	4%	5%
10	1.34	1.48	1.63
11	1.38	1.54	1.71
12	1.43	1.60	1.80
13	1.47	1.67	1.89
14	1.51	1.73	1.98
15	1.56	1.80	2.08

Step 3: Meeting Your Income Needs

In retirement, most people receive income from three sources—employer pension plans, Social Security, and personal savings. In the following calculation, you estimate what you can expect from employer pensions and Social Security. This is compared to your estimated retirement income needs to determine what you must provide from personal savings.

The Social Security Administration sends an annual statement of earnings history and benefits estimate to every wage earner. You may also phone (800) SSA-1213 or visit the Social Security web site (www.ssa.gov) to request a customized benefits estimate. Also, your employer's pension plan administrator will provide an estimate of your pension benefits.

Step 3a: Estimated Income from Social Security and Pensions

1. Your estimated annual pension at planned retirement   _____

2. Partner's estimated annual pension at planned retirement   _____

3. Estimated Social Security benefit   _____

Total   _____

Table 2: Estimated Social Security Benefits

Age at Retirement	Annual Earnings				
	$20,000	$30,000	$45,000	$60,000	$75,000
62	8,800	11,500	15,000	16,900	17,900
63	9,900	13,000	16,900	19,000	20,200
64	11,100	14,600	18,900	21,300	22,700
65	12,400	16,300	21,000	23,700	25,400

(Assumes age-55 male with maximum contributions.)
Source: My Social Security Calculator; www.TeamNPCA.org

The amount of personal savings you will need to fund your retirement depends on several variables including inflation, return on investments, and how long you will live. You already have an assumption about inflation. You should continue to use this number. You can expect investment returns to exceed inflation by 3–4 percent. You can be conservative and add 3 percent to your assumed inflation rate or be optimistic and add 4 percent. You can estimate your life expectancy from Table 3, which is based on the IRS life expectancy tables. A brief look at the table shows that for planning purposes, it is reasonable to plan to age 90 unless you have reason to adjust this number either up or down.

Table 3: Estimated Length of Retirement

Age at Planned Retirement	Individuals	Couples of Same Age
55	28 years	34 years
60	24 years	30 years
65	20 years	25 years
70	16 years	21 years

Step 3b: Estimated Personal Savings Needed to Fund Retirement

1. Estimated income needs in future dollars   _____

2. Less estimated income from pensions and Social Security   _____

3. Differences to be provided from personal savings   _____

4. Times factor from Table 4   × _____

5. Estimated personal savings required at retirement   _____

Table 4: Factors for Estimating Savings Required at Retirement

Years of Retirement	Net Rate of Return*		
	2%	**3%**	**4%**
11	9.79	9.25	8.76
12	10.58	9.95	9.39
13	11.35	10.93	9.99
14	12.11	11.30	10.56
15	12.85	11.94	11.12
16	13.58	12.56	11.65

Years of Retirement	Net Rate of Return*		
	2%	3%	4%
17	14.29	13.17	12.17
18	14.99	13.75	12.66
19	15.68	14.32	13.13
20	16.35	14.88	13.59
21	17.01	15.42	14.03
22	17.66	15.94	14.45
23	18.29	16.44	14.86
24	18.91	16.94	15.25
25	19.52	17.41	15.62
26	20.12	17.88	15.98
27	20.71	18.33	16.33
28	21.28	18.76	16.66
29	21.84	19.19	16.98
30	22.40	19.60	17.29
31	22.94	20.00	17.59
32	23.47	20.39	17.88
33	23.99	20.77	18.14
34	24.50	21.13	18.41
35	25.00	21.49	18.66
36	25.48	21.80	18.88
37	25.93	22.08	19.09
38	26.32	22.34	19.27
39	26.67	22.59	19.46
40	26.98	22.84	19.65

*Assumed rate of return minus assumed inflation rate.

This calculation gives you an idea of the capital you must accumulate to fund your estimated retirement income needs. However, there is one more issue to consider. Most pensions are not indexed for inflation. Therefore, you need to calculate the additional capital required to maintain your pension's purchasing power.

Step 3c: Maintaining Your Pension's Purchasing Power

1. Estimated annual pension at planned retirement   _____

2. Times factor from Table 5   × _____

3. Additional savings required to maintain   _____
   purchasing power of pension

Table 5: Factors to Calculate Savings at Retirement to Maintain Purchasing Power of Pension

Years of Retirement	3% Inflation Rate of Return				4% Inflation Rate of Return				5% Inflation Rate of Return			
	6%	7%	8%	9%	6%	7%	8%	9%	6%	7%	8%	9%
11	1.21	1.13	1.07	1.00	1.66	1.56	1.46	1.38	2.14	2.00	1.88	1.77
12	1.41	1.32	1.23	1.15	1.94	1.81	1.69	1.59	2.51	2.34	2.19	2.04
13	1.62	1.51	1.40	1.30	2.24	2.08	1.93	1.80	2.91	2.69	2.50	2.33
14	1.84	1.70	1.57	1.46	2.55	2.36	2.18	2.02	3.32	3.06	2.83	2.62
15	2.07	1.90	1.75	1.61	2.88	2.64	2.43	2.24	3.75	3.44	3.16	2.91
16	2.30	2.10	1.92	1.76	3.21	2.93	2.68	2.46	4.20	3.83	3.50	3.21
17	2.54	2.30	2.10	1.92	3.55	3.23	2.93	2.68	4.67	4.23	3.85	3.51
18	2.78	2.51	2.28	2.07	3.91	3.53	3.19	2.89	5.15	4.64	4.20	3.80
19	3.03	2.72	2.45	2.22	4.27	3.83	3.45	3.11	5.64	5.06	4.55	4.10
20	3.23	2.93	2.63	2.36	4.63	4.14	3.70	3.33	6.15	5.48	4.90	4.40

Table 5: Factors to Calculate Savings at Retirement to Maintain Purchasing Power of Pension

Years of Retirement	3% Inflation Rate of Return				4% Inflation Rate of Return				5% Inflation Rate of Return			
	6%	7%	8%	9%	6%	7%	8%	9%	6%	7%	8%	9%
21	3.53	3.14	2.80	2.51	5.00	4.44	3.96	3.54	6.66	5.91	5.26	4.69
22	3.78	3.35	2.97	2.65	5.35	4.75	4.21	3.75	7.19	6.34	5.61	4.99
23	4.04	3.55	3.14	2.78	5.76	5.06	4.47	3.95	7.72	6.78	5.97	5.28
24	4.29	3.76	3.30	2.92	6.14	5.37	4.71	4.16	8.26	7.21	6.32	5.56
25	4.55	3.96	3.47	3.05	6.53	5.68	4.96	4.35	8.81	7.65	6.67	5.84
26	4.80	4.16	3.63	3.18	6.92	5.99	5.20	4.55	9.37	8.09	7.02	6.12
27	5.05	4.36	3.78	3.30	7.31	6.29	5.44	4.74	9.93	8.53	7.36	6.39
28	5.31	4.56	3.94	3.42	7.70	6.59	5.68	4.92	10.50	8.97	7.71	6.66
29	5.56	4.75	4.09	3.53	8.09	6.89	5.91	5.10	11.07	9.41	8.05	6.92
30	5.81	4.94	4.23	2.64	8.48	7.19	6.14	5.27	11.64	9.85	8.38	7.18
31	6.06	5.13	4.37	3.75	8.87	7.49	6.36	5.44	12.22	10.28	8.72	7.43
32	6.31	5.31	4.51	3.86	9.26	7.78	6.58	5.61	12.80	10.72	9.04	7.67
33	6.55	5.50	4.65	3.96	9.65	8.07	6.79	5.76	13.39	11.15	9.36	7.91
34	6.79	5.67	4.78	4.05	10.04	8.35	7.00	5.92	13.97	11.58	9.67	8.14
35	7.03	5.85	4.90	4.14	10.42	8.63	7.21	6.07	14.56	12.01	9.98	8.37
36	7.26	6.02	5.03	4.23	10.81	8.91	7.41	6.21	15.15	12.43	10.29	8.59
37	7.50	6.19	5.14	4.32	11.19	9.18	7.60	6.32	15.74	12.85	10.58	8.81
38	7.73	6.34	5.26	4.40	11.57	9.45	7.79	6.49	16.32	13.26	10.88	9.02
39	7.96	6.50	5.37	4.48	11.94	9.71	7.98	6.62	16.91	13.68	11.17	9.22
40	8.18	6.69	5.48	4.55	12.31	9.97	8.16	6.74	17.50	14.08	11.46	9.42

Step 4: Adjusting for Early Retirement

If you plan to retire before you're eligible for immediate Social Security benefits, you need to provide additional savings to help meet your income needs until you qualify for Social Security. Typically, those retiring before age 62 find it to their advantage to begin drawing benefits at age 62, or the earliest age at which they qualify. For workers born before 1938, age-62 benefits are 80 percent of the age-65 full benefits. Workers born in 1938 and later qualify for full benefits at a later age.

Step 4: Early Retirement Supplement for Social Security

1. Years of retirement prior to age 62   _____

2. Estimated age 62 Social Security benefits   _____

3. Times factor from Table 6   × _____

4. Savings needed at retirement to provide the   _____
     equivalent to estimated Social Security

Table 6: Factors to Estimate Savings Needed to Provide Social Security Equivalent for Early Retirement

Years of Retirement Prior to Age 62	Net Rate of Return		
	3%	4%	5%
1	0.98	0.97	.96
2	1.94	1.89	1.86
3	2.88	2.83	2.78
4	3.81	3.72	3.63
5	4.71	4.58	4.45
6	5.60	5.42	5.24
7	6.49	6.23	6.00
8	7.33	7.02	6.73
9	8.16	7.79	7.44
10	8.98	8.53	8.11

You can now summarize the savings required to fund your retirement income needs.

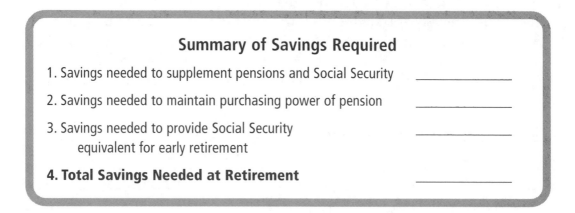

Summary of Savings Required

1. Savings needed to supplement pensions and Social Security   _____

2. Savings needed to maintain purchasing power of pension   _____

3. Savings needed to provide Social Security
    equivalent for early retirement   _____

4. Total Savings Needed at Retirement   _____

Step 5: What You Have Today

You probably have some savings already set aside. But, considering the years until you retire, inflation, and return on investments, do you have enough now and are you adding enough each year?

In this section, you inventory your retirement assets, project them to the year you plan to retire, compare the results to the total savings required at retirement, and calculate the additional amount you must save each year to meet your retirement income needs.

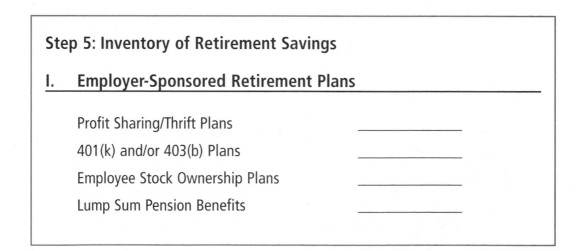

Step 5: Inventory of Retirement Savings

I.　Employer-Sponsored Retirement Plans

    Profit Sharing/Thrift Plans   _____

    401(k) and/or 403(b) Plans   _____

    Employee Stock Ownership Plans   _____

    Lump Sum Pension Benefits   _____

II. Other Tax-Deferred Retirement Plans

Individual Retirement Accounts (IRAs)   _____

Keogh Plans and SEPs   _____

Tax-Deferred Annuities   _____

III. Other Retirement Savings

Money Market Accounts   _____

Certificates of Deposit   _____

U.S. Government Securities   _____

Stocks and stock mutual funds   _____

Bonds and bond mutual funds   _____

Partnership interests   _____

Business interests   _____

Deferred compensation   _____

Real estate investments   _____

Net equity from sale of residence   _____

Net equity from sale of vacation home   _____

Other retirement savings   _____

Total Savings for Retirement   _____

Fewer payments to be made at retirement   –_____

Net savings in today's dollars   _____

Times factor from Table 7   ×_____

Net Savings in Future Dollars   _____

Table 7: Retirement Savings Growth Factors

Years to Retirement	Assumed Rate of Return			
	6%	7%	8%	9%
10	1.79	1.97	2.16	2.37
11	1.90	2.11	2.33	2.58
12	2.01	2.25	2.52	2.81
13	2.13	2.41	2.72	3.07
14	2.26	2.58	2.94	3.80
15	2.40	2.76	3.17	3.64

Step 6: Savings Required to Meet Your Goal

You now have the information necessary to determine your savings goal between now and retirement. This is the difference between Total Savings Required at Retirement and Net Savings for Retirement in Future Dollars.

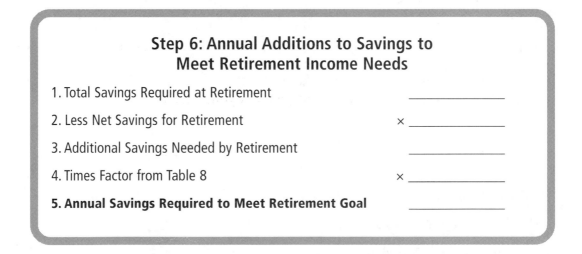

Step 6: Annual Additions to Savings to Meet Retirement Income Needs

1. Total Savings Required at Retirement   _____

2. Less Net Savings for Retirement   × _____

3. Additional Savings Needed by Retirement   _____

4. Times Factor from Table 8   × _____

5. Annual Savings Required to Meet Retirement Goal   _____

Table 8: Factors for Determining Annual Savings

Years to Retirement	Assumed Rate of Return			
	6%	7%	8%	9%
10	.075	.072	.069	.066
11	.066	.063	.060	.057
12	.059	.056	.053	.051
13	.052	.050	.047	.044
14	.047	.044	.041	.038
15	.042	.040	.037	.034

As a result of these calculations, you should have a good idea of your prospects for a financially secure retirement. However, if the amount required to fund your retirement income needs seems out of reach, here are some alternatives:

■ Delay retirement a few years to allow more time to add to your savings and reduce the number of years for which you need to provide.

■ Review your post-retirement budget for expenses that can be reduced.

■ Review your assumptions about rates of return on your savings. Perhaps a bit more risk is required.

■ Consider working part-time to supplement your income.

KEY POINTS

- With planning and commitment, you can have a financially secure retirement.

- Making a post-retirement budget is a good place to start the planning process. From the budget, you can determine your financial needs.

- Most retirements are funded with a combination of pension income, Social Security, and personal savings.

- You can estimate pension income and Social Security and then determine what is required from personal savings.

- Don't overlook inflation in your calculations. It will continue to be a factor in the economy.

- Plans must be updated as new information is available.

Things to Do

Instructions: In the space below, list the things you want to do as a result of reading this chapter. Then, choose a target date for completing each of your action items.

Action Item	Target Date

CHAPTER 17

INVESTING YOUR RETIREMENT SAVINGS

Never invest your money in anything that eats or needs repairing.

—**Billy Rose**

If there is a key to successful investing, it is to keep it simple and go for the long term. This is a tough strategy to maintain because so many financial advisors try to sell investment opportunities that are too complex for the average person. And, if you don't understand it, you likely will make wrong decisions about it. The average investor will do well with a couple of good stock mutual funds until nearing retirement. Then, gradually move a portion of savings to U.S. Treasury securities and/or tax-exempt bonds, depending on income tax bracket.

There are three basic principles of investing: 1) risk and how risk regulates the rate of return, 2) how diversification moderates risk, and 3) growth through compounding, which is even better when it is tax deferred.

THE ELEMENTS OF RISK

Any investment strategy has some risk. Even if you put your savings in a safe deposit box, you will lose as inflation erodes its purchasing power. To earn a positive net rate of return, you must take some risk.

There are four types of risk to plan around in developing your savings strategy:

- *Market Risk:* This is the risk that you will not be able to sell your investment for what you paid for it.

- *Business Risk:* This is the risk that the business you have invested in will not do well.

- *Interest Rate Risk:* This is the risk that your investment will decline in value as interest rates fluctuate.

- *Liquidity Risk:* This is the risk that you will not be able to get your money from the investment when you need it.

There is a direct relationship between risk and the rate of potential return. Just like the lottery, when the potential return is high, so is the risk. You should understand the different types of risk and how they affect rates of return. Take only as much risk as you need to meet your savings goal.

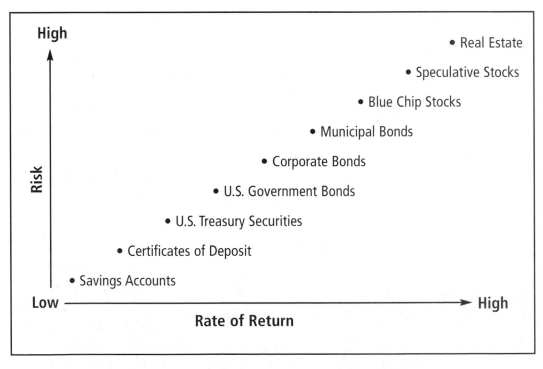

Relationship Between Risk and Rate of Return

DIVERSIFICATION SPREADS THE RISK

Diversification is the best way to moderate risk. It is done on two levels. The first is asset allocation—spreading your savings among three basic categories: cash equivalents, income investments, and growth investments. The portion of your total investment in each category depends on your savings goal and the time available. Asset allocation will help moderate market risk. When you need to withdraw savings you can choose the category that is best at the time.

Further diversification within categories minimizes exposure to business risk. It recognizes that within an asset category some investments will do well while others will not. Unfortunately, you don't know ahead of time which ones to choose. Consider the following example of a diversified investment of $100,000:

Investment		Value 25 years later
$20,000	total loss	0
20,000	0% return	$20,000
20,000	5% return	7,720
20,000	10% return	216,700
20,000	15% return	658,380
Total value of portfolio		**$962,800 (9-1/2%)**

Interest rate risk affects investments such as preferred stocks, utility stocks, bonds and U.S. Treasury securities. To minimize exposure, concentrate on top quality investments and hold until maturity.

Liquidity risk is greatest with real estate. As a general rule, only invest in real estate when you can wait until the right time to get your money back.

THE MAGIC OF COMPOUNDING

There is no other source with the potential to contribute as much to your savings as compound interest—not you, nor your employer. But to get maximum benefit, you need to start early. For example, if you want to have a million dollars when you retire at age 65, you can use the Rule of 72 to calculate the savings you need at different ages. (The Rule of 72 states that interest rate divided into 72 will give the number of years it takes to double an investment.) If you can earn nine percent on your investment, it will double every eight years without adding to principal and assuming you don't withdraw anything.

Age 65	$1,000,000
57	500,000
49	250,000
41	125,000
33	62,500

Another vivid example of the benefit of time with compound interest is shown in the following table. One person starts contributing $2,000 at age 25 to a tax-deferred savings plan but stops contributing at age 34. The other person starts at age 35 and continues through age 64. The one who started earlier, but stopped after only 10 years, ends up with considerably more money at age 65.

	Example A			Example B	
Age	Paid in	Year-end Balance		Paid in	Year-end Balance
25	$2,000	$2,108		0	0
30	12,000	16,401		0	0
35	20,000	36,102		2,000	2,180
40	20,000	55,547		12,000	16,401
45	20,000	85,466		22,000	38,282
50	20,000	131,499		32,000	71,948
55	20,000	202,328		42,000	123,747
60	20,000	311,307		52,000	203,447
64	20,000	439,435		60,000	297,151

DETERMINING AN INVESTMENT STRATEGY

Four factors should be considered when deciding on your investment strategy. Here are a few thoughts on each.

What is your objective? Consider the importance of stability of principal, predictability of income, and capital growth. These must be considered against the risk and reward potential of the three categories of investment alternatives. To have maximum stability of principal, you could invest in cash equivalents.

However, your income would be unpredictable due to the variation in short-term interest rates, and inflation could erode your purchasing power.

For higher predictability of income, you could invest in bonds. To do so would require you to take on interest rate risk in the event you need to dip into your savings before some bonds reached maturity. There would also be some exposure to loss of purchasing power through inflation although not as severe as with cash equivalent investments.

You could put your savings in stocks or a stock mutual fund. These choices have provided substantial growth of both income and capital over long periods of time. But, with wide, unpredictable price swings you would be exposed to market risk if you needed to draw from savings in excess of current dividends.

How long do you have? Time gives you two advantages. If you have time, you can wait out swings in the stock market. And, if you have time, you can often settle for a lower rate of return because the effects of compounding will work more to your favor. Therefore, the time you have before you need to spend your savings and the flexibility, if any, you have on withdrawing money will point you toward particular classes of investments.

What is your risk tolerance? Investors can be labeled as either conservative, moderate, or aggressive depending on the amount of risk they can comfortably handle. The rule: Don't take on more risk than you can sleep with. Lying awake nights worrying about your savings is no way to either anticipate or enjoy your retirement.

What are your financial circumstances? If you have ample savings to cover your needs, you may be able to take additional risk and not substantially affect your financial status. However, if you have limited resources, it might be better to concentrate on less risky investments in order to preserve what you have.

Allocating Your Savings Among the Choices

Many investment choices are available. Some guarantee the return of capital with interest after a set time period. Others make no guarantees. This leaves many people unsure about where to invest their retirement savings. Those too concerned with preserving capital see their purchasing power eroded by inflation. Those too concerned with maximizing returns to build capital may see their savings disappear to risky investments. Here are examples of investment opportunities in each of the asset allocation categories. There are other, more complex, investments available. But, for the novice, this list should be sufficient.

Cash Equivalent Investments

- Savings accounts

- Certificates of Deposit (1 year or less)

- U.S. Treasury bills

- U.S. government bonds

- Money market accounts

Income Investments

- Certificates of deposit (more than 1 year)

- U.S. Treasury notes and bonds

- Municipal bonds

- Corporate bonds

- Bond mutual funds

- Preferred stocks

- Fixed annuities

Growth Investments

- Common stocks

- Stock mutual funds

- Variable annuities

- Real estate

Seldom do the experts agree completely on the percentage of one's savings to be invested in cash equivalents, income, and growth investments. However, there is general agreement that as you grow older you should shift some from growth to income. Here are three examples for three different ages.

	Age of Investor		
Asset Category	**Forties**	**Fifties**	**Sixties**
Cash Equivalents	10%	10%	25%
Income Investments	25%	50%	60%
Growth Investments	65%	40%	15%

Examples of Asset Allocation

GUIDELINES FOR REACHING YOUR GOAL

People who experience the most success in saving for a financially secure retirement follow some specific guidelines. See if you are guided by a successful strategy.

- Start by eliminating all consumer debt.

- Set up a regular program to add to your savings monthly. Use payroll deductions, systematic transfers from your checking account, or (at least) marks on your calendar to send in a check.

- Make full use of tax-deferred savings. Contribute the maximum to IRAs for both you and your life partner.

- Take full advantage of employer-sponsored plans. These plans not only offer tax-deferred compounding, but frequently offer employer matching of all or a portion of your contributions.

- Don't spend your retirement savings on other things. If you change employers, roll your retirement savings over into an IRA or your new employer's retirement plan.

- Before retirement, invest for growth. After retirement, shift into income investments to conserve capital and meet income needs.

MUTUAL FUNDS

A mutual fund is an investment company that pools the money of many investors and invests it on their behalf. Based on a fund's stated objective, the money is invested in stocks, bonds, money market securities, or a combination of these. At the end of 2004, there were about 8,000 mutual funds with 267 million accounts worth in excess of $8.1 trillion. All investments have an element of risk. Mutual funds are no different. And, with so many choices, great care should be exercised to find a fund that is right for you.

Mutual Fund Charges

There are four types of potential charges to mutual fund investors. Some funds have front-end loads of two percent to eight percent of your initial investment. This generally goes to pay a commission to the person who sold you the fund. Some funds have back-end loads of one percent to six percent on money taken out. Often these charges are on a declining schedule so that if you leave your money with the fund for, say, five years, there is no longer a charge. No-load funds do not impose these charges. All funds charge an administration fee for handling your investments although the charge varies, usually rising to 1.5 percent. Some funds impose a 12b-1 charge. This is a Securities and Exchange Commission regulation that allows a fund to pass on certain advertising and marketing expenses. Many funds include these expenses as part of their administration fee. When considering a mutual fund, be sure to consider all the costs against the fund's performance history. What have been the net results?

Information on Mutual Funds

To help sort through the enormous array of choices, turn to the information services available. Good resources include *Investor's Guide and Mutual Fund Directory* available from the No-Load Mutual Fund Association, 11 Penn Plaza, Suite 2204, New York City, NY 10001, and *The Guide to Mutual Funds* available from the Investment Company Institute, 1600 M Street NW, Suite 600, Washington, DC 20036. Morningstar, Inc. does a complete analytical report on all mutual funds biweekly and rates fund performance. The service is too expensive for the average investor, but check with your local library or banker for a copy. Morningstar reports are also available on the Internet at www.morningstar.com. Finally, *Money, Kiplinger, Business Week, Consumer Reports,* and *Forbes* rank mutual fund performance at least once a year.

Reasons for Investing in Mutual Funds

Mutual funds appeal to such a large number of investors for many valid reasons. Here are the ones most often cited.

Diversification: Your investment is pooled with others and spread among a large number of securities. This reduces the potential for any one investment having a significant negative effect on the total portfolio.

Professional Management: Few investors have the time or knowledge to analyze companies and securities, study forces that influence the economy, and assess trends in financial markets. With mutual funds, individual investors gain access to professional portfolio management at bargain rates.

Liquidity: Mutual fund shares can be sold at any time at their current market value. They are subject to market risk.

Convenience: You can add to your mutual fund holdings at any time. Additionally, record-keeping is simplified by the periodic reports and tax information provided. Withdrawals are also convenient. Many funds will mail you a monthly check while others offer check-writing privileges.

Affordability: The minimum initial investment for most funds is between $500 and $2,500. Additional investments are usually a minimum of $50. However, a few funds will accept $25 additions as long as a regular investment program is set up.

Regulation: Mutual funds are regulated by a number of federal and state laws. They are also subject to the regulations of the Securities and Exchange Commission. This has led to a high level of confidence among mutual fund investors that they will be treated according to the published materials issued by the funds.

Flexibility: Many mutual fund families such as Vanguard, T. Rowe Price, and Fidelity allow investors to move savings among their different funds without charge. Some others charge a modest exchange fee. This permits investors to change their investments, as their financial needs change.

Types of Stock Funds

Stock mutual funds are generally classified as income, growth and income, or growth funds. Income funds invest in common and preferred stocks of established companies that have a history of paying above-average dividends. Growth and income funds invest in the stock of blue chip companies that combine steady growth with good dividends. Growth funds invest in common stock of companies whose earnings have grown faster than the rate of inflation or the general economy and they reinvest most of their earnings in further growth.

An easy way to invest in stock mutual funds is to buy an indexed fund. These funds invest in all the stocks of the group they are attempting to duplicate, such as the Standard & Poor's 500. As a result, administration fees are minimal.

HIRING A FINANCIAL ADVISOR

At some point, you will probably need the services of a financial advisor. Depending on your understanding of financial matters, you may need answers to tax questions or a complete saving and spending plan. When you start looking for a financial advisor, you will find no shortage of candidates. However, finding one that meets your needs may be a challenge.

Types of Certifications

Start by understanding the various certifications you will encounter.

Certified Financial Planner (CFP): This designation is awarded to anyone who passes a series of tests, has at least three years' experience, an undergraduate degree, and has completed a curriculum of study outlined by the International Board of Standards and Practices of Certified Financial Planners. Fifteen hours of continuing education are required each year.

Chartered Financial Consultant (ChFC): This certification is granted by the American College in Bryn Mawr, PA. There is a comprehensive course of study followed by 10 two-hour exams. The American College also grants a graduate degree in financial services.

Accredited Personal Financial Specialist (APFS): This designation is issued by the American Institute of Certified Public Accountants. Recipients must be Certified Public Accountants (CPA), then pass a one-day exam and have at least 750 hours of experience in personal financial planning in the three preceding years. Twenty-four hours of continuing education directly related to personal financial planning are required each year.

Methods of Compensation

Financial advisors are paid for their services in one of the following three ways. It is important to understand ahead of time how an advisor is paid.

Hourly Fee: Fee-only advisors charge for the time spent with a client and working on the client's business. Total charges can become substantial for a comprehensive plan and implementation.

Sales Commissions: Some advisors offer free planning service with an expectation of making a commission on the investments you select. If you choose this type of advisor, be sure of his or her qualifications and that the investments offered fit your needs.

Combination: Some advisors calculate a fee based on the time spent on your business. Then, you may choose to pay the fee and go elsewhere to implement your plan; or, if you buy investments from the advisor, any commissions received are credited to your account. Most people prefer this approach as it offers some savings along with freedom to choose who handles their investments.

Good financial planning is a combination of analysis and application tailored to your specific needs and circumstances. It is not a sales approach for marketing investment products. Therefore, you need to sort out the method of compensation that best suits your situation.

Choosing an Advisor

When you decide to engage the services of a financial advisor, start by checking with others for recommendations. Then, schedule meetings with two or three to see which one best fits your needs. Here are some questions to ask on your first visit.

- *What are your background and experience?* Look for someone who has been in the business 10 years or more.

- *What degrees and designations do you hold?* Look for someone who holds one of the three designations mentioned earlier. While they are not guarantees of qualifications, they are indicators of education and experience.

■ *Do you consult other professionals?* Seldom is one person an expert in everything. Expect an advisor to consult with a CPA, insurance specialist, investment advisor, estate attorney, and a tax attorney in developing a comprehensive plan.

■ *How do you charge for your services?* You need to know if there is any chance of advice being tainted with greed.

■ *What are your typical client's financial circumstances?* You want an advisor who deals with clients similar to you.

Sources of Candidates

The names of qualified advisors in your area can be obtained from the Financial Planning Association at (800) 282-PLAN. You might also want to contact the Society of Financial Service Professionals at (800) 243-2258 and the American Institute of Certified Public Accountants at (800) 862-4272.

PROFESSIONAL MONEY MANAGERS

If your retirement savings is $250,000 or more, you should consider professional money management. A professional money manager will handle your investment account according to your instructions. You will pay a fee for this service, but the benefits may be well worth the cost.

The first thing a professional money manager does is help you define your goals and risk tolerance. This information is converted into a long-term strategy that can sustain you through various markets. From this preliminary work, an investment plan is formed that accommodates both your long-term goals and short-term needs, based on your tolerance for risk.

A professional manager has the time, training, and temperament to manage your assets successfully—qualities you may not possess. A trained professional takes the emotionality out of investing, knows the appropriate investment vehicles to achieve your goals, and can manage risk within your portfolio by choosing the proper balance of investment choices. This service will cost from one to two percent of your account balance annually.

When choosing a professional money manager, become acquainted with the management team that will handle your account. Look at how long they've been in business, the size of accounts they handle, and their track record. You want someone who handles accounts similar to yours and has demonstrated success. Also, find out about coverage under the Securities Investor Protection Corporation (SIPC) and any additional protection provided through insurance.

INVESTMENT TIPS

It takes capital, time, and professional advice to build a good individual portfolio. Some people are better suited to do this than others. Keeping your money hard at work with good results is not easy, but if you choose to manage your own investments, here are some tips that should prove helpful.

Tip #1: Stay within your comfort zone. To most people, sleep is more important than gambling for a higher return on an investment. Your comfort zone may move toward the conservative in the years ahead.

Tip #2: No one has all the answers. Financial markets are influenced by so many factors that no one can predict beyond an educated guess.

Tip #3: Seek professional help. Make your own decisions. Second opinions are advisable. Refrain from becoming dependent on one advisor.

Tip #4: Work as a team with your life partner. Two heads are better than one. Should anything happen to one of you, the other is better prepared to take over.

Tip #5: Stay current. If changes are required, you will be in a position to take action before you get hurt. You can't tuck your investments away in a safe deposit box and expect them to take care of themselves.

Tip #6: No matter how much you know about investments, keep learning. What was a good investment last week may be a poor one today. The financial world is constantly changing. If you can't keep in touch, make sure you have advisors who do.

KEY POINTS

- There is a direct relationship between risk and the potential rate of return.
- Diversification is the best way to moderate risk.
- Compound interest is an important ally of the long-term investor.
- In making investments, it's important to discover and stay within your comfort zone.
- Stick to investments you understand.
- Mutual funds offer excellent investment opportunities for the average investor.
- Choose a qualified, experienced professional as your financial advisor if you plan to manage your own assets. Otherwise, select a professional money manager.

Things to Do

Instructions: In the space below, list the things you want to do as a result of reading this chapter. Then, choose a target date for completing each of your action items.

Action Item	Target Date

CHAPTER 18

SPENDING YOUR RETIREMENT SAVINGS

He had so much money he could afford to look poor.

—Edgar Wallace

Is it possible to plan your retirement so you can live with style and still break even at the end? All you need to do is spend your income and nest egg at just the right rate. Intriguing?

Most retirees want their money—at least part of it—to outlast them to provide a cushion for late-in-life contingencies. Under no conditions do they want to be dependent on others. To achieve the right balance requires some clever planning plus a little luck.

Everything on financial planning seems to relate to creating and enhancing retirement income. The emphasis is on having *enough* money. This is Phase I. At some point you need to consider how to use what you have accumulated (no matter how small). This is Phase II. Wise spending to enrich retirement, not saving, is perhaps the real financial challenge.

To start you thinking about Phase II (spending), the following strategies may be worth considering. Read all nine before deciding which one is best suited to your desires, philosophy, values, and financial situation. The more you discuss these options, the better. To be happy with your ultimate choice it should fall within your personal comfort zone and have a positive impact on your lifestyle.

Following a discussion of the nine strategies, additional information on tapping your home equity for retirement living expenses, tools for estimating your spending level, and tax rules and penalties that affect your tax-deferred retirement accounts are discussed. All of these items are important to your Phase II planning.

THE SQUEEZE-AND-SPEND STRATEGY

Retired people with limited incomes and small nest eggs do not have a wide range of strategies. Nevertheless, one is required. In fact, it could be argued that the less money accumulated in Phase I, the more a good plan for Phase II can accomplish. The squeeze-and-spend strategy says that you should make renewed efforts to squeeze out more disposable income from your present income and what you save should be spent on things that put more style in your life. Live it up within your limitations. This approach may appear to be high risk, but remember you are spending money you would otherwise not have unless you economized. Therefore, enjoy!

Advantages to this strategy:

Check if you agree

☐ *Fun to live dangerously.* Not all retirees are conservative. Many enjoy living it up.

☐ *Provides a motivating goal.* Saving money to receive immediate rewards is motivating to some people.

☐ *Nothing to lose.* When your retirement income is modest and you cannot do anything about it, why worry?

Disadvantages to this strategy:

☐ *No feeling of security.* To live without a small cushion falls outside the comfort zone of many retirees.

☐ *No contingency fund.* If the TV needs repairing, you can't pay the bill until you save something.

☐ *Dependency on government.* Without a cushion, it might be necessary to ask for help from a social service agency.

THE SQUEEZE-AND-SAVE STRATEGY

This plan is similar to squeeze-and-spend and also applies to retirees with modest incomes. It is specifically designed for those who enjoy saving more than spending and are happy building a nest egg. Splurging is not their style. They prefer to cover themselves with a security blanket of savings. Some go to extremes and deny themselves necessities like a proper diet. Spending money hurts these people, especially when they worry about inflation.

Advantages to this strategy:

Check if you agree

☐ *Provides a feeling of financial security.* Money in the bank provides peace of mind.

☐ *A motivating goal for some.* Saving money is a reward in itself for some individuals.

☐ *Money available for emergencies.* Provides a sense of independence no matter what happens.

Disadvantages to this strategy:

☐ *Loss of immediate rewards.* People who save rather than spend lead more restrictive lifestyles.

☐ *Possibility of fewer friends.* A few individuals are so motivated to save that they chase their friends away. They often turn down social events because of the cost.

☐ *Money saved may be worth less later.* Under inflationary conditions, money saved now will buy less later.

THE MODEST-CUSHION-AND-RELAX STRATEGY

It's easy to envy those adopting this strategy. Frequently these retirees calculate how much money they think they will need for a comfortable cushion. They then invest or bank that sum and relax. Once they have their personal cushion, they cease to worry about money. From that point on they buy necessities, pay bills, and enjoy life, spending whatever their monthly retirement income may be.

They tell themselves, "I had a savings goal in mind and reached it. That is all the cushion I need."

There are psychological advantages to this worry-free strategy. The critics, however, claim that today it is unrealistic to count on anything but a very large cushion.

Advantages to this strategy:

Check if you agree

☐ *Provides both security and discretionary income.* For many it seems to be the right combination. You can have your cake and eat it, too.

☐ *Cushion earns additional money.* Properly invested savings should grow.

☐ *Spending discretionary money is more fun.* With a cushion, it's easier to enjoy spending money foolishly.

Disadvantages to this strategy:

☐ *Cushion investments can turn sour.* Some people lose a good cushion through unwise investments.

☐ *Figuring the right amount may be a problem.* Some retirees keep changing their minds when they get close to a predetermined cushion amount. They never reach a point where they can relax and start spending.

☐ *Spending cushion money for emergencies is difficult.* A cushion is designed for unexpected expenses, but many find it painful to use when the time comes.

THE BIG-CUSHION/SAVE-SAVE STRATEGY

Retirees subscribing to this strategy often do so with little forethought. They probably had good luck during Phase I (accumulating wealth). They enjoyed the process so much and their egos were so gratified that they have trouble switching to Phase II. No matter how large their cushion, it is never enough. As a result, they spend their retirement investing and reinvesting. They frequently live very frugally. Even though they know they can't take it with them, they enjoy making it too much to give it up. Investing and saving become not means to an end but ends in themselves. Often these people are wealthy and, ultimately, wish they had given more consideration to other strategies.

Advantages to this strategy:

Check if you agree

☐ *Excellent sense of security.* Although big-cushion people frequently admit they are hooked on money, they say the size of their security blanket is responsible for most of their happiness.

☐ *Ego rewarding.* Making and saving money is a form of personal fulfillment for some. It is how they get their "kicks."

☐ *They are usually happy with their lifestyles.* Spending more money on themselves would not fall within their comfort zone.

Disadvantages to this strategy:

☐ *Preoccupation with money.* Many use valuable leisure time to earn more money than they can ever spend.

☐ *Money has a destructive hold on some people.* A few miss out on the special rewards of retirement because their lives are centered around making more money instead of enjoying it.

☐ *Excessive worry.* The bigger the cushion, the more some people worry. They worry about losing it or what to do with it. A few agonize over leaving it to those who either don't deserve it or won't appreciate it. Money can be a burden to some.

THE CAPITAL-PROTECTION/SPEND-INTEREST STRATEGY

Members of this group seek a balance between saving and spending during retirement years. This strategy is a variation on the previous one, but the differences are significant. Those who adopt the capital-protection package enjoyed success in Phase I. They establish a cut-off date on earning and saving, however, and promise themselves to begin spending their income without disturbing their capital.

No matter how large or small their capital may be, it is sacred. It is their security blanket. Those who adopt this strategy can often be found on cruise ships or the golf course. The moment they return from one trip, they calculate next year's trip accordingly. These people are often happy with their solution, feeling they have the best of both worlds. It seldom occurs to them that they could begin to dip into their capital and take an extra trip or buy a luxury item they have always wanted.

Advantages to this strategy:

Check if you agree

☐ *Right combination for some.* Those who don't mind having their capital grow smaller because of inflation and want more money to spend now have a good solution.

☐ *Easy decision.* It is not a complicated strategy that requires constant review. It is simple to implement.

☐ *Cushion can be any size.* This strategy makes sense for a millionaire or a person with only a few thousand dollars.

Disadvantages to this strategy:

☐ *Inflexible.* Investment portfolios need to be updated. Those who adopt this plan often see their investments deteriorate.

☐ *Capital might disappear.* If a retiree neglects the portfolio long enough, and if inflation is great enough, the cushion could become insignificant.

☐ *Insecure without it.* Some are so hooked on this strategy that they never spend any of their capital.

THE ACTUARIAL STRATEGY

This strategy is designed to take you as far as you can go—but not much further. The actuarial strategy involves spending capital at a regular clip so that little or nothing is left over for children, friends, or charitable institutions.

For example, as a widow of 65, you can, according to the actuarial tables, anticipate 19.5 more years. (This figure will probably increase in the future.) Your income from Social Security or company pension will remain relatively constant no matter how long you live. It is possible for you to plan on spending your capital (and the income it produces) over a specified time period—so much per month or year.

You must take into account the fact that, as you dip into your capital, the income it produces will diminish. This strategy can be a high risk. If you have a partner, the calculations are more complex, and you may want to talk to a financial expert before embarking on the actuarial strategy.

Advantages of this strategy:

Check if you agree

☐ *Retirement years more enjoyable.* If spending money will make you happier, then the advantage is you can spend it while you will enjoy it most.

☐ *Might eliminate estate taxes.* The government can't take something from you if it is spent in advance.

☐ *Excellent plan if it works.* Winding up close to breaking even is a dream of many. If this is your dream and it works, you can take satisfaction from beating the system.

Disadvantages to this strategy:

☐ *Plan might leave you stranded.* You could wind up broke and insecure.

☐ *You might want your security blanket back.* Once you spend most of your capital, remorse might set in and ruin your later years.

☐ *Actuarial tables are for large groups.* As an individual, you may outlive the tables by many years. If this happens, you will have lost your security blanket.

THE BIG-SCARE CONTINGENCY STRATEGY

This strategy is a supplemental strategy frequently called into play when something unexpected happens. For example, if a retiree who is an advocate of the big-cushion/save-save strategy encounters a serious medical problem, he might decide to spend part of his cushion while he will still enjoy it. "Why not live it up in case I won't be around?" You may know members of this group, who take hurried trips around the world. The big-scare plan is, in essence, a speed-up strategy. You do some things you had always planned to do, but you do them sooner and faster. As with all strategies, some risk is involved. You might, for example, go on an all-out, once-in-a-lifetime spending spree and then discover that your medical condition was a false alarm. Should this happen, a reverse contingency plan might be required.

Advantages to this strategy:

Check if you agree

☐ *Dreams can still come true.* A few people seem to have a delightful last fling by spending their savings quickly.

☐ *Satisfaction in living an accelerated lifestyle.* Even under such circumstances, a big splurge can be fun.

☐ *Going first class for a short time is better than never going first class at all.* Sitting on your capital under these circumstances is not a good alternative.

Disadvantages to this strategy:

☐ *The uncertainty of it all.* How much better it is to speed up without a health problem.

☐ *Money not spent as well.* People are more likely to make poor choices under such pressures.

☐ *Too much pressure.* The danger of trying to crowd too much into a short period can be counterproductive.

THE SHARE-THE-WEALTH STRATEGY

This happy plan can easily be incorporated with others. It is popular for all retirees, but especially appealing to those more advanced in years. This strategy advocates giving away money or belongings while you're still around to enjoy the process. Used in a sensible way, this strategy can provide gratification to the giver and a special reward to those who receive the gifts. There are also tax advantages when you give your money away.

Some people wait until a scare of some sort before embarking on this strategy. Some risks are involved. For example, some individuals might enjoy the process so much they get carried away. Also, it can be a mistake to give children too much too soon. Finally, it is not a good plan for those who might get upset watching how some of their gifts are used.

Advantages to this strategy:

Check if you agree

- ☐ *Protects estate.* Under the Gift Tax laws, it is possible to give $11,000 per year to each beneficiary without being taxed. There are other savings.

- ☐ *Gain more attention.* Those who receive money often show appreciation while you are still around.

- ☐ *Life plan more complete.* The distribution of money ahead of time provides most with a feeling of fulfillment.

Disadvantages to this strategy:

- ☐ *May be premature.* Some retirees get carried away with their generosity and discover they have needlessly lost some freedom and control.

- ☐ *May not be fully appreciated.* If you give money and it is not fully appreciated, remorse can set in.

- ☐ *May do children more harm than good.* Giving money too soon can cause children to not reach their potential because they have too much protection.

THE DELAY-OPTION STRATEGY

Some people consider all the various retirement strategies but never make a choice. They always seem poised to make a decision, but they delay and delay. Their rationale is that life changes too fast. "Why adopt a strategy today that may not meet my needs tomorrow?" "Why lock into a plan that I'm not sure I'll be happy with?"

These people point to new tax laws, family realignments, and their own changing lifestyles as justification. You hear them say, "The best way to stay in control is to remain flexible and change with the times. The best strategy of all is knowing the available options in order to make the best decision when the proper time comes."

Advantages to this strategy:

Check if you agree

☐ *You don't lock yourself in.* You can adjust to changing conditions on a monthly basis.

☐ *No plan is better than a bad one.* Some become disenchanted when their plans don't work. The longer you wait, the less chance of disappointment.

☐ *A lack of plan can still be a running plan.* Those who think a good deal about financial strategies have, in effect, a running plan. That is, they are thinking as they go. Because of this, they can come up with a plan quickly if necessary.

Disadvantages to this strategy:

☐ *Plan needed for ultimate fulfillment.* The purpose of a strategy is to help you enjoy retirement years more, not less.

☐ *Quick plans are risky.* Those who wait too long may be forced into an ill-advised emergency plan.

☐ *Procrastination creates inner pressure.* Those who delay continue to carry the problem with them. Those who design a plan release these pressures and enjoy life more.

TAPPING YOUR HOME EQUITY

As you consider your retirement income needs, don't overlook the equity in your home as a source of income. There are four options for tapping the equity in your home. The first two require a move. The other two allow you to remain in your present home.

Trade Down

Many people approaching retirement have experienced enormous appreciation in their home's value. Selling such a home and buying a cheaper one can leave a substantial sum of money to meet current living expenses.

The Taxpayer Relief Act of 1997 provides special tax treatment for gains on the sale of primary residences. Couples can exclude up to $500,000 of profit from taxation while singles can exclude up to $250,000. To qualify, you must have occupied the home at least two years during the five years prior to the sale, with some exceptions. The full exclusion is available once every two years. These new rules are especially good news for people approaching retirement who want to buy or rent a less expensive home.

Sell and Rent

The real estate market has changed to the extent that home ownership is not necessarily the best financial option. You may come out ahead by selling your home and renting either a house, apartment, or condo. This option frees all of your home equity for living expenses.

To calculate a financial analysis of owning versus renting, add up all the costs associated with home ownership. This includes the direct costs of taxes, insurance, and maintenance, plus the opportunity cost of earnings on the capital tied up in the home. Then, compare this figure to what it would cost you to rent adequate housing.

Reverse Mortgage

A reverse mortgage is a home equity loan. It can be granted only on homes that are mortgage free. Rather than making payments to the mortgage company, the mortgage company makes payments to you. As a result, you receive monthly income based on the value of your home as long as you live, or, in some cases, for a specified number of years. The money you receive is tax free since it is a loan rather than income. At the end of the term, or when you move or die, the loan must be repaid, including accumulated interest—usually by selling your home.

At this time, reverse mortgages are not available in all states. Check with your local banker, if interested.

Sale-Leaseback

Typically, in a sale-leaseback, you sell your home to someone at an agreed-upon price but continue to live in it by paying monthly rent. The new owner becomes responsible for paying taxes, insurance, and maintenance. This arrangement gives you the value of your home to use for current living expenses without requiring you to move. Sale-leasebacks can be arranged with investors, family members, community organizations, churches, and charities.

TOOLS TO HELP PLAN YOUR SPENDING

How long will your money last? Running out of money is perhaps the biggest fear retirees have. This is understandable. People are retiring younger, living longer, and dealing with continually rising living expenses. Uncertainty over future inflation and investment returns only adds to the problem. Here are two tools to help you implement whichever strategy you choose to follow.

The Constant Withdrawal Plan

If your preferred strategy includes spending capital, a plan for judicious spending will allow you to supplement other income to provide an enjoyable retirement. You must work with a couple of unknowns—how long you will need income and what future rate of return you can expect—but sufficient data help you make educated guesses on these. Consider the following table.

How Long Your Capital Will Last						
Annual Withdrawal of Original Capital	Average Annual Return					
	5%	6%	7%	8%	9%	10%
5%						
6%	36 yr					
7%	25	33 yr				
8%	20	23	30 yr			
9%	16	18	22	28 yr		
10%	14	15	17	20	26 yr	
11%	12	13	14	16	19	25 yr
12%	10	11	11	12	14	16 yr

The Increasing Withdrawal Plan

If you want to be sure something is left when you die, here's a plan that will work for you. Harvard University's endowment fund developed a spending guideline in 1973 to ensure a person wouldn't prematurely run out of money. The rule assumes a balanced portfolio allocated half to stocks and half to bonds and cash equivalents. It limits the first-year withdrawal to four percent of the portfolio's total value. Then, in each following year, increase this amount by the previous year's rate of inflation. Continue in this manner from year to year. For example, if you have a $500,000 portfolio, you could withdraw $20,000 in the first year. If the rate of inflation were 3.5 percent that year, you could withdraw $20,700 the second year.

Even in the high-inflation, poor-return environment of the 1970s, this guideline allowed a retiree to withdraw more each year, in line with inflation, without depleting savings.

Today's computer technology makes it easy to combine this approach with one designed to deplete capital. With assumptions on inflation, rate of return, and longevity, a withdrawal schedule can be set up. Such a schedule will increase each year by your assumed rate of inflation and carry you through the specified number of years. With such a spending plan, it is imperative that you monitor your assumptions and make adjustments as required. One simple way to do this is to calculate a capital balance for each year into the future. Then, compare your actual balance to this figure.

TAX-DEFERRED SAVINGS AND THE TAX LAWS

As you consider a spending plan for your retirement savings, you must be aware of several tax rules. A qualified tax accountant or attorney can guide you through this maze of taxes and penalties.

Income Tax

Withdrawals from tax-deferred plans are taxed as ordinary income in the year received under federal and state income tax laws. A systematic withdrawal plan may reduce your tax liability in the long run by keeping you out of the top tax brackets in later years.

Inheritance Tax

The balance in your retirement savings becomes a part of your estate at the time of your death. You can leave an unlimited estate to a spouse. If you aren't married, you may find a significant portion of your savings going to pay inheritance tax. A withdrawal plan that moves money from tax-deferred accounts to a trust could save your estate a good deal of money.

Penalty Taxes

Tax laws encourage you to save for your retirement. But these same laws penalize you severely if you don't follow the rules. Tax-deferred retirement savings are meant to be used during your lifetime and the lifetime of your qualified beneficiary. To avoid being penalized, you must not take out too much or too little, too soon or too late. These restrictions may encourage you to take out more than you need or less than you would like to.

Early Withdrawal Penalty. There is a 10-percent penalty for taking money out of your tax-deferred retirement accounts before age 59-1/2. But there are two exceptions. One is if you retire at age 55 or later, are disabled, or die. The other is if you receive your money in a series of substantially equal periodic payments. If you choose this route, you must stay with the program at least five years or until you reach age 59-1/2.

Minimum Required Distribution Penalty. You must begin withdrawing from your tax-deferred accounts in the year you reach age 70-1/2. (The first withdrawal may be delayed until the first quarter of the following year.) Withdrawals must be sufficient to deplete the account during your lifetime or the combined lifetimes of you and a qualified beneficiary. If you fail to make the minimum withdrawal, a penalty equal to 50 percent of the difference between your actual withdrawal and the minimum withdrawal will be imposed. Clearly, you should avoid this penalty. Also, it probably is not wise to wait until the deadline to make your first withdrawal because you will end up having two withdrawals that year (age 70-1/2 and age 71 withdrawals). This probably will push you into a higher income-tax bracket for that year. Calculating your minimum required distribution is relatively simple. Locate your age in the table below and divide the amount in your qualified plans at the end of the previous year by the figure shown. For example, if you had $250,000 in your qualified plan at the end of last year and you are age 70, divide $250,000 by 27.4. This yields a minimum required distribution for the current year of $9,124.09. The table assumes that you have a beneficiary no more than 10 years younger than you. If your sole beneficiary is a spouse who is more than 10 years younger than you, there is a different calculation method.

Age	Divisor	Age	Divisor	Age	Divisor
70	27.4	85	14.8	100	6.3
71	26.5	86	14.1	101	5.9
72	25.6	87	13.4	102	5.5
73	24.7	88	12.7	103	5.2
74	23.8	89	12.0	104	4.9
75	22.9	90	11.4	105	4.5
76	22.0	91	10.8	106	4.2
77	21.2	92	10.2	107	3.9
78	20.3	93	9.6	108	3.7
79	19.5	94	9.1	109	3.4
80	18.7	95	8.6	110	3.1
81	17.9	96	8.1	111	2.9
82	17.1	97	7.6	112	2.6
83	16.3	98	7.1	113	2.4
84	15.5	99	6.7	114	2.1
				115+	1.9

YOUR LONG-TERM FINANCIAL STRATEGY

Now that you have reviewed the strategies, options, and tax rules, what seems like the best approach for you? It's unlikely that one of the strategies presented will be exactly right for you. Based on your comfort zone, you should be able to combine elements of two or more into a plan with which you can live. You're invited to use the box below to summarize your plan.

My Retirement Spending Strategy

The plan I like best is:

☐ Squeeze and Spend

☐ Modest Cushion and Relax

☐ Actuarial Strategy

☐ Spread the Wealth

☐ Capital Protection/Spend Interest

☐ Squeeze and Save

☐ Big Cushion/Save Save

☐ Big Scare Contingency Plan

☐ Delay Option

Issues that are important to me when planning my post-retirement spending:

_____

_____

_____

_____

_____

KEY POINTS

- Phase I is pre-retirement financial planning. Phase II is a strategy to spend money after retiring.

- Your spending strategy must meet your needs and fit with your philosophy and comfort zone.

- How you learn to spend money after retiring is critical to the quality of life you will enjoy.

- Your home may represent a substantial financial resource to help meet your retirement income needs.

- There are tools available to help you design a spending plan that meets your objectives.

- Tax rules affecting tax-deferred retirement savings must be taken into account when planning your Phase II strategy.

Things to Do

Instructions: In the space below, list the things you want to do as a result of reading this chapter. Then, choose a target date for completing each of your action items.

Action Item	Target Date

CHAPTER 19

ESTATE PLANNING

The power of perpetuating our property in our families is one of the most valuable and interesting circumstances belonging to it.

—Edmund Burke

The facts—you have things; you will die; someone will get your things. Through estate planning, you can direct the distribution of your things so that they go to the right people, in the right amount, and at the right time. You can also arrange matters so your heirs pay a minimum amount of probate costs and estate taxes.

REACTIONS TO ESTATE PLANNING

When confronted with the issue of estate planning, people react in predictable ways. Here are four typical reactions.

The Delayers

These people dread the process so much that they either postpone it too long or handle it in such a cursory way that it brings little or no satisfaction. They say, "It's such an ugly subject that I just can't get around to doing anything at this point. Besides, what's the hurry? Laws keep changing, and I'll have plenty of time later. All it takes is a few hours, and I'm going to be around for a while."

The Worriers

These individuals agonize over every detail of the plan until they drive themselves and their lawyers to distraction. Then, when the work is complete, they continue to make unnecessary changes. "Since making a will 10 years ago, I have changed it six times myself, plus one major overhaul suggested by my lawyer. Now I wish I had waited longer. Think of the money and agony I would have saved." Worriers include those who make too many (but sometimes necessary) changes and those who make temperamental changes. Unfortunately, some people adjust their wills or trust documents based on the current status of their relationship with beneficiaries. Lawyers who deal with estates can provide juicy examples.

The Realists

These people accept the need for a will or a trust and deal with it in an open, forthright manner. They see the process as important and don't delay beyond a reasonable time. They understand there is no such thing as a perfect instrument and therefore don't agonize over it. Realists recognize changes should be made only when necessary. "I feel good that our will is made, but we still have to be realistic and change it now and then. It will be easier when our adult children settle down. Every time there's a divorce, we are forced to rethink the distribution of our estate."

The Opportunists

It is possible to be realistic yet still make the process a once-in-a-lifetime opportunity. These individuals view the preparation of a will or trust as a chance to pull their families closer together. They do this through open communication with the beneficiaries ahead of time. They state their views and then listen. In doing this, they accomplish their estate-distribution goals and strengthen relationships at the same time. When completed, the will or trust is more meaningful to all. "You can't imagine the difference in the relationships with our children since we started talking openly about our estate. They know our feelings and desires, and we know theirs. For example, they want us to enjoy ourselves first; whatever is left, they will use wisely. Best of all, we have avoided holding money over their heads to gain a change in their behavior. They seem to respect us for this. We are still in control, but they know they are part of the family and have a voice. When it comes to estate planning, it's the best approach."

If you have yet to make arrangements for the distribution of your estate, or your present will needs revision, now is the time to act. Obviously, the more you know about the legal aspects, the better you can communicate to your lawyer and the more you will satisfy your special desires and dreams. The following pretest will help you get started.

METHODS OF DISTRIBUTION

There are several ways you can direct the distribution of your estate. Most people use more than one, depending on the nature of the asset and individual circumstances.

Property Titling. Property (such as stocks, bonds, certificates of deposit, or real estate) held in joint tenancy with rights of survivorship automatically passes to the joint owner upon your death. This property is not subject to probate. If the property was acquired before 1977, the property's full value is included in your estate for tax purposes. For property acquired after that date, only your share of the property is included in your estate. Property held as tenancy in common does not follow these rules. In this case, you can leave your share to whomever you wish and it is subject to probate.

Designation of Beneficiary. Life insurance proceeds, U.S. savings bonds, and balances in employer retirement plans, Individual Retirement Accounts, or Keogh accounts pass directly to named beneficiaries. The asset is not subject to probate but is included in the estate for tax purposes. Also, bank accounts can have a "pay-on-death" person named to receive the proceeds of the accounts after your death.

Pretest for Estate Planning

Check your responses with the answers provided to ensure that any misunderstandings are immediately corrected. If wills and trusts are new to you, you may miss several questions. You may also be surprised by how much you already know.

True	False	
☐	☐	1. Only the wealthy need wills.
☐	☐	2. A primary purpose of a will is to help you specify and delineate your bequests.

True   False

☐   ☐   3. *In testate* is the legal phrase for dying without a will. It means the state will process your estate according to its laws.

☐   ☐   4. Once you have a will, nothing you own can pass to a person outside it.

☐   ☐   5. A holographic (hand-written) will does not require witnesses.

☐   ☐   6. In a joint-tenancy arrangement, one party automatically becomes sole owner upon the death of the other party.

☐   ☐   7. A no-risk approach to preparing a will is to buy a standard form from a stationery store and fill it out yourself.

☐   ☐   8. If you have an attorney draw up your will, it's a good idea to settle on the fee at the first meeting. For existing clients, attorneys usually do wills at a nominal sum.

☐   ☐   9. If you are single and have $100,000 in your estate, you should not investigate a trust.

☐   ☐   10. To the courts, a common disaster means one spouse dies ahead of the other.

☐   ☐   11. A trust is a legal document by which you transfer assets such as money or real estate to a trustee to manage for any beneficiary or beneficiaries named.

☐   ☐   12. A testamentary trust is considered part of your will and passes through probate.

☐   ☐   13. One potential of a trust is to provide money to a beneficiary in small amounts so he or she will not make foolish spending mistakes and use his or her part of the estate too quickly.

☐   ☐   14. The executor and trustees are one and the same.

☐ ☐ 15. You cannot change an irrevocable trust.

☐ ☐ 16. It is always best to have a friend as an executor or trustee because he knows your wishes better than a professional.

☐ ☐ 17. A codicil is the style of handwriting you use to sign your name to a will.

☐ ☐ 18. Under current laws, there are no tax advantages to the preparation of a trust.

☐ ☐ 19. An executor's job is finished once an estate is settled.

☐ ☐ 20. A trust is never part of a will.

Total Correct _____

Answers: (1) F (a will is equally important in the settlement of any estate); (2) T; (3) T (you want to avoid this); (4) F; (5) T (there are many ways you can do this legally); (6) T; (7) F (it's wise to work with an attorney whose fees for preparing wills are usually very reasonable); (8) T (don't be afraid to ask; it's a good idea); (9) F (anyone with a sizable estate might benefit from looking into trusts); (10) F (a common disaster is when both spouses die at the same time); (11) T; (12) T; (13) T; (14) F (you discover the difference in the chapter); (15) T; (16) F (selecting an executor or a trustee is a personal choice; sometimes it's better to have a professional, but a fee would be involved); (17) F (a codicil is a legal addition to a will); (18) F (there are still many tax advantages); (19) T; (20) F (although independent, it is still part of the will).

Will. A will is a set of instructions to your personal representative (called an executor) on how to handle things. Your representative collects anything owed to you, pays anything owed by you (including taxes and expenses of probate), files tax returns, and distributes any remaining assets to the people you designate in the amount and at the time you specify. You also can nominate a guardian for any minor children. These activities are carried out under the supervision of a probate court. All property that passes under a will is subject to probate and is included in the estate, along with other taxable property, for estate tax purposes.

Trust. A trust agreement designates someone you choose (called a trustee) to hold property you transfer to the trust on behalf of a beneficiary. Property distributed through a trust is not subject to probate. The estate tax advantages are limited and vary depending upon the type of trust.

Other. There are two other methods of property distribution. One deals with the distribution of community property in the nine community property states. If you live in one of these states, half of all possessions acquired during marriage (except gifts and inheritances) belongs to your spouse. This property is not subject to probate nor is it subject to estate tax. The other method deals with the distribution of property when there is no will or other valid distributive instrument. Individual state laws vary. But, the probate court will distribute your property according to the law. Your surviving spouse will not receive all of your property. It is distributed either among your spouse and children or directly to your children. All property is subject to estate tax.

ESTATE PLANNING

Shortly you will have an opportunity to prepare a form you can use as a planning device. Completing this form in advance could save you money if you visit a lawyer who charges by the hour. It also demonstrates that you are not an ordinary client, but one who is more in charge. This may result in your receiving better attention. Finally, it should mean you wind up with a better plan.

Here are some ideas to help you to prepare your form.

List Your Assets. Refer to your net worth statement prepared in Chapter 16 and record all assets at current market value. List any insurance policies at face value rather than cash-surrender value.

Know Forms of Ownership. Knowing the form of your assets' ownership saves you considerable time. To discover this, you may need to make a trip to your safe-deposit box.

Know Designated Beneficiaries. Check all assets that allow for a beneficiary to be designated and verify that the current designations are consistent with your wishes. This includes life insurance policies, annuities, tax-deferred savings plans, bank accounts, and brokerage accounts.

Name a Trustee. This is a person or institution that you designate under a trust document to manage your property for your beneficiaries. A trustee and an executor can be the same person. You can be your own trustee.

Name an Executor. This is the individual or firm that executes your will after your death. Your executor can be:

■ Family member

■ Friend

■ Professional (attorney, accountant)

■ Trust department in a bank

A professional or trust department is likely to have more expertise than a relative or friend and may be more capable of dealing impartially with sensitive issues that develop. Executors get one fee; attorneys get another.

With this minimal background, you are now ready to complete the following form. If it means digging out papers and policies, it will be time well spent. When the form is complete, you can look forward to a more fruitful meeting with your attorney because you have done your homework.

Pre-consultation Form

This form is to be completed by those preparing or updating their estate plans before the first appointment with a lawyer. Do it in pencil so changes can be made easily.

1. Refer to your financial statement in completing the following:

Asset	Value	Date Acquired	Marital Status at Time	Form of Ownership

2. List names of intended beneficiaries and other data. For tax purposes, it is important for your attorney to know the line of succession between you and your beneficiaries. Normally, but not always, people list their lineal descendants in order and then add others. Your attorney's advice will be significant here.

Beneficiary   Relationship   Amount of Money or % of Estate   Specific Assets*

_____

_____

_____

_____

_____

_____

3. Alternative distribution in case both spouses are killed in a common disaster or something happens to a primary beneficiary. This is optional but a good idea to plan for in the unlikely event it might happen.

Beneficiary   Relationship   Amount of Money or % of Estate   Specific Assets*

_____

_____

_____

_____

_____

_____

4. After careful investigation, list the names of your executor and alternate in the spaces below.

Executor

Name: _____

Address: _____

_____

Telephone: _____

Alternate Executor

Name: _____

Address: _____

_____

Telephone: _____

*You may list separate pieces of property, specific jewelry, automobiles, or any tangible asset you have. Your lawyer may suggest this be consolidated on a separate list outside the actual will. If you do this, keep in mind that specific bequests are not only difficult to list but also subject to whimsical changes that annoy attorneys. Give your list careful thought to avoid unnecessary changes. Many people simplify their lists by giving things away ahead of time.

Congratulations! You are now ready to make an appointment with the lawyer of your choice. Your meeting should be viewed as positive and educational. Once your will has been completed, keep it in a safe place where your executor, spouse, or closest beneficiary can get to it easily and quickly. Your safe-deposit box may or may not be appropriate. Check with your attorney on this. Copies may be desirable for your spouse or others directly involved.

KEEPING YOUR PLANS UPDATED

Soon it will be possible for people, in concert with their attorneys, to maintain wills and other estate planning documents on a home computer. This would make them easily changeable and provide other advantages. Even though not presently realistic, your will or trust should be viewed as an ongoing document, not a once-in-a-lifetime creation forever sealed and stored in a secret place. It needs to be updated periodically because of such possibilities as the following:

- You might have a change of mind.

- You might receive an inheritance or other asset not previously covered.

- A marriage, birth, adoption, divorce, or death might occur.

- New laws may be passed.

Life is not predictable, especially among beneficiaries. Your life may seem predictable to you, but this may not be so with younger members of your family. They may also be more conditioned to the fact that divorce can happen in all age groups—even yours.

Caution: Never make changes directly on the face of your written will. Such changes could invalidate it. The best way to make an addition is to use a typewritten, legal codicil (an extra page or more that can explain, add, or delete provisions in the will itself). To be valid, it must meet the same legal requirements as the will. This is another reason to maintain a good relationship with your lawyer.

PROTECTING YOUR ESTATE FROM UNNECESSARY EXPENSES

You have worked hard to accumulate and protect your estate, so you probably want to pass much of it to your heirs or beneficiaries. Protecting your estate normally moves you into a higher level of money management and often requires the advice of professionals—tax specialists, lawyers, or trust officers. Keep in mind that although you can obtain good information from an accountant or trust officer, only a lawyer can draft a will. To avoid extra expenses, you may want to go directly to an attorney.

Federal estate tax rates start at 37 percent on taxable estates (over $1,500,000 in 2005) and go up to 55 percent on very large estates. In addition, 18 states collect inheritance taxes. The result can be a sizable portion of a modest estate going to the government.

Federal law has three features you can use to minimize estate taxes:

1. Amounts left to qualified charities are deductible from the estate before calculating a tax liability.

2. There is a unified tax credit of $555,800 (in 2005) that everyone can use. (This is the amount of tax due on a taxable estate of $1,500,000.)

3. There is an unlimited marital deduction that allows you to leave any amount to your spouse tax free. (This process could greatly increase taxes at the time of your spouse's death.)

Scheduled Increases in the Unified Tax Credit

Year	Exempt Amount	Credit
2006 through 2008	$2,000,000	$780,800
2009 & thereafter	3,500,000	1,455,800

Probate is a public process that can be expensive and time consuming. Administrative and legal costs can run from 5 percent to 10 percent of the gross estate. This includes accountant, appraisal, and attorney fees, as well as court costs. Typical probate takes four to eight months but can run longer if the will is contested or you own property out of state. These costs and delays can place an undue burden on your family.

Retirees respond well to lectures, forums, and articles that discuss how to avoid probate. They seem interested in any technique that will help them beat the system. The more you can learn about legal ways to accomplish this, the better. One area to pay particular attention to—political debates about estate tax. A major decision is to find the right professional to help you. This person should know current federal and state estate-tax laws as well as recent applicable court cases. The right person will help you develop the estate plan you want—a plan that both takes advantage of tax provisions and accomplishes your wishes in the disposal of your estate. No easy assignment!

DEVELOPING A PLAN

You can develop a plan that guarantees that the right people get your property and, at the same time, keeps probate costs and estate taxes to a minimum. Here are some steps to take:

1. Check the beneficiary designations you have on file for your life insurance, employer retirement plan, Individual Retirement Account, or Keogh plan. Be sure the current designations are consistent with your wishes.

2. See an estate attorney to draw up a will. Even though you may use other methods to transfer the bulk of your estate, you need a will for two reasons: so you don't neglect to title all of your property properly, and in case you need to appoint a guardian for minor children.

3a. If your gross estate is well under the exempt amount, change the title on real estate and financial holdings to joint tenancy with right of survivorship. This allows the property to pass to the joint owner without probate. The unified tax credit eliminates any estate taxes.

3b. If your estate, including life insurance, is nearing the exempt amount, see an estate attorney and set up a revocable living trust with a testamentary trust that kicks in at your death. Your attorney will help design the trust so that you pass the maximum allowable to your children when your spouse dies. Until then, your spouse has full use of it. Anything over $600,000 goes directly to your spouse and comes under the unlimited marital deduction. This avoids probate and takes maximum advantage of estate tax credits.

3c. If your estate is more than twice the exempt amount, follow the plan outlined under 3b and consider reducing your estate by giving property to heirs or charity while you are living. You and your spouse can each give up to $11,000 a year to as many people as you wish without gift tax consequences. If you don't want someone to have the property immediately, set up an irrevocable living trust. Also, consider leaving some of your estate to charity upon your death.

SETTING UP A TRUST

A trust is a way to leave your money so that it avoids probate, takes full advantage of tax benefits, and accomplishes what you desire either before or after you are gone. In a trust, you assign part or all of your estate to a trustee or trustees to manage and distribute in a manner prescribed by you. It is a way to control the release of your money after your death. This can be done to protect and enhance the lives of others, usually those dear to you. Things are prearranged for your beneficiaries because you won't be around to do it yourself.

In other words, a trust can be any arrangement you choose that maintains and distributes your estate. It is your money, so it is your responsibility to call the shots. Arrangements, however, can be highly complicated.

Testamentary versus Living Trusts

A testamentary trust is a separate, sophisticated addition to your will. You designate the purpose and specifics in your will and also designate a trustee. When you die, the testamentary trust goes into effect and carries out your wishes.

A so-called living trust is not a specific part of your will. You draft it outside your will, but refer to it inside your will so both work in tandem. A trust can be designed to either end after a period of time or continue after your death. It is whatever you wish as long as you understand the tax implications. A living trust can be either revocable or irrevocable. If revocable, you retain the right to change the terms of the trust, or even end it, during your lifetime. In other words, you remain in charge. If you establish an irrevocable trust, you cannot change the terms or end it. Though inflexible, an irrevocable trust does offer special tax advantages.

Structure versus Flexibility in a Trust

The basic problem in setting up any trust is the uncertainty of what will happen in the future. It is possible to spend hours developing an arrangement that does not ultimately accomplish your desires because of some unanticipated change. On the other hand, if you simply leave your estate to beneficiaries hoping they will spend the money according to your wishes, it might not happen that way, either.

Many people like trusts because it is possible to make a more direct contribution to their grandchildren. It is not that they mistrust their children; they simply feel better knowing provisions are made for grandchildren in the event of a divorce or if their children are unsuccessful in building estates of their own.

Once again, the more advance thinking you do, the better prepared you will be when you consult your lawyer. Spouses need to discuss things ahead of time to avoid arguments in the presence of their attorney. No one, including your lawyer, should do your thinking for you.

Naming a Trustee

The individual you designate as an executor can also be designated as your trustee. Selecting a trustee involves many of the same considerations as selecting an executor. However, there is a difference between the two. An executor's job is finished once an estate is settled. This usually happens within a year or two. A trust can continue for many years. This means that the trustee acquires an almost permanent obligation.

You can choose a personal friend, relative, professional, or the trust department of an institution as your trustee. There are advantages and disadvantages to each. A personal friend may know and understand you and the beneficiaries, but may not be experienced with investments. A professional may not know you or your beneficiaries, but have the experience. A trust department in a bank won't move away or die. It also has a staff of professionals. Finally, the cost of a trust must be taken into consideration. The choice is yours.

If you name a personal acquaintance or relative as trustee of a living trust, the fee will be whatever is agreed upon—often no fee at all. Professional trustees, however, receive fees that are either a set amount or a percent of the trust's assets. Fees should be discussed and negotiated ahead of time.

LETTERS OF INSTRUCTION

After you have completed your will and trust arrangements, you will probably want to prepare a letter of instruction for your beneficiaries. This letter is a guide to make it easier for your family to close out your affairs. Although not a legal document, it should be in agreement with the terms of your will. You may want to check with your attorney on this matter. This letter of instruction may be written or placed on audio or video tape. Most people write a letter.

Here is some information you may want to consider as you prepare your letter of instruction. Use it as your outline.

People to be notified of death: Certain people and institutions need to be notified of your death, including your attorney, executor, trustee, and tax specialist, to name a few. Also, your Social Security office needs to know. Special friends will want to know as soon as possible. Providing names, titles, addresses, and telephone numbers will make it easier for the individual who assumes this responsibility. Take time in preparing this list. You will probably include your inner-circle support group of relatives and close friends. These individuals can provide emotional support if needed.

Advance funeral arrangements: You have the freedom to make all your own arrangements. Make sure you communicate them, providing all necessary details. Include a reminder that the funeral director provide multiple copies of the death certificate for processing insurance and Social Security claims.

Location of personal papers: Provide all the help you can here. Give the exact location of your personal documents, including birth certificate, marriage certificate, diplomas, military papers, and so on. It's a good idea to gather these in a single location.

Bank accounts: List all checking and savings accounts by name of institution, address where the account is located, type of account, and account number. Also, give the location of canceled checks and statements.

Credit cards: List by issuer and card number. Make sure the payer is provided access to accounts. Ask that these accounts be paid immediately and cards destroyed.

Loans: List all loans and other accounts payable by lender. Give full information on terms, payments, collateral, and so forth.

Money owed you: List all debts, first trust deeds, and other forms of loans owed to you. Provide all details.

Special survivors' benefits: List possible sources of benefits not named in the will— Social Security, veteran's, employee, pension, retirement, fraternal associations, and so on. Others may not think of these benefits as they go through your papers.

Deed and mortgage papers: Most people keep these vital documents in their safe-deposit boxes. If you do, also provide the location of the box and key and a list of the box's contents.

Insurance policies: List all life, auto, home, veteran's medical, and other insurance policies. Name the agent(s) and give the location of these documents. Describe any loans you may have taken out against said policies.

Vehicles: Tell where registration and other papers may be found for all motor vehicles or boats you own. Provide location of all keys and special instructions.

Taxes: Provide the location of your federal and state income-tax returns for the past three years. Name your tax consultant. Give special instructions if necessary.

Investments: For some people, this can be most important. List all stocks, bonds, certificates of deposit, IRA or Keogh accounts, and other investments. Include issuer name and cost to you. Also indicate where items are located. Identify your stockbroker and other agents. If you have any gold coins or silver bars that constitute an investment, provide location and details.

Valuables: Make certain you have a complete list of all jewelry and other valuables (china, glassware, art pieces, etc.). Tell where things are located. This list may also include the names of those to whom articles should be given. Often this list is a part of the will itself (on a separate list of personal property).

Trusts: List any trust you have established and give the name and address of the trustee—very important!

Miscellaneous: There will be other documents you should include. Think of them and prepare a list.

A NOVEL IDEA

If you are looking for an enjoyable way to distribute your personal possessions ahead of time, you might consider throwing a label party. It works like this: Invite your children (or perhaps special friends) to your home for a party. Provide a stack of gummed labels with invitee names printed on them. After preliminary instructions, ask them to work out, through discussion, who wants what property you wish to pass along. Once agreements have been reached, they can place their label on each item (where it cannot be seen). After the party, you can enjoy their choices and back up their selections with a list.

Estimate the Value of Your Estate

Note: Your estate includes all assets over which you have control.

1. Real estate _____

2. Investments _____

3. Retirement plans _____

4. Life insurance _____

5. Household furnishings _____

6. Automobiles, boats, RVs, etc. _____

7. Sporting equipment _____

8. Tools and equipment _____

9. Furs and jewelry _____

10. Art and collectibles _____

11. Other _____

Total Gross Estate _____

Outstanding debts – _____

Funeral & administrative expenses – _____

Adjusted Gross Estate _____

Charitable Bequests – _____

Marital Deduction – _____

Taxable Estate _____

KEY POINTS

■ Estate planning is making sure that your property goes to the right people when you die.

■ Property can be passed on to others by several different methods.

■ Quality estate planning also considers ways to minimize the cost of probate and estate taxes.

■ Individual circumstances such as multiple marriages and large estates often require special measures to achieve the desired results.

■ The process of estate planning can be a positive experience and add to your quality of life.

Things to Do

Instructions: In the space below, list the things you want to do as a result of reading this chapter. Then, choose a target date for completing each of your action items.

Action Item	Target Date

CHAPTER 20

INSURANCE

Science may have found a cure for most evils, but it has found no remedy for the worst of them all—the apathy of human beings.

—**Helen Keller**

As you near retirement, protecting yourself and your possessions takes on a new dimension. For example, health insurance becomes increasingly important. Although you may take fewer risks, you still need more insurance protection because accident and health problems tend to accelerate as you grow older.

A Definition of Insurance

Insurance is accepting a small loss now (premium payment) to prevent a potentially larger loss in the future. If you take out a policy to protect yourself against a loss (such as theft), in a sense, you win if you are robbed. You were smart enough to protect yourself. On the other hand, if you paid the premium for 20 years and were never robbed, you still won because you transferred the risk at a small cost and gained peace of mind. Insurance is a way to transfer risk and worry to another so you come out ahead. No time is more important to transfer worry than when you retire.

INSURANCE GOALS

Your objective is to develop an insurance package that accomplishes the following goals.

GOAL 1: Greater Peace of Mind. The secret is to be able to look down the road recognizing real risks, but not creating ones that are not there. When a risk is identified, you should pass it along to an insurance company and then relax. No part of life, especially retirement, is totally worry free, but the more worries you can transfer to insurance companies, the better.

GOAL 2: Less Confusion and Frustration. For most people, insurance contracts are hard to understand. There are too many clauses, too many exclusions, and too much small print. Many capable people throw up their hands in defeat. This chapter should help simplify the problem.

GOAL 3: Money Saved. Senior discounts provide opportunities to stretch insurance dollars if you select the right policies and avoid duplication. Saving dollars in areas where you need less insurance means you get more protection where your need is greater.

GOAL 4: More Help from Insurance Agents. Among professional people, your insurance agent should stand beside your medical doctor and lawyer. The more you learn about insurance, the more effective you will be in building a sound, rewarding relationship with your agent. The better your relationship, the more help you should receive.

MANAGING RISKS

There are three ways to manage risks. The best plan takes all three into account and develops a strategy that fits your personal financial situation.

Take all Possible Preventive Measures

If the time comes when you become a little unsteady on your feet, you should have enough common sense to stay off roofs and out of slippery bathtubs. If necessary, buy a cane and use it with style. If your eyesight begins to dim, recognize that driving at night is risky and plan daytime driving trips when possible.

Unless you take common sense precautions, all the insurance in the world can be meaningless. Insurance only cushions risks with money after something bad happens. To live with style, your objective should be to keep accidents and illnesses from happening in the first place. Take a risk-management approach—that is, avoid risks without hurting your lifestyle and then transfer the remaining risks to others. Like other aspects of life, risks can be managed.

Become Self Insured

The more money you have, the easier this is to do. For example, you might buy dental insurance. But perhaps your dentist does not choose to participate in such a plan. The policy is good only if you switch dentists. Solution? Insure yourself. Instead of paying, say $15, into a policy each month, use the money to build a kitty for future dental bills. Such a fund becomes a self-insurance policy.

Self insurance works best when the risk is small. Deductibles are, in a sense, self insurance. The more money you have, the higher the deductible can be. If you can afford to pay the first $2,500 of medical expenses each year, a deductible of this amount will greatly lower your monthly medical insurance premium.

Transfer the Risk to an Insurance Company

Do this by entering into a contract that costs a little each month as protection against a possible loss. You might never have enough money to rebuild your home if it burned, so you pay a company each month to assume that risk. When thousands of others do this, you receive the protection you seek at a low cost.

Transferring risk may sound easy. All you need is to find the right policy, for the right need, at the right cost. Write a check once a year and hope nothing happens. Of course, it is more complicated than this. When you retire, you must find policies that cover new risks or close gaps in existing ones. Policies can be deceptive. You may think you are fully covered when you're not. There are sometimes exclusions that limit your policy. Also, you must consider cost. It's impossible to live with style if you spend all your discretionary income on insurance premiums.

TYPES OF RISK

You face a number of risks in the process of daily living. You can generally cover many of them from current assets through self insurance, but here are six that you should consider insuring against.

Property Damage. This is the insurance you have on your car, home, and other personal property to repair or replace it if damaged by fire, storm, theft, or the negligence of someone else. When buying this type insurance, consider carefully the relationship between premium cost and deductibles. By assuming some of the risk through a higher deductible, you can reduce your premium.

Disability. If you are a 42-year-old man, you are four times more likely to become disabled for three months or longer before retirement than you are to die. This can be devastating for your retirement plans. However, after retirement, you probably won't need to continue this coverage. Check with your employer to see what coverage is available under a group plan. Also, investigate Social Security disability benefits and how your employer's plan coordinates with these benefits. You may find you have sufficient coverage or you may need to buy additional insurance until you retire.

Death. Life insurance is an important part of an overall financial plan, but see it for what it is. Don't get led into buying life insurance as an investment. Sales commissions and administrative costs run high. In retirement, minimize coverage since you will have other assets to cover living costs for survivors. Look into converting existing whole life policies to paid-up insurance. If you have a policy that pays dividends, consider having the dividend applied to the premium. One insurance feature that is attractive to retired couples is the "second-to-die" policy. This policy provides cash to help with estate taxes and thus eliminates the need to sell other assets when the estate passes to children.

Lawsuit. In today's lawsuit-prone society, sufficient liability insurance is a must. To protect your assets and your future, buy an umbrella liability policy. This policy kicks in after your car or homeowner's liability limits are exhausted. Premiums are quite reasonable.

Medical Expenses. Everyone is aware of the high cost of medical care. A major illness or injury could easily wipe out years of savings. Your employer or professional society may offer a group plan. If so, it is probably your best option. If you must buy medical insurance on your own, look for a high-deductible, catastrophic policy. Premiums are so expensive on private policies that you probably can only afford to insure against major risk. When you become eligible for Medicare, consider a Medigap policy if you feel you can't afford to pay the costs not covered by Medicare. These will be deductibles, co-payments of 20 percent of approved charges, charges in excess of the Medicare allowable (if your doctor doesn't accept Medicare assignment), and prescription drugs taken at home that exceed the amount covered by Medicare.

Long-term Care. Only five percent of people between ages 75 and 84 are in nursing homes. However, the percentage increases to 19 percent in the 85 and over age group. Seventy to 80 percent of nursing home residents use up their capital in a year or so. Long-term care insurance is available to help with these expenses. Premiums for this coverage increase with age. So, if you are considering it, buy it before the age of 60. As with any insurance, tailor a policy to balance benefits and premiums. Consider coverage that has inflation adjustment built in, has a lengthy waiting period (90 days), and covers Alzheimer's disease. You should also include home care as well as nursing home care so you won't be forced to leave your home until you physically have to.

An alternative to long-term care insurance is a financially sound life-care community. These communities, located throughout the country, provide care for residents as needed. Typically, there are three levels of care—independent living, assisted living, and custodial care. There is an entrance fee of several thousands of dollars and a monthly charge consistent with the level of care provided. While these communities are not inexpensive, residents are assured of the care they need throughout their lifetimes.

MEETING YOUR INSURANCE NEEDS

To properly meet your insurance needs, you must first take stock of the coverage you have and then consider what you have versus the coverage you need. This will help you identify any gaps in your coverage. Review all of your existing policies and then complete the Insurance Assessment Questionnaire. After reviewing the tips and warning that follow, you will be prepared to shop for the coverage you need.

Insurance Assessment Questionnaire

1. Is your insurance coverage adequate?   **Yes**   **No**

   Medical Insurance (including dental and vision)   ☐   ☐

   If not, what changes do you need to make?

   _____

   Long-term Care Insurance   ☐   ☐

   If not, what changes do you need to make?

   _____

   Disability Insurance   ☐   ☐

   If not, what changes do you need to make?

   _____

   Life Insurance   ☐   ☐

   If not, what change do you need to make?

   _____

   Property Casualty Insurance   ☐   ☐

   If not, what changes do you need to make?

   _____

   Liability Insurance   ☐   ☐

   If not, what changes do you need to make?

   _____

2. Are you making maximum use of group plans?   ☐   ☐

   If not, what plans do you need to investigate?

   _____

Tips on Shopping for Insurance

If you agree with the tip, place a checkmark in the square on the left of it.

☐ *Always compare.* In buying any new insurance policy, compare the two that you feel provide the best protection. Only after a step-by-step comparison should you make your choice.

☐ *Buy only what you need and can afford.* Duplicate coverage is not only costly but confusing as well. Keep your insurance program as uncomplicated as possible, but still get the protection you need. Don't fill the same gap twice.

☐ *Look for major exclusions.* Unless you cover the big risk you want to eliminate, forget it. You've got to get what you buy, or you've been misled. Ask your agent to write out exclusions.

☐ *Beware of a replacement offer.* If someone tries to replace your policy, be suspicious—especially in health insurance. Have someone who is qualified help you make a comparison.

☐ *Question policies with maximum ceilings.* If a company puts a low limit on how much they will pay, they are, in effect, leaving the risk with you. If their payoff is low, it may not be worthwhile.

☐ *Ensure your renewal rights.* If you cannot retain a policy as you get older, then you are only buying temporary protection and have not effectively transferred the risk.

☐ *Be aware that only private companies supplement Medicare.* Do not be misled that the government is protecting you when you deal with private companies. State insurance departments provide standards for insurance firms, but you are on your own when you deal with anything other than Medicare.

☐ *Take enough time to do research.* We sometimes buy something just to get it done. This frequently creates more stress at a later date. Be sure of what you are buying before you act.

☐ *When possible, deal with a single, reliable insurance agent.* Choose insurance agents the same way you choose lawyers or doctors. Seek one who enjoys working with people. Do not deal with anyone who is not sympathetic to your special needs as a retiree.

Special Warning: Normally, you are not eligible for Medicare unless you qualify for Social Security and reach the age of 65. This can mean that if you are in your forties or fifties and not under Social Security, you might consider moonlighting in a job that could provide you with this coverage; see Chapter 6. Also, those who retire before they reach the age of 65 should make sure they have adequate medical coverage between the date they retire and the date they become 65. Covering this time span is so important that it sometimes determines when an individual retires.

If you plan to retire before becoming eligible for Medicare and your employer doesn't provide retiree medical insurance, you need to know about the Consolidated Omnibus Budget Reconciliation Act of 1986. The act, called COBRA, includes much more than budget reconciliation. One of its provisions extends medical coverage in employers' group plans for employees who leave the payroll. So, you could pay the full cost plus a two-percent administration fee and continue coverage for up to 18 months after retiring. Then your employer's group plan must allow you to convert your group coverage to a private policy. While these provisions don't give you any price advantage, they do guarantee coverage without having to pass a medical exam.

KEY POINTS

- The first goal of insurance is to protect your financial resources. The second is to provide peace of mind.

- You should plan to cover small risks from current assets and insure against large risks.

- Larger deductibles will lower your premium costs.

- Health care costs represent potentially high risks for retired people.

- Medicare is the primary health care insurance for those over age 65.

- Most people on Medicare either buy Medigap insurance or join an HMO.

Things to Do

Instructions: In the space below, list the things you want to do as a result of reading this chapter. Then, choose a target date for completing each of your action items.

Action Item	Target Date

PART VI

LIVING ARRANGEMENTS

This section covers living arrangements after you retire, including both location and type of housing. When you complete it, you will have a better understanding of the choices available to you. And, you will know whether you want to stay in your present home or move to a new one.

CHAPTER 21

CHOOSING WHERE TO LIVE

A person travels the world over in search of what he needs and returns home to find it.

—George Moore

One of your biggest retirement decisions will be where to live. Do you stay where you are? Move to Florida? Have a mobile home in Oregon or a condo in California? There are many options.

Everything thus far has been leading you to this point. By now, you should have a solid foundation on which to make the best decision. The bad news is that you may still have to make it.

HOW TO CHOOSE WHERE TO LIVE

Choosing a new place to live, or deciding to stay where you are, can be a challenging experience. You can make it easier, however, by starting early and thinking through your retirement plans.

What do you want out of retirement? Do you want to move? Do you want to stay where you are for part of the year and spend the rest of the year someplace else? Do you plan to travel? Do you plan to work either full- or part time? In what activities do you plan to engage? Do you have a dream place in mind? What does your life partner want? When you begin by thinking about and discussing these issues, your retirement location decision will be easier. The basic message is: Plan around the activities and lifestyle you wish to pursue in retirement and make sure the location you choose will support them.

Researching location options can be the most enjoyable part of retirement planning. Take a two-step approach to picking a potential location. Start by reading books and magazine articles. There is a wealth of information available. You can consider places based on how they rate on such issues as cost of living, climate, services and activities available, crime rate, and employment opportunities.

As you collect information, you'll need to set up a file and organize your material. Use file folders for storing copies of articles, brochures, and notes. Consider organizing your files by cities, states, or specific communities.

After reading about several possible locations, select a few to visit. Be sure to visit during the less popular season of the year. You want to see the Gulf Coast in the summer and New England in the winter. The better you know a place during its off season, the better you can evaluate it as a potential retirement location. Here are some tips for your visits:

Go on fact-finding trips, not vacations. Even if you are using vacation time, take a few days and get practical. Visit the chamber of commerce, read the local newspaper, check out health care facilities, visit supermarkets and shopping malls, and attend church or synagogue.

Think long term. Remember, you may be spending the rest of your life here. What is the attitude of old-timers toward newcomers? Do the locals resent retirees moving into their community? Does the place offer the activities and environment you need for a truly satisfying retirement?

Be practical. You are what you are. You may change, but chances are you won't. Make your selection based on what you already enjoy doing plus what you think you might like to do in the future.

Make your own decision. Real estate salespeople and chamber of commerce employees tend to paint too rosy a picture. Filter what they tell you. Broaden your research base by talking to others. Ask questions and then make up your own mind. Don't be sold by some overzealous community representative.

WHAT TO LOOK FOR

You will meet your personal needs and your decision will fit within your comfort zone if you make a list of things that are important to you. Here are some points to consider:

Climate. What do you enjoy and what can you tolerate? Many people prefer a mild temperature with moderate humidity. Others are just as happy in the humid Gulf Coast; the hot desert; the cool, rainy northwest; or the cold, snowy winters of the north. Is this an important issue for you? If so, what do you find acceptable?

Geography. Do you look forward to living on the seashore or lake front? What about the desert versus mountains? Do you favor a rural setting, a small town, or a larger city? These are important considerations to some.

Travel. How convenient is travel into and out of the area? You will want to visit your children and grandchildren, or have them visit you. You may plan to travel during your retirement. Is there an airport in the community? Is the interstate highway system nearby?

People. Most retirees like to live where there are other retirees. It is easier to get involved socially in an area with a large number of newcomers.

Crime. Read local newspapers to get a feel for the crime rate. Go to the library and look up crime figures for the community. They are usually published in reference books.

Recreational and Cultural Facilities. What do you like to do and can you do it here? If you play golf, is there a reasonably priced golf course available? What about a community theatre and an arts center? Is there a local college that offers courses to seniors? Does the college offer plays and concerts for the community?

Housing. Does the community offer the type of neighborhoods and housing you would like to live in? If so, tour the neighborhood and look at houses. What is the cost and availability of housing? Also consider property taxes and maintenance costs. If you don't plan to buy, are there reasonable rentals available? Are there systems in place to deter crime? What about fire protection?

Services. Does the community offer what you need in terms of medical facilities, a place of worship, and shopping?

Public Transportation: Does the community offer adequate public transportation service? Many communities provide either free or low-cost transportation designed especially for seniors.

Cost of Living. Look for low food and energy costs. Check local property, income, and sales taxes. For example, you pay no state income tax in Alaska, Florida, Nevada, South Dakota, Texas, Washington, and Wyoming. However, these savings may be offset by higher property and sales taxes. Work to get a true and accurate picture of total costs. Avoid the trap of assuming that all costs are low, especially if one or two categories such as food and housing are.

Quality of Life. You will find quality of life tradeoffs among large cities, small towns, and rural areas. Consider traffic, crime, and congestion versus museums, theaters, and shopping. What is important to your quality of life?

CHOICES TO CONSIDER

In a 1990 survey, 86 percent of older Americans said they wanted to stay in their present home and, in fact, 70 percent do. Of those who move, most stay within their community, some return to their "home" community, and a few move to the Sun Belt states. Of those moving to the Sun Belt states, many return to their home communities within five years.

Relocating can be either a great adventure or a big mistake, depending on how carefully you assess your needs and plan to meet them. Here are several options that work for different retirees. Which one appeals to you?

Stay Where You Are

Although most dream of a distant retirement paradise, after careful analysis, some retirees wisely opt to stay close to their roots. They discover paradise in their own backyard. The fact is, there is no perfect place. What really makes a place enjoyable is a combination of factors unique to you. Most important are the availability of supportive relationships with family and friends and the opportunity to engage in meaningful activities. What about you? Do you already live in paradise or is it time to consider a new location?

Maintain Two Residences

Geese aren't the only ones that go south for the winter and north for the summer. Many retirees are learning that they can enjoy their home community during its ideal season and then get away during the less desirable time of year. For those living in the north, it means going to Florida, Texas, or Arizona for the winter.

The same idea leads those in locales with hot summers to head to the mountains during the summer months.

Whether you rent or buy your second home, there are problems associated with maintaining two residences—things that you don't run into living in only one home. Here are a few to consider:

■ Extra things are required for the second home. You'll need two sets of the things that make living comfortable—appliances, pots and pans, telephones, and possibly even cars.

■ Security is a concern at the house you are not occupying. Insurance premiums may be higher if you only occupy a place part time.

■ There will be minor hassles such as getting mail at both places and figuring out how to get the important stuff to you. Also, you'll need two sets of doctors.

■ Travel costs can get expensive depending on the distance between the two places.

Move to Another Area

You just might be part of the small percentage that finds relocation the answer to a satisfying retirement. This is particularly true if your employer has moved you during the course of your career and you haven't lived in your present location very long. You may still have family and friends in another area who you're anxious to rejoin. Or, if your present location doesn't support the activities and lifestyle you plan to pursue, relocation can be necessary. Finally, if there are significant negatives associated with your present locale such as climate, crime, or high living costs, relocation can be the basis for a more enjoyable retirement. The most popular areas in the United States for retirees are the Ozark Mountains of Arkansas and Missouri, the Gulf Coast of Florida, the Pacific Northwest, and the Research Triangle of North Carolina.

Some people believe that only when you leave your pre-retirement environment does a full retirement transition take place. When you remain in the same geographic location with the same habits, responsibilities, and associations, retirement may work. When you make a major relocation the transition forces you to replace old habits and retirement eventually becomes more fulfilling. This notion deserves serious discussion and consideration. However, it shouldn't be accepted without extreme caution and careful research.

Move to a Retirement Community

The standard retirement community is a community of adults, usually over 50 years old. Many are located in the Sun Belt states. Their major attraction is the recreational facilities they offer, ranging from clubhouses, golf courses, and tennis courts to swimming pools. A wide range of planned activities are offered for residents. Housing tends to be relatively inexpensive and there is a group of people of similar ages and backgrounds to count as your new friends.

Many of these communities are located some distance from cities, making it inconvenient for shopping, obtaining medical care, and going to worship. There are annual fees for the maintenance of common facilities. If you don't play golf, you still pay for the golf course maintenance. This could be considered wasteful if you don't take advantage of everything the community has to offer. Also, fees may escalate in the future.

If you are considering such a location, it is better to buy into a well-established community. You avoid the disappointment of unfulfilled promises, and you can see just how well things are being kept up.

Move Abroad

About 400,000 Social Security checks are mailed outside the U.S. each month. This is not an accurate estimate of the number of U.S. citizens who have retired abroad, because some checks go to foreigners who earned benefits while working in the U.S. and many U.S. citizens have their benefits directly deposited into their U.S. bank account. But, it does show that a great many have chosen to live abroad in retirement.

Unless you have lived abroad, you probably have no idea of the potential problems you can face. You are no longer in your home country; you are no longer the same as everyone else. If you are thinking about a place where English is not the official language, consider your ability to read the newspaper, go shopping, and talk to your neighbors. If you can't communicate in the local language, you can feel very isolated. Of course, there are communities made up entirely of U.S. retirees in other countries if you want to feel more at home in a distant land.

Retiring abroad can have advantages. Among them are the opportunity to immerse yourself in another culture, and see and experience the historic and geographic features of the country. You might find that it is cheaper to live abroad than in the U.S.

Some of the more popular countries for U.S. retirees are Mexico, Canada, the Philippines, and Costa Rica. By far, the nation with the largest population of U.S. retirees is Mexico. More than 1,000,000 live there, attracted by its low cost of living. Canada attracts U.S. retirees with its natural beauty, more sedate lifestyle, and cosmopolitan cities. The Philippines is popular with retired military personnel, who have experience with the area and with Philippine-Americans. Its main attractions are beautiful geography, lush tropical settings, and a rich cultural past. Costa Rica is a free and stable democracy that enjoys peace. (It is one of the few nations in the world without an army, and has the highest literacy rate in the Western world.) It is a beautiful country with moderate temperatures, and there is no tax on pensions or other income from abroad.

Become a Modern-Day Nomad

Some retirees choose to sell their homes and most of their possessions and hit the road in an RV. This choice is not for people who are into structure and routine. Living space is limited and there is a lot of togetherness. But, it affords you the opportunity to see the country at your own pace and choose the part of the country by the seasons. And, for the socially oriented, new friends await you at each new RV park.

The Good Sam Club, headquartered in Englewood, Colorado, provides a wide range of support services for RVers, including mail forwarding. You can visit the Web site at www.GoodSamClub.com. Learn more about the full-time RVing lifestyle by visiting www.FullTimeRVer.com.

WHERE-TO-RETIRE EXERCISE

The following exercise allows you to structure a preliminary analysis of your present location and two others you have chosen as potential retirement sites. After working through it, you will have a better understanding of how these three choices compare.

Step 1: Rate all factors on where you now live. Write a number from 1 to 10 in the appropriate box in the exercise. (10 is the highest rating; 1 is the lowest.)

Step 2: Select two other locations you have investigated. Write these locations in the boxes under Options 1 and 2.

Step 3: Rate each of these locations and compare them to the rating of the place where you now live.

Step 4: Some of the factors may be far more critical to your needs than others and should, therefore, be given more weight in your personal analysis. Check the factors that are very important to you.

Where to Retire: Preliminary Analysis of Geographical Locations

Check if very important	Factors to be rated	Where you live now	Option 1 (city) _____	Option 2 (city) _____
☐	1. *What is the climate from a health standpoint?* Is the climate good for you? Less demanding, with less chance of illness? Might it extend your life? A rating of 10 is the healthiest of all climates.	☐	☐	☐
☐	2. *What is the climate from a cost standpoint?* Would it reduce your utility bills? Are clothing costs less? Under this category, it is probably more expensive to live in Michigan than in Texas.	☐	☐	☐
☐	3. *Does the geographical area fit your comfort zone?* Do you enjoy changes in seasons? Are mountains more attractive to you than beaches? Would you fit the local culture? West Palm Beach, Florida, is vastly different from Albuquerque, New Mexico. Give high ratings to those areas that best fit your personal comfort zone.	☐	☐	☐

Check if very important	Factors to be rated	Where you live now	Option 1 (city) _____	Option 2 (city) _____
☐	4. *What about housing?* Could you afford the kind of housing you want? How do costs compare to where you are now? What would it cost to move? Preliminary housing cost comparisons may be made by writing for a local newspaper. Make certain you have accurate data before rating this significant factor.	☐	☐	☐
☐	5. *What about other expenses?* The cost of consumer goods or tax rates are examples. Prices vary. Some states do not have income taxes. Sales taxes are lower in some areas. A high rating indicates lower prices.	☐	☐	☐
☐	6. *Are your kind of leisure activities available?* Can you enjoy them year round? Do they cost less? The quality of your retirement years can depend heavily on your leisure activities.	☐	☐	☐
☐	7. *What about medical facilities?* Would you be close to the best possible help? If you belong to an HMO, does it have a facility at the new location? Would you need to change doctors? Do you have a special health problem?	☐	☐	☐

Check if very important	Factors to be rated	Where you live now	Option 1 (city)	Option 2 (city)
☐	8. *Would you be able to build a new inner circle easily?* Would you be with your kind of people? People in New England can be different from those in California. Would you be quickly accepted in a new environment?	☐	☐	☐
☐	9. *What about transportation?* Is public transportation available if you need it? Would transportation be a low or high factor?	☐	☐	☐
☐	10. *Other factors?* Would you be near friends and relatives you would choose? Would you be closer or farther away from your special vacation spots? Would you be too isolated for friends to visit? Give this a general rating based on what has not already been covered. A high rating indicates you are still enthusiastic; a low rating indicates you may be changing your mind.	☐	☐	☐
Totals		☐	☐	☐

If you rated where you live now higher than your options, you are saying there may be more advantages in staying where you are rather than in moving. If either option is rated higher, this signals that more investigation is desirable, including perhaps a trip to make specific comparisons.

A geographical move is a decision that should be made only after lengthy, careful, and complete analysis. Several months' time is recommended, including visits during different seasons so you can verify all significant factors. Many retirees recommend living in a new area for several months as renters until you are sure.

KEY POINTS

- Retirement presents the opportunity to live anywhere you choose.
- Your retirement location must support your retirement activities and lifestyle.
- If you plan to relocate, carefully investigate potential options before making a final decision.
- Consider renting at your new location for a few months before making a final decision.

Things to Do

Instructions: In the space below, list the things you want to do as a result of reading this chapter. Then, choose a target date for completing each of your action items.

Action Item	Target Date

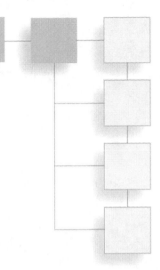

CHAPTER 22

RETIREMENT LIVING OPTIONS

Be it ever so humble, there's no place like home.

—J. Howard Payne

When you have settled on a geographic preference, your attention can turn to the kind of housing or living environment that is best for you. (In fact, these decisions are often made together.) Should you move to a condo, mobile home park, or retirement center, or stay where you are? Some of the many options are shown in the following illustration.

WHERE TO BEGIN

As you consider the plethora of questions and options open to you, there are three major categories of concerns to address.

Available Choices

To assist you in taking your first step, it is helpful to reduce the many possibilities to four broad and basic choices.

Typical Residential Living. In addition to freestanding homes, this category should include apartments, duplexes, town homes, and condominiums where people of all ages reside. Over 70 percent of retirees live in these accommodations.

Retirement Centers. There are all kinds of adult (over age 50) retirement centers in all parts of the country. Some are small mobile home parks with few amenities. Others are elaborate. Some are planned communities like Sun City in Arizona. Others are like Leisure World in California. Some provide a wide assortment of recreational services—golf courses, swimming pools, exercise rooms, auditoriums, emergency nursing care, and so on. Most charge monthly fees, which often include maintenance of common grounds and other services. Various property arrangements (own, lease, rent) can apply.

Continuing Care Retirement Community. A CCRC facility (often called a LifeCare operation) usually provides everything a sophisticated retirement center offers but may also have an around-the-clock, long-term care facility (similar to a so-called nursing center). Some even have assisted living accommodations—a step between independent living and full care. All of this plus some housekeeping assistance and one or more meals per day are provided for one regular fee. It is the goal of most CCRC operations to provide care for the rest of your life with as many amenities as possible. All such facilities have complex entrance fee arrangements and are supervised by state governments. Some are religiously based and non-profit; others are privately owned and developed. Many couples view the centers as insurance for the future, knowing that if one partner needs special care, the other can remain independent and be close by to provide personal support.

Other Choices. Any adult living arrangement that does not fit comfortably into the first three options should be included in this category. In other words, if you have an unusual accommodation already in mind (RV park, your own boat, etc.) it goes here.

Things to Consider

As you evaluate the possibilities, please keep the following in mind.

- **Your health is the Joker in the retirement deck.** Do your planning based upon good health, but keep in mind that the further you move into your retirement years, the more attractive some living options become.

- **Unless you have accumulated considerable capital and have a high retirement income, a few options may be out of reach.** Your ultimate choice should be one that fits into your financial comfort zone. In doing your preliminary research, seek an option that will be a good financial investment.

- **Independence can be a matter of interpretation.** For example, those who choose residential living may consider themselves independent because they accept a minimum of services from others. Those who choose to live in a retirement community may consider themselves independent because they need not spend time performing home-maintenance services and therefore are free to travel more.

- **Those with life partners may need two living options.** One option is as a two-member team, another as a single person should one lose her or his partner.

- **Once a decision has been made, all choices will be home.** Who can say whether living permanently in an RV is less of a home than a traditional residence?

■ **Keep in mind that you might wish to make two or more moves during your retirement years.** For example, you may wish to live your first 10 or so years in your present residence, move to a smaller condominium for the next five or so, and then move into a retirement center or Continuing Care Retirement Community. The more you think in these terms, the more realistic you will be.

Some General Rules for Choosing Where to Live

As you consider various alternatives, these general rules will help you make a decision that is right for you.

■ Before deciding to move, make sure advantages measurably outweigh disadvantages.

■ You alone should make the final decision. Do not be overly influenced by relatives, friends, or promoters. (Remember, the grass always looks greener on the other side.)

■ Protect your freedom with a passion. Any move that causes you to lose freedom or makes your world smaller may not be worth the apparent security it brings.

■ Take culture shock seriously. Culture shock—the disorientation that occurs when moving from one area to another—requires adjustment. There is also a necessary adjustment when you move from your private home to a different living environment. There will be new neighbors, new social situations, and new rules to follow. This culture shock is possible in your own community when you move from your home into a retirement center.

SEVEN RETIREMENT LIVING OPTIONS

Summarized in this section are seven common retirement living options. Read the description of each with its advantages and disadvantages. Check the appropriate boxes as you analyze the possibilities.

Is Your Home Still Your Castle?

If you own your home, you might be happier staying there. More and more gerontology specialists advocate this, and there seems to be a trend in this direction.

There can be a lot of happiness in your own backyard. Sometimes, though, it is wise to move: Neighborhoods change or you change. Study the following advantages and disadvantages of living in your own home, and check items important to you. Write in any you feel are missing.

Advantages:

■ Your image is tied to your home. People you love identify you with being there.

■ You feel more in charge in your own home.

■ You have more privacy and space in your own home. You don't have to listen to someone else's plumbing.

■ You retain more of your possessions.

■ You can keep your pets.

■ Other: _____

_____

Disadvantages:

■ Home ownership is often more expensive (taxes, maintenance, etc.).

■ Maintenance takes time, and you may worry or do too much yourself.

■ Security risks may be higher.

■ It may be more difficult to take trips.

■ Until you sell your home, you can't take advantage of the tax break that excludes capital gains taxes on homes selling for up to $500,000 for couples or $250,000 for individuals.

■ Other: _____

_____

☐ *My decision is to stay put, for now.*   ☐ *I need to seriously investigate other options.*

Would You Be Happier Renting?

Some retirees are very happy in rented apartments. The reason is that they are not tied down with homeowner responsibilities. They can select the neighborhood they prefer in the community they like. They can also stay close to their inner circle without the problems of maintaining their own home.

Advantages:

- Moving to a new apartment is usually easy.

- Maintenance is the responsibility of the owner.

- Apartments require no capital investment.

- Credits are available for tax purposes.

- Apartments with special facilities (swimming pools and health clubs) are often available.

- Other: _____

_____

Disadvantages:

- Landlords can be uncooperative and difficult.

- Rent increases are always possible.

- Neighbors living too close can be a problem.

- Apartments build no equity.

- Other: _____

_____

☐ *No thanks—apartment living is not for me.*   ☐ *I have an open mind and will investigate.*

What About a Condominium?

If you own your home, you might be able to sell it, buy a nice condo at a lower price, and invest the difference. Many do this and feel they have done the right thing. Condominium life can have style!

Maintenance is normally not required. You are responsible for things inside your unit, but nothing on the outside. You will have a deed and/or mortgage and pay real estate taxes. But you join with other owners to pay for outside maintenance, including recreational areas, landscaping, and even roofing. There are many elegant condominium facilities in the United States. All have their own special requirements, and almost all have a homeowner's association in which you automatically become a member.

Advantages:

- Usually safer than an isolated, private dwelling.

- Easier to leave for long trips because there is less to care for.

- Special facilities are often available—pool, sauna, recreation rooms, tennis courts.

- More likely to have neighbors your own age and social level.

- Easier to meet new people.

- Other: _____

_____

Disadvantages:

- There are rules to follow and association involvement.

- Normally you have less room, which may force you to sell some of your possessions.

- Your assessment fees can increase.

- Your neighbors are not always compatible.

- There are often restrictions on pets.

▪ Other: _____

_____

☐ *A condominium*   ☐ *Much more investigation*
   is a best bet.   *is called for.*

Mobile-Home Living Can Be Nifty

A growing number of retirees are living happily in adult mobile parks, some of which are quite elegant. The homes are really prefabricated houses, and some have two or three bedrooms. Mobile homes normally cost less than condominiums or single-dwelling houses. Often you can sell a private home, buy a mobile home, and bank the difference.

Advantages:

▪ Less capital investment is required.

▪ There are many parks from which to select.

▪ Security protection can be excellent.

▪ Your neighbors are often in your comfort zone.

▪ There can be excellent recreational facilities or locally sponsored social events.

▪ Other: _____

_____

Disadvantages:

▪ Neighbors can be too close.

▪ Usually some restrictions prevail—for example, pets may not be permitted.

▪ Park owners can raise rent on space.

▪ Like neighborhoods, parks can deteriorate.

- ■ Sometimes it is difficult to get into good parks.

- ■ Other: _____

_____

☐ *Mobile home living is not my cup of tea.*   ☐ *I need to investigate this option.*

Retirement Centers Are in Vogue

Many retirees are so enthusiastic about retirement centers, they have closed their eyes to other possibilities. Retirement centers can come in all sizes, varieties, and prices. Many have medical centers. Large ones often have churches, organized social activities, golf, swimming, and tennis. Compared to adult condominiums and mobile-home parks, retirement centers are more self contained.

Advantages:

- ■ Retirement centers offer greater security.

- ■ More facilities, especially medical, are available.

- ■ You have less worry and feel more secure as you grow older. You have easier access to inside facilities.

- ■ Different centers fit most pocketbooks.

- ■ Other: _____

_____

Disadvantages:

- ■ There are many restrictions.

- ■ Generally no pets are allowed.

- ■ Centers are like a closed world.

- ■ There are fewer young people around.

- Sometimes it is difficult to get any of your money back if you change your mind and want to move out.

- Other: _____

_____

☐ *I'm not the retirement*   ☐ *I'm going to do a*
center kind.   *complete investigation.*

Should You Apply for Government-Sponsored Housing?

If your income is modest, government housing could be the best step to take. If you can find a place and the list is not too long, you might want to act in a hurry.

Advantages:

- Lower costs are often adjusted to your income.

- Each facility must meet government specifications.

- There are few responsibilities.

- Government housing is usually close to public transportation.

- Government facilities are normally secure.

- Other: _____

_____

Disadvantages:

- Being accepted can be difficult.

- Like most things connected with government, there are many restrictions.

- Rooms are usually small.

- There is often a hotel atmosphere.

- There is some loss of freedom.

▪ Other: _____

_____

☐ *Government housing*   ☐ *I'm going to look into this.*
  is not for me.

Life-Care Centers Have Special Attractions

There are centers that provide full or life care. This usually means that, with a sizable investment, you can enter a community with the intention of staying there the rest of your life. You may be totally able when you enter; but later, when you need greater—even custodial—care, the facility is prepared to care for you. Some are very attractive, and often they are connected with a religious denomination.

Advantages:

▪ You can receive the greatest possible care and security.

▪ Life-care centers can provide peace of mind.

▪ Other residents are usually in the same comfort zone.

▪ Centers potentially eliminate future difficult decisions.

▪ Often less concern is required by your family.

▪ Activities may fit your needs better than other retirement options.

▪ Other: _____

_____

Disadvantages:

▪ Centers cost money. Often a sizable investment is required. In some cases you turn over a part of your estate.

▪ The age level is usually more advanced.

▪ Often people lose more freedom than expected.

- The decision can be almost irrevocable because of financial commitments.

- It is difficult to find the perfect center.

- There is a possibility the organization will go bankrupt.

- Other: _____

_____

☐ *I could become*
   interested at a later date.   ☐ *I'm going to spend*
                                         some investigating.

RETIREMENT LIVING DECISION PROCESS

Now that you have considered the advantages and disadvantages of several retirement living options, the following process will help bring everything together. It starts by helping you decide what is important in your retirement living arrangements. Then, it has you evaluate at least five alternative arrangements against your list of important factors.

Take Your Positive Attitude with You

If you decide to make a major move, take your positive attitude with you. More than anything else, it will help make your move successful. Here are some further tips:

- Within reason, take your prized possessions with you. They help make a new location seem more like home.

- Once settled, get involved in a number of civic, athletic, social, or church activities.

- The sooner you make new friends, or rebuild an inner-circle support group, the better.

- The people you meet will do more than anything else to make your new environment a happy one.

Weigh and Decide

Listed below are 10 factors to take into consideration as you evaluate your many options. A few will be far more important to you than others. Because of this, you are asked to prioritize the five most important to you. To do this, write the number 1 in the box opposite the desire most important to you. Then select the second most important and write the number 2.

Continue to weigh and decide until you have chosen your five most important considerations. Once accomplished, satisfying these desires will help you make choices within your comfort zone. In doing this, it is strongly recommended that life partners make their choices independently so they can be matched and discussed later.

Please read all 10 factors carefully before taking your first 5 choices.

☐ ***Refusing to Give Up Important Things.*** One reason many people never move away from their pre-retirement residence is because they do not wish to give up pets, extra space, extra cars, possessions like workshop equipment, and so forth. Are you willing to simplify your life by giving up some of the priceless things that currently make your living environment comfortable? If not, this factor deserves a top choice.

☐ ***Safety Factors.*** Wherever you intend to live after retirement, you want to feel safe, secure, and relaxed. Although single residences can be made safer (alarm systems, barred windows, safety doors, having a large dog, etc.), if your neighborhood is deteriorating it may no longer be in your comfort zone. This factor, if sufficiently important, may be a top five priority for you.

☐ ***Staying Close to Children, Family, or Friends.*** Some retirees who would prefer living in a retirement center of some kind remain in their homes in order to stay close to their children. Others prefer to start a new life away from family and friends. You need to dig down deeply within yourself in deciding if staying close to your family and friends is a priority with you. If so, you will want to enter a number from 1 to 5 in the box.

☐ ***Becoming a Burden on Your Family.*** Interviews indicate that a primary reason many retirees opt to move into retirement centers is because they do not wish to be dependent upon the help of other family members. This may be a change over the way previous generations have felt. Depending upon how strongly you feel about this factor, you may wish to include it in your top five choices.

☐ ***Social Aspects.*** Some people wish to "get away from it all" upon retirement. They are not comfortable living close to others. Still others want the sense of community that can be found in small towns or retirement centers. They want to mix with others and enjoy social activities such as bridge, dancing, golf, etc. Do you need to be around people? If so, give this factor careful consideration.

☐ ***Adjusting to a Purpose.*** For retirees who have strong goals to reach, their living option may be determined by what they hope to achieve. For example, many painters and writers like to live in art colonies. Environmentalists often prefer wilderness locations. Pet lovers seek extra space with few restrictions. In short, a purpose can dictate a special lifestyle, which can influence living accommodations. Is this a priority for you?

☐ ***Maintenance Responsibility.*** Some people enjoy having large homes and gardens and doing fix-it chores. Others would much prefer living in a retirement center where there are no maintenance responsibilities. Regardless of your preference, this may or may not be a priority factor for you.

☐ ***Convenience Factor.*** A mountain retreat may have poetic advantages but inconvenience is a high price to pay for living in isolated places. Generally speaking, the more isolated your living accommodations, the farther you must travel for medical attention, shopping, and recreational activities. Does convenience outweigh a wilderness existence? If so, you may want to check this as a priority factor.

☐   ***Health Factor.*** Some communities make it easy for people to grow old in their own home by providing services such as Meals on Wheels, home nursing care, housekeeping assistance, and so on. Retirement centers often go further. It may not be a critical factor during early retirement years, but it can become increasingly important later. In looking over the factors under consideration, does this one merit a priority check?

☐   ***Miscellaneous.*** Now that you are more familiar with the complexity of making a post-retirement living environment decision, please ask yourself these questions: How important is having peace of mind or mental comfort? Is a long life important to me? Is there such a thing as a happiness factor? *If there is a factor not listed above that is most important to you, list it below and place a check in the box.* This factor should receive a high priority in making your final decisions.

_____

_____

Congratulations! You have identified five key desires you wish to satisfy. It is now time to weigh these desires against your living options. The following steps are recommended.

Step 1: On a sheet of paper, list a minimum of five living arrangements that interest you.

Step 2: Opposite this list, write the five desires you wish to satisfy most. List others if you wish.

Step 3: Based upon how well each living option satisfies your desires, reduce the number to three.

Step 4: Enter your first, second, and third choices in the box below.

Step 5: Match your choices against your anticipated retirement date, age at the time, and life expectancy to see if your choices are progressive in nature.

Go slowly and be sure of yourself. Keep in mind that no one can go through this mental process for you. Only you can make the ultimate decision that will fit best into your comfort zone.

If you have a life partner, work independently so you match and discuss results later. This can be fun and sometimes revealing!

MY RETIREMENT LIVING CHOICES

1. _____

2. _____

3. _____

CONCLUSION

Whatever your ultimate decisions may be, please take these suggestions into consideration.

- You have only started your research. Additional and continuous investigation is recommended. Take vacations at locations where you might like to reside. Visit retirement centers of all kinds. Start a file on possibilities.

- Only you know your comfort zones. Compromises should be minor and then only between life partners. Keep in mind that there is no perfect living environment. All possibilities have advantages and disadvantages.

- Timing is critical to making any change. Many couples desire to move into a retirement center of some kind early so that if one partner doesn't make it as long as the other, the remaining partner is more settled and secure.

- When the time comes to make a move, financial factors may rule out certain options but keep an open mind until that time arrives.

- Do not permit anyone to overly influence you in any direction. It may be your toughest retirement decision, so satisfy yourself. If you have a life partner, do all of your research together until you reach the best possible solution.

When you ultimately discover those options that fall within your comfort zone, don't fear making a decision. You have earned the right to build an exciting retirement lifestyle in your present home or undertake new adventures in different living environments as you choose.

Good luck!

KEY POINTS

■ Some retirees choose to make two or more moves as their interests and health change.

■ Most older people prefer to remain independent in their own home as long as possible.

■ Some retirees prefer to give up the responsibility and financial burden of home ownership.

■ Before making a move, be sure the advantages outweigh the disadvantages.

■ Make your own decision. Don't be influenced by others.

■ Be sure your living arrangements support your retirement activities and lifestyle.

Things to Do

Instructions: In the space below, list the things you want to do as a result of reading this chapter. Then, choose a target date for completing each of your action items.

Action Item	Target Date

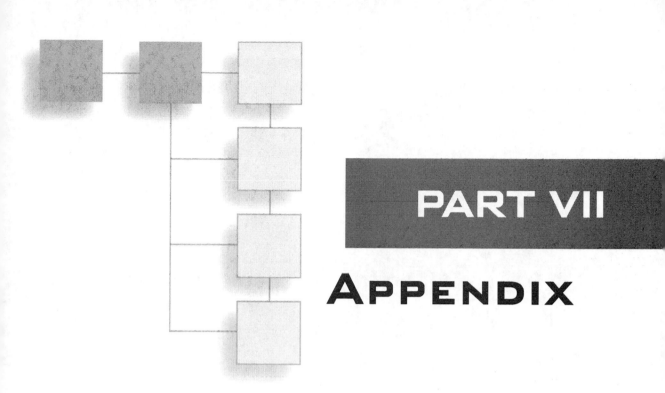

PART VII

APPENDIX

APPENDIX A

INVENTORY OF RETIREMENT ACTIVITIES (IRA)

This easy, self-scoring survey can help you make the most of your retirement years.

This Inventory of Retirement Activities (IRA) could be an important way to enhance your retirement years. It can help you develop interests worthy of your retirement leisure hours—activities that fit your personality and provide satisfaction.

There are three parts to the exercise: ranking your activity preferences, constructing and interpreting your personal profile, and comparing your profile with others—especially a life partner or friend. Complete one step at a time; please do not jump ahead.

Reproduction of any part of this instrument is expressly prohibited. Separate copies may be ordered.

PART 1: PREFERENCE INVENTORY SCALE

Rate each statement in each box by circling an appropriate number.

- 10 indicates that you look forward with great enthusiasm to participating in the activity.

- 9, 8, or 7 indicates high interest in the activity. You thoroughly enjoy it.

- 6 to 4 indicates moderate interest. Time permitting, you would enjoy the activity.

- 3 or 2 signifies limited interest. You would probably engage in the activity only to make another person happy.

- 1 says you would not participate under any circumstances.

If you are currently working, rate the items as if you were retired. As you complete each statement, assume your financial condition makes the activity affordable.

This is not a test, so there are no wrong answers. Work quickly; first impressions will probably give you the best results.

IRA—Box 1

Statement	Scale
1. Enjoying a sunset from a foreign shore	10 9 8 7 6 5 4 3 2 1
2. Playing competitive outdoor games	10 9 8 7 6 5 4 3 2 1
3. Participating in church or temple activities	10 9 8 7 6 5 4 3 2 1
4. Using a drill, skill saw, sewing machine, or other craft activities	10 9 8 7 6 5 4 3 2 1
5. Painting, sketching, designing, writing, or other creative activities	10 9 8 7 6 5 4 3 2 1
6. Camping, backpacking, or other wilderness activities	10 9 8 7 6 5 4 3 2 1
7. Demonstrating pride of ownership through home improvements	10 9 8 7 6 5 4 3 2 1

IRA—Box 1 *(continued)*

Statement	Scale
8. Planning a festive party or attending one	10 9 8 7 6 5 4 3 2 1
9. Listening to music alone	10 9 8 7 6 5 4 3 2 1
10. Playing a game for fun, prizes, or money	10 9 8 7 6 5 4 3 2 1
11. Watching the five o'clock news	10 9 8 7 6 5 4 3 2 1
12. Browsing in a bookstore or library	10 9 8 7 6 5 4 3 2 1
13. Dealing with investments as a leisure activity	10 9 8 7 6 5 4 3 2 1
14. Having fun with children, grandchildren, nieces, nephews	10 9 8 7 6 5 4 3 2 1
15. Earning as much money as Social Security allows	10 9 8 7 6 5 4 3 2 1
16. Volunteering services to a cause	10 9 8 7 6 5 4 3 2 1
17. Visiting an art gallery or museum	10 9 8 7 6 5 4 3 2 1
18. Having an intriguing conversation with a neighbor or friend	10 9 8 7 6 5 4 3 2 1

IRA—Box 2

Statement	Scale
1. Getting away from it all—staying at a resort, taking a cruise, etc.	10 9 8 7 6 5 4 3 2 1
2. Participating in sports or taking part in a physical-conditioning program	10 9 8 7 6 5 4 3 2 1
3. Contributing to the welfare of others through a religious organization	10 9 8 7 6 5 4 3 2 1
4. Working creatively with wood, fabric, leather, or other materials	10 9 8 7 6 5 4 3 2 1

IRA—Box 2 *(continued)*

Statement	Scale
5. Blocking out time to satisfy creative needs	10 9 8 7 6 5 4 3 2 1
6. Enjoying nature	10 9 8 7 6 5 4 3 2 1
7. Working in a garden or other home-related activity	10 9 8 7 6 5 4 3 2 1
8. Meeting members of the opposite sex in a social setting	10 9 8 7 6 5 4 3 2 1
9. Reading an interesting book	10 9 8 7 6 5 4 3 2 1
10. Playing bridge, poker, or other inside games	10 9 8 7 6 5 4 3 2 1
11. Watching television in bed before going to sleep	10 9 8 7 6 5 4 3 2 1
12. Reading mystery stories, westerns, or historical novels	10 9 8 7 6 5 4 3 2 1
13. Turning to the financial page first	10 9 8 7 6 5 4 3 2 1
14. Entertaining favorite relatives	10 9 8 7 6 5 4 3 2 1
15. Earning money in preference to a retirement leisure activity	10 9 8 7 6 5 4 3 2 1
16. Participating in community activities	10 9 8 7 6 5 4 3 2 1
17. Reading about concerts, ballets, or musicals	10 9 8 7 6 5 4 3 2 1
18. Having coffee or cocktails with a good friend	10 9 8 7 6 5 4 3 2 1

IRA—Box 3

Statement	Scale
1. Participating in an activity in locales such as mountains, deserts, or other scenic areas, local or abroad	10 9 8 7 6 5 4 3 2 1
2. Staying active—walking, jogging, or biking in pleasant surroundings	10 9 8 7 6 5 4 3 2 1
3. Attending religious retreats or events	10 9 8 7 6 5 4 3 2 1

IRA—Box 3 *(continued)*

Statement	Scale
4. Building something with my hands	10 9 8 7 6 5 4 3 2 1
5. Taking courses in art, music, writing, or crafts to enhance my creative skills	10 9 8 7 6 5 4 3 2 1
6. Owning a recreational vehicle	10 9 8 7 6 5 4 3 2 1
7. Being a homebody—enjoying crafts, hobbies, television, comforts	10 9 8 7 6 5 4 3 2 1
8. Having people contacts—spending time with a congenial group	10 9 8 7 6 5 4 3 2 1
9. Doing special things alone	10 9 8 7 6 5 4 3 2 1
10. Going to Las Vegas, spending time at a racetrack, playing bingo	10 9 8 7 6 5 4 3 2 1
11. Watching a TV special, sporting event, or situation comedy	10 9 8 7 6 5 4 3 2 1
12. Turning to the book section in a publication	10 9 8 7 6 5 4 3 2 1
13. Following the stock market or checking on my other investments	10 9 8 7 6 5 4 3 2 1
14. Attending family gatherings	10 9 8 7 6 5 4 3 2 1
15. Earning dollars after retirement—odd jobs, consulting, self-owned business	10 9 8 7 6 5 4 3 2 1
16. Engaging in community activities—Meals on Wheels, hospital auxiliary	10 9 8 7 6 5 4 3 2 1
17. Attending a play or musical comedy	10 9 8 7 6 5 4 3 2 1
18. Talking privately about an interesting subject	10 9 8 7 6 5 4 3 2 1

PART II: CONSTRUCTING AND INTERPRETING YOUR PERSONAL PROFILE

Now that you have indicated your activity preferences, you have the fun of constructing your personal profile.

Step 1

Study the accompanying profile diagram for a moment. The scale from 0 to 30 on the left measures the level of your interests; the labels across the top identify your activity interest.

Step 2

Total your responses to question number 1 in each of the preceding three IRA boxes and enter this number at the bottom of column 1 (travel). You may want to use a scratch pad or calculator. Continue this process until you have entered the correct number at the bottom of each of the 18 columns.

Step 3

On the scale for each column locate the number equal to your total and draw a line across the column.

It is now time to evaluate your profile. Like personality, it is uniquely yours and should be studied carefully. Here are some tips that will help you interpret it:

- The more high-interest categories you have, the more exciting your retirement can be. If you have only a few, study others you might like to develop.

- Categories 1, 2, 3, 8, 10, 14, 15, 16, 17, and 18 involve considerable human contact; categories 4, 5, 6, 7, 11, and 13 are low-social activities. Often a mix of the two is best.

- Retirement is a perfect time to develop new interests. A higher interest than you expected in any activity could be a signal it is waiting to be developed.

- Significant interrelationships may exist between your interests. High travel and social interests suggest you might enjoy group tours or cruises more than independent travel. A high hobby or home interest may indicate your greatest happiness is at home and not on the road. A high sports interest can reinforce a love for the outdoors. Look for other correlations in your profile. You may find some surprises that allow you to understand yourself better.

▪ According to Dr. G. Frederic Kuder, who developed the Kuder Preference Vocational Record, interest patterns tend to be relatively stable. This does not mean medium- or low-interest activities cannot be developed. For example, at a later date, perhaps when your health may not permit you to pursue a previous high-interest choice, another may be substituted.

		High Interest	Medium Interest	Low Interest	
Private Communications	18				
Culture/Education	17				
Volunteer Work	16				
Working	15				
Family	14				
Investments	13				
Reading	12				
Television	11				
Games	10				
Time Alone	9				
Social	8				
Home	7				
Outdoors	6				
Hobbies (Artistic)	5				
Hobbies (Mechanical)	4				
Religious Activities	3				
Sports/Exercise	2				
Travel	1				

30   25   20   15   10   5   0   **Total**

If you sense the exercise did not fully identify or highlight a special interest of yours, rely on your judgment. Such an interest can easily be added to your profile.

PART III: COMPARING PROFILES

Life partners can learn some interesting things about each other's interests by each completing an Inventory of Retirement Activities and discussing the results. You may find areas of common interests that open up new opportunities for time together. Or, you may find areas where there are no interests in common that offer opportunities for time alone. In either case, knowing each other's interests will lead to greater understanding and appreciation of each as individuals.

Common Interest

Life partners and friends can discover, through a comparison of their individual profiles, that they share interests they were not aware existed. One wife learned her husband had a higher social interest than she anticipated; with his involvement, she initiated more social situations. A husband learned his wife showed higher interest in outdoor activities than he had imagined. After some discussion, they purchased a camper and enjoyed some great trips together.

Capitalizing on common interests (even when one is high and the other moderate) is the best way for two people to make the most of retirement. A profile comparison can reveal compatible interests that bring enjoyment to both parties.

Contrasting Interests

A profile comparison can also show polarized interests. For example, one person may show a high interest in artistic hobbies while the other shows none at all. However, the person with the low artistic interest might be high in sports or games. Solution? A comfortable tradeoff. To make the most of retirement, one person should permit the other to enjoy his or her favorite activity. Not all interests can or should be shared. For example, one partner with a high interest in religion not shared by the other spent evenings at church while her partner scheduled time at a fraternal club. Each person had the freedom and time to pursue divergent interests.

Conflicting Situations

Some retirement activities need to be shared more than others. It is difficult when one person likes to travel but the other does not or when one person likes to go out socially and the other prefers solitude. In these situations, some give and take is necessary. When each person gives a little, good things often happen. Many an individual, through encouragement from a life partner, discovers the joys of social activity or the outdoors. One party learns from the other. When this happens, both individuals come out ahead.

Be enthusiastic about your high-interest activities, and continue to develop those in lower categories. Doing this should provide you with a more fulfilling retirement. Good luck!

RETIREMENT PLANNING GUIDE

Planning is essential to achievement. It clarifies the steps necessary to reach your goal and it establishes an order and time requirement for carrying out those steps. This very act of writing down your plans will heighten your commitment to follow through and experience the satisfaction of reaching your goal.

A fulfilling retirement will include most, if not all, of the elements covered in this book and take into account your specific health and financial circumstances. To make sure you cover all of the bases, look over the categories on this planning form. Then review the work you did at the end of Chapter 1 plus your Things to Do lists at the end of the other chapters.

You are asked to set specific goals in each of the planning categories. Be sure these goals are specific. For example, don't say, "My goal is to be financially secure in retirement." Instead, say, "My goal is to have a $2,500 a month income, in today's dollars."

1. My Vision of Retirement

A perfect retirement for me will include: _____

_____

_____

_____

_____

_____

2. When I Plan to Retire

I plan to retire on: _____

In order to meet this schedule, I will need to do the following:

Action Steps	*Target Date*
_____	_____
_____	_____
_____	_____
_____	_____

3. Pursuing My Dream

Goal: _____

_____

Action Steps	*Target Date*
_____	_____
_____	_____
_____	_____
_____	_____

4. Retirement Activities

Goal: _____

_____

Action Steps	*Target Date*
_____	_____
_____	_____
_____	_____
_____	_____

5. Health and Wellness

Goal: _____

_____

Action Steps	*Target Date*
_____	_____
_____	_____
_____	_____
_____	_____

6. Relationships

Goal: _____

_____

Action Steps	*Target Date*
_____	_____
_____	_____
_____	_____
_____	_____

7. Finances

Goal: _____

_____

Action Steps	*Target Date*
_____	_____
_____	_____
_____	_____
_____	_____

8. Living Arrangements

Goal: _____

_____

Action Steps	*Target Date*
_____	_____
_____	_____
_____	_____
_____	_____

Summary

Summarize your action steps in chronological order. This will make it easier to monitor your progress. Then, schedule follow-up reviews for the next year.

Schedule of Action Steps

Action Steps	*Target Date*
_____	_____
_____	_____
_____	_____
_____	_____
_____	_____
_____	_____
_____	_____
_____	_____
_____	_____

Follow-up Schedule

Follow-up creates an effective way to prod yourself to action. If you have a life partner, include your partner in your review and follow-up.

3-month review date: _____

6-month review date: _____

12-month review date: _____

Notes on Follow-up Reviews

Following each of your reviews, write a brief summary of your progress. Note progress made toward your goals, things that have changed, and problems you have encountered.

Summary of 3-month Review

Summary of 6-month Review

_____

_____

_____

_____

_____

_____

_____

_____

_____

_____

_____

Summary of 12-month Review

_____

_____

_____

_____

_____

_____

_____

_____

_____

_____

_____

Appendix C

Additional Resources

Finances

Carlson, Robert C. *The New Rules of Retirement* (Hoboken, NJ: John Wiley & Sons, Inc. 2004).

Clifford, Denis and Cora Jordan. *Plan Your Estate* (Berkeley, CA: Nolo Press, 2002).

Flores, Dan L. *The Retirement Revolution: A Strategic Guide to Understanding and Investing Lump-Sum Distributions from Qualified Plans* (Kosciusko, MS: Writers Advantage, 2003).

Howells, John. *Retirement on a Shoestring* (Guilford, CT: Globe Pequot Press, 2002).

Malaspina, Margaret A. *Cracking Your Retirement Nest Egg (Without Scrambling Your Finances)* (New York City, NY: Bloomberg Press, 2002).

Schwab, Charles R. *You're Fifty—Now What? Investing for the Second Half of Your Life* (New York City, NY: Crown Publishing Group, 2002).

Slesnick, Twila and John C. Suttle. *Creating Your Own Retirement Plan: A Guide to Keoghs and IRAs for the Self-Employed* (Berkeley, CA: Nolo Press, 2002).

Living Arrangements

Cullinane, Jan and Cathy Fitzgerald. *The New Retirement: The Ultimate Guide for the Rest of Your Life* (New York City, NY: Rodale Press, Inc., 2004).

Evans, Eva G. and Richard L. Fox. *America's Best Low-Tax Retirement Towns: Where to Move to, and from, to Slash Your Taxes in Retirement* (Houston, TX: Vacation Publications, 2002).

Howells, John. *Where to Retire: America's Best and Most Affordable Places*, Fifth Edition (Guilford, CT: Globe Pequot Press, 2003).

United Seniors Health Council. *Planning for Long-Term Care* (New York City, NY: McGraw-Hill, 2002).

Young, Heather M. and Rheba deTornyay. *Choices: Making a Good Move to a Retirement Community* (Seattle, WA: ERA Care Communities, 2001).

Health

Koenig, Harold George. *Purpose and Power in Retirement: New Opportunities for Meaning and Significance* (Radnor, PA: Templeton Foundation, 2002).

Wei, Jeanne Y. and Sue Levkoff. *Aging Well: The Complete Guide to Physical and Emotional Health* (Hoboken, NJ: John Wiley & Sons, 2001).

Internet Sites

www.founders.com
Web site for the Dreyfus Founders Fund. Excellent source for retirement-planning information and tools. (Many funds require you to be an investor to access their planning tools. This one does not.)

www.fidelity.com
Web site for Fidelity Funds. Another excellent information and tools source that does not require you to be an investor.

www.morningstar.com
Web site of Morningstar Investor Services. A great source for financial information and planning tools.

www.ici.org/factbook/index.html
Web site of *Investment Company Fact Book* provided by the Investment Company Institute. Everything you want to know about mutual funds generally—not specific funds.

www.ssa.gov
Web site of the Social Security Administration. Good source of information and online application for Social Security benefits.

www.TeamNCPA.org
Web site of the National Center for Policy Analysis. An excellent calculator for Social Security benefits.

INDEX